HYPER SCAPE ™

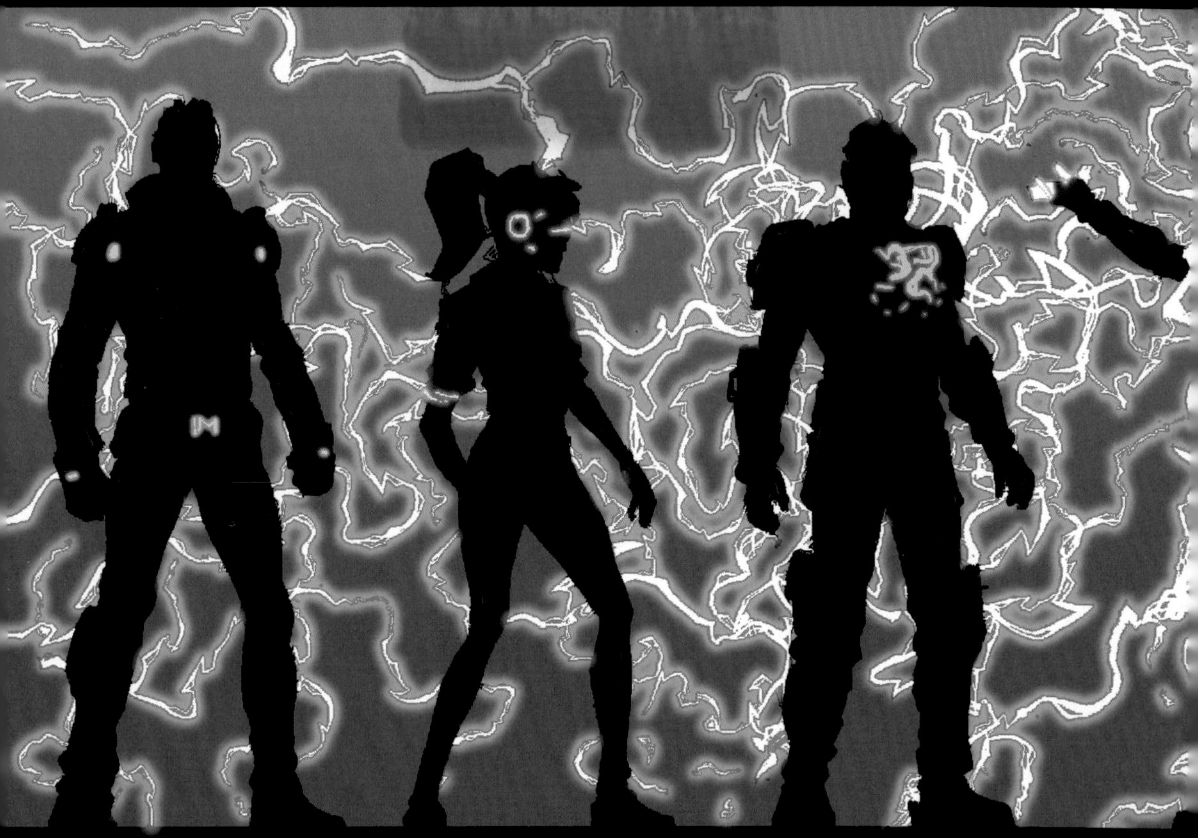

HYPER SCAPE™

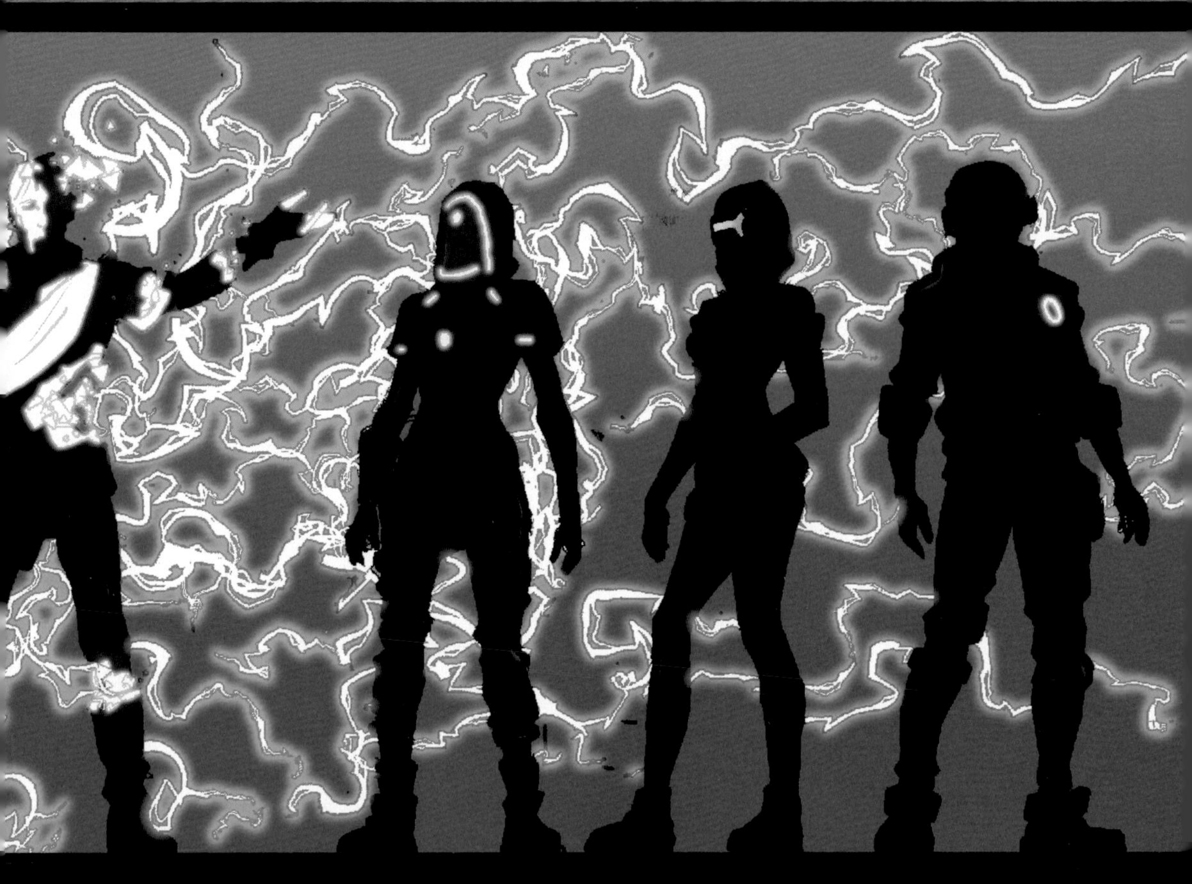

president and publisher MIKE RICHARDSON

editors FREDDYE MILLER, DAVE MARSHALL   associate editor JUDY KHUU

assistant editors ROSE WEITZ, KONNER KNUDSEN

designer PATRICK SATTERFIELD   digital art technician ANN GRAY

senior producer – ubisoft GRAEME JENNINGS

creative director – ubisoft JEAN-CHRISTOPHE GUYOT   graphic art director – ubisoft MICKAEL LABAT

associate producer – ubisoft MARIE-JOSEE OUELLET   production manager – ubisoft YAN CHARRON

Published by Dark Horse Books
A division of Dark Horse Comics LLC
10956 SE Main Street
Milwaukie, OR 97222

First edition: January 2022
Ebook ISBN 978-1-50672-071-5
Trade Paperback ISBN 978-1-50672-070-8

1 3 5 7 9 10 8 6 4 2
Printed in China

DarkHorse.com   Facebook.com/DarkHorseComics   Twitter.com/DarkHorseComics

To find a comics shop in your area, visit comicshoplocator.com

HYPER SCAPE

This volume collects issues #1–#6 of the Dark Horse comic book series *Hyper Scape*, published September 2020–September 2021.

Library of Congress Cataloging-in-Publication Data

Names: Emgård, Christofer, writer. | Guzmán, Gabriel, 1975- artist. |
    Atiyeh, Michael, colourist | Betancourt, Jimmy, letterer.
Title: Hyper scape / writer, Christofer Emgård ; artist, Gabriel Guzmán ;
    colors, Michael Atiyeh ; letters, Jimmy Betancourt.
Description: Milwaukie, OR : Dark Horse Books, 2022. | "This volume
    collects issues #1-#6 of the Dark Horse digital comic book series HYPER
    SCAPE, published September 2020-September 2021."
Identifiers: LCCN 2021029607 (print) | LCCN 2021029608 (ebook) | ISBN
    9781506720708 (trade paperback) | ISBN 9781506720715 (ebook)
Subjects: LCGFT: Science fiction comics.
Classification: LCC PN6728.H97 E44 2022 (print) | LCC PN6728.H97 (ebook)
    | DDC 741.5/973--dc23
LC record available at https://lccn.loc.gov/2021029607
LC ebook record available at https://lccn.loc.gov/2021029608

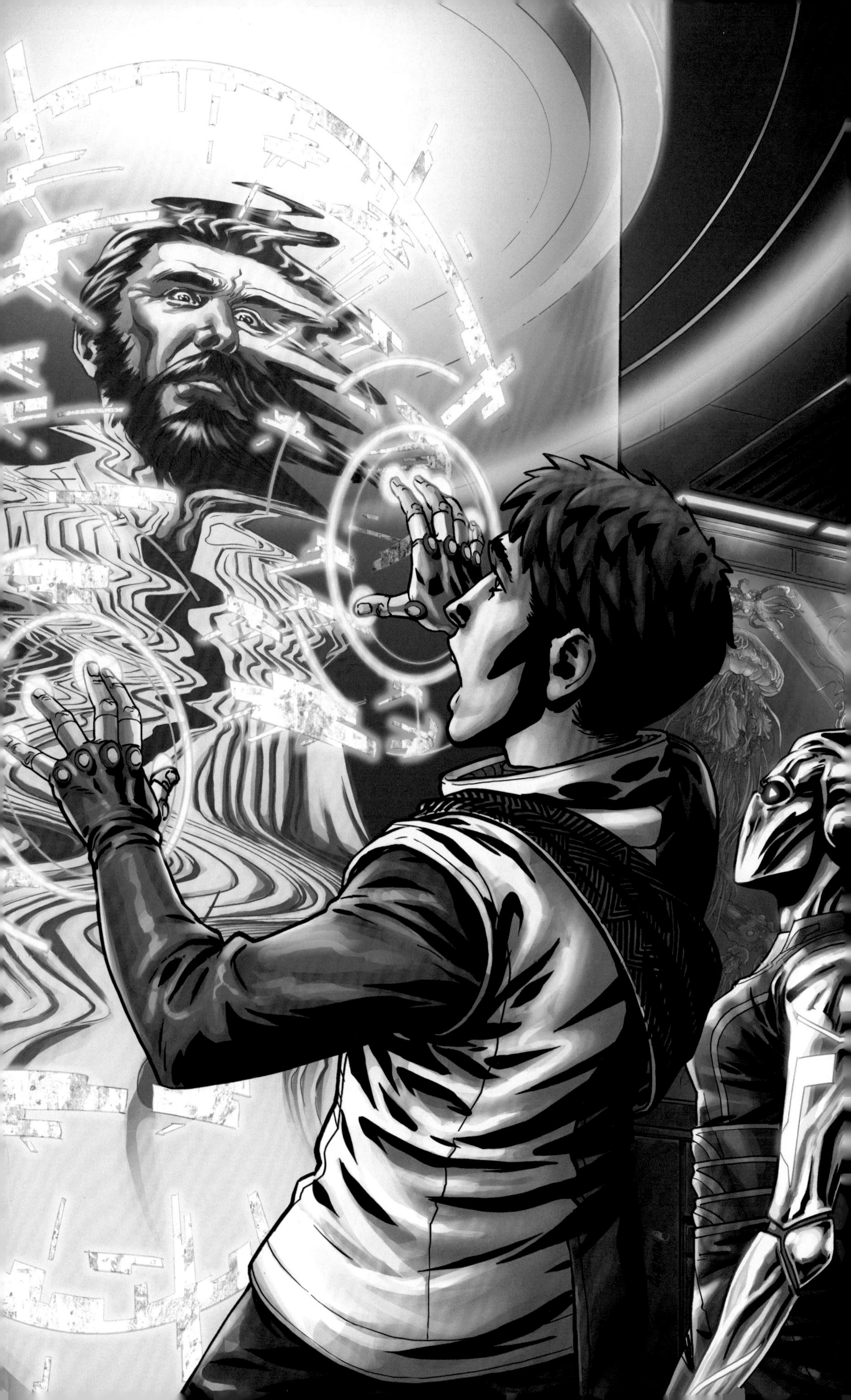

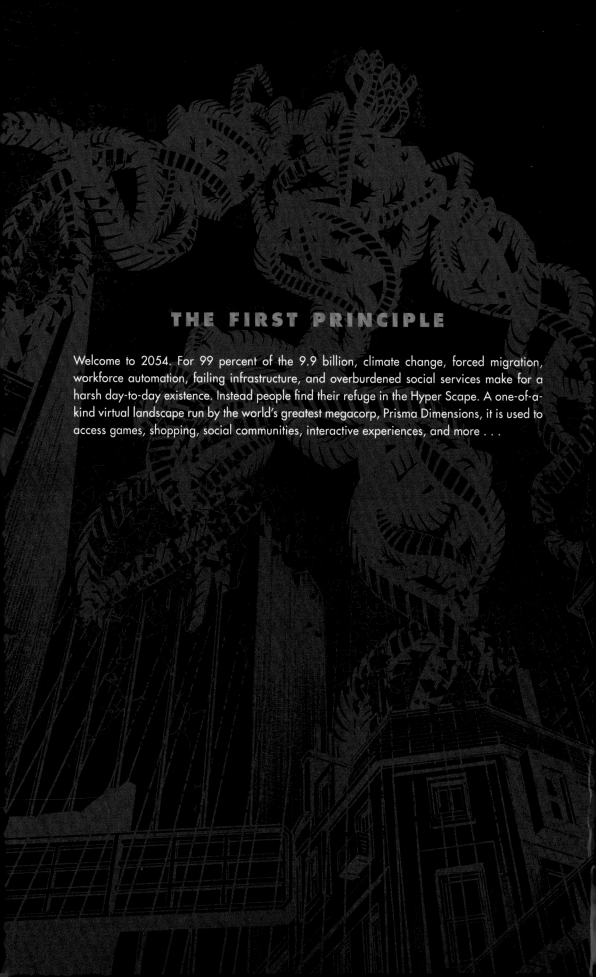

THE FIRST PRINCIPLE

Welcome to 2054. For 99 percent of the 9.9 billion, climate change, forced migration, workforce automation, failing infrastructure, and overburdened social services make for a harsh day-to-day existence. Instead people find their refuge in the Hyper Scape. A one-of-a-kind virtual landscape run by the world's greatest megacorp, Prisma Dimensions, it is used to access games, shopping, social communities, interactive experiences, and more . . .

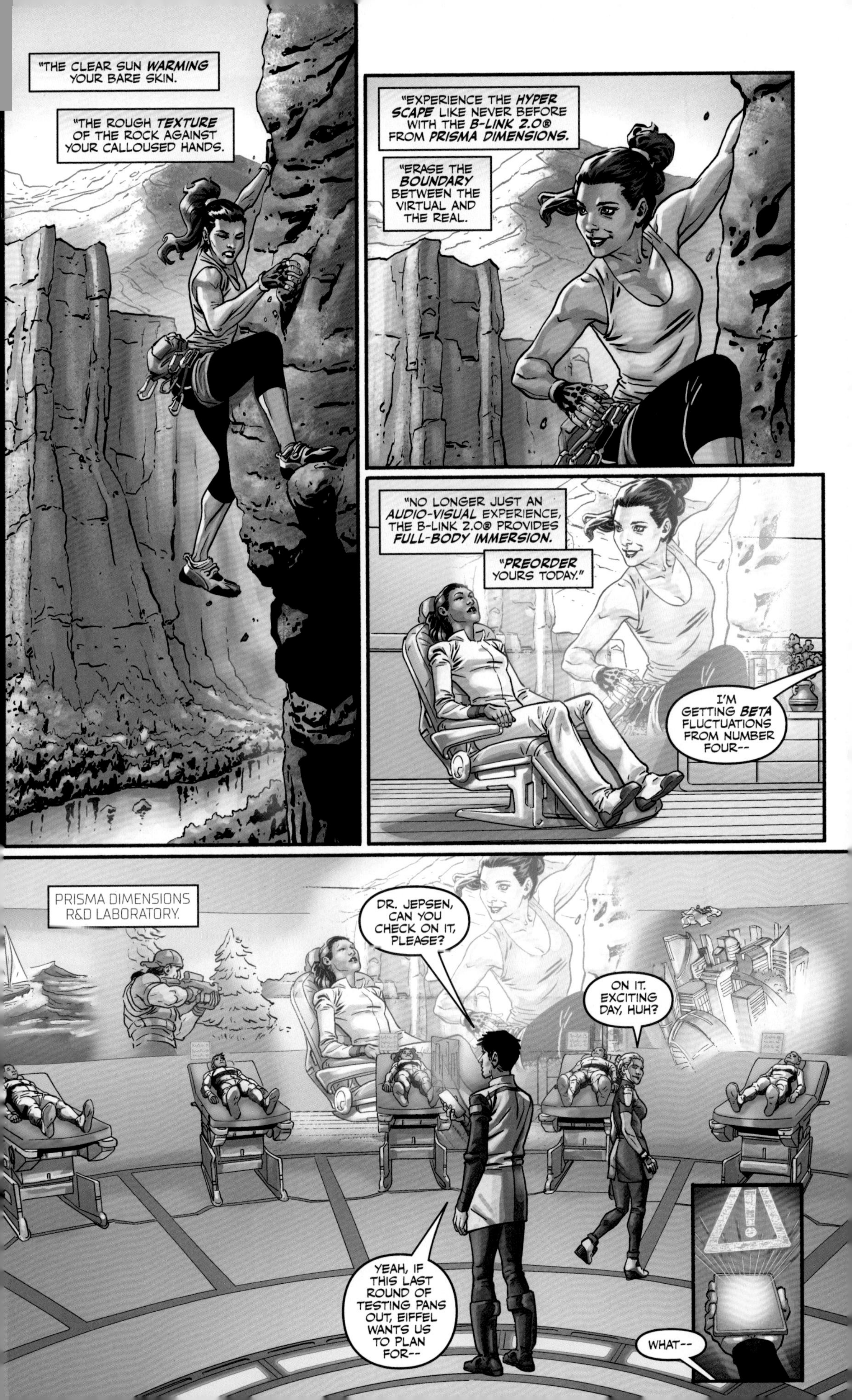
"THE CLEAR SUN WARMING YOUR BARE SKIN.
"THE ROUGH TEXTURE OF THE ROCK AGAINST YOUR CALLOUSED HANDS.
"EXPERIENCE THE HYPER SCAPE LIKE NEVER BEFORE WITH THE B-LINK 2.0® FROM PRISMA DIMENSIONS.
"ERASE THE BOUNDARY BETWEEN THE VIRTUAL AND THE REAL.
"NO LONGER JUST AN AUDIO-VISUAL EXPERIENCE, THE B-LINK 2.0® PROVIDES FULL-BODY IMMERSION.
"PREORDER YOURS TODAY."
I'M GETTING BETA FLUCTUATIONS FROM NUMBER FOUR--
PRISMA DIMENSIONS R&D LABORATORY.
DR. JEPSEN, CAN YOU CHECK ON IT, PLEASE?
ON IT. EXCITING DAY, HUH?
YEAH, IF THIS LAST ROUND OF TESTING PANS OUT, EIFFEL WANTS US TO PLAN FOR--
WHAT--

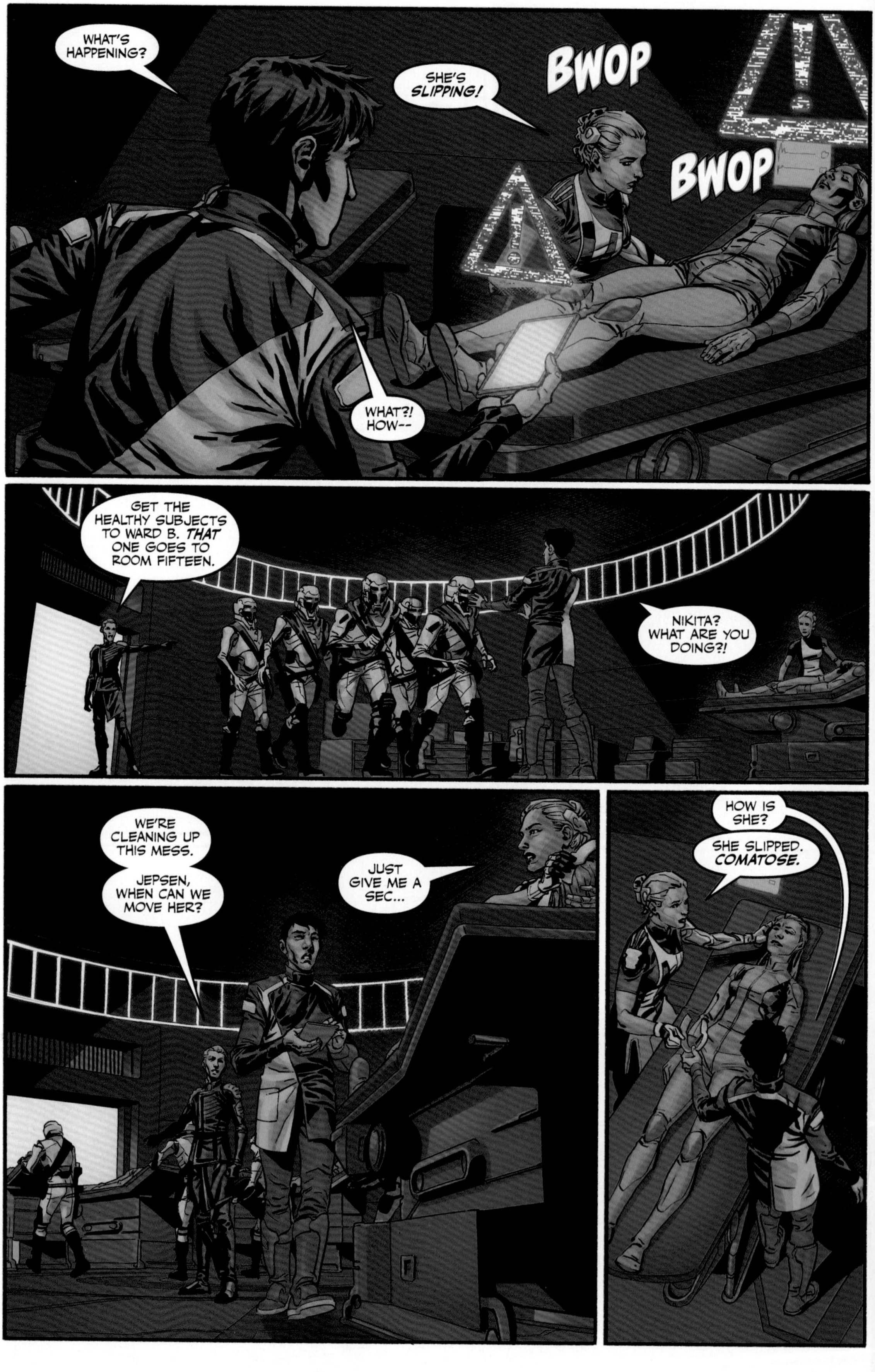
WHAT'S HAPPENING?
SHE'S SLIPPING!
BWOP
BWOP
WHAT?! HOW--
GET THE HEALTHY SUBJECTS TO WARD B. THAT ONE GOES TO ROOM FIFTEEN.
NIKITA? WHAT ARE YOU DOING?!
WE'RE CLEANING UP THIS MESS.
JEPSEN, WHEN CAN WE MOVE HER?
JUST GIVE ME A SEC...
HOW IS SHE?
SHE SLIPPED. COMATOSE.

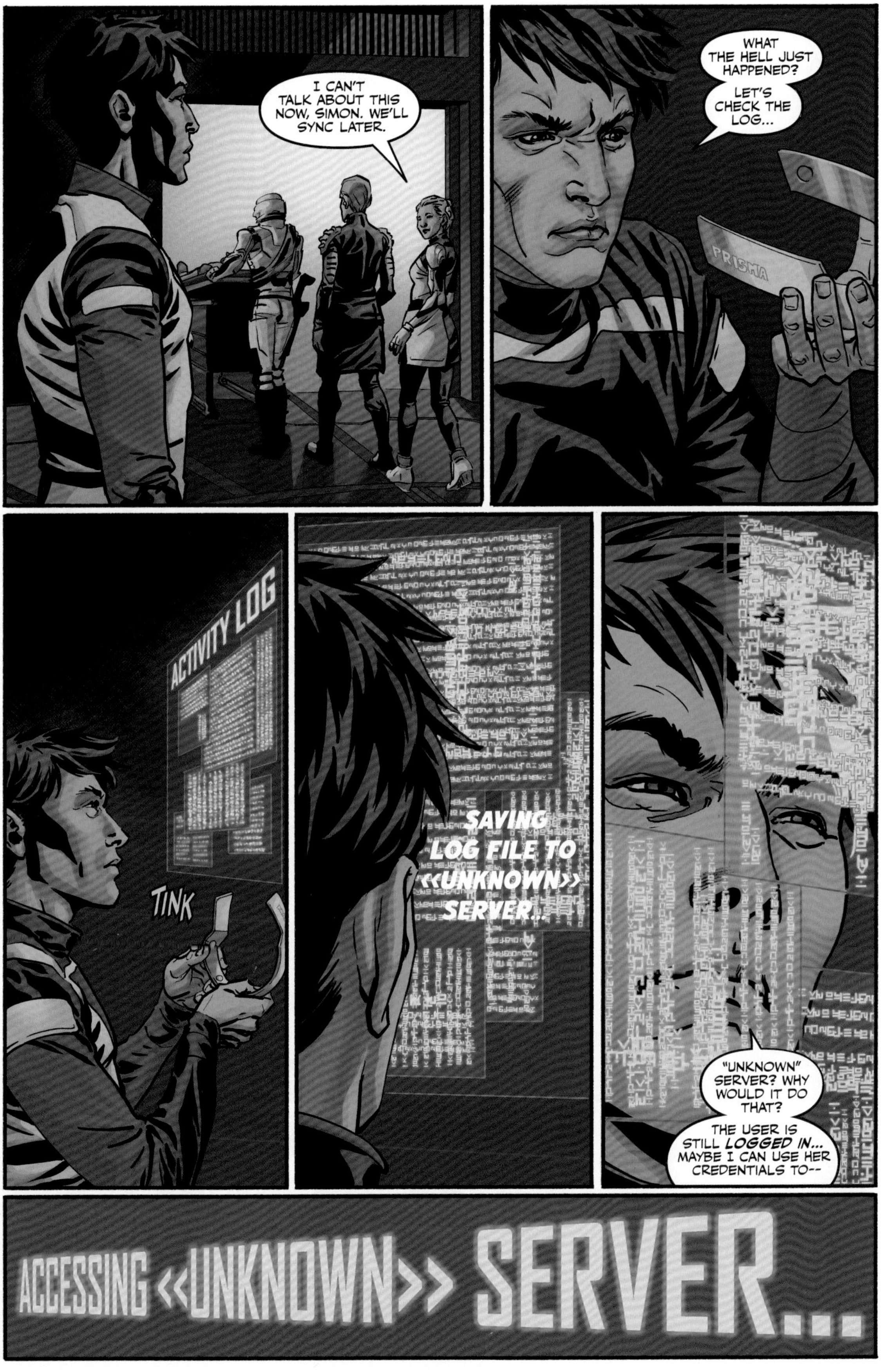
I CAN'T TALK ABOUT THIS NOW, SIMON. WE'LL SYNC LATER.
WHAT THE HELL JUST HAPPENED?
LET'S CHECK THE LOG...
PRISMA
ACTIVITY LOG
TINK
SAVING LOG FILE TO «UNKNOWN» SERVER...
"UNKNOWN" SERVER? WHY WOULD IT DO THAT?
THE USER IS STILL *LOGGED IN*... MAYBE I CAN USE HER CREDENTIALS TO--
ACCESSING «UNKNOWN» SERVER...

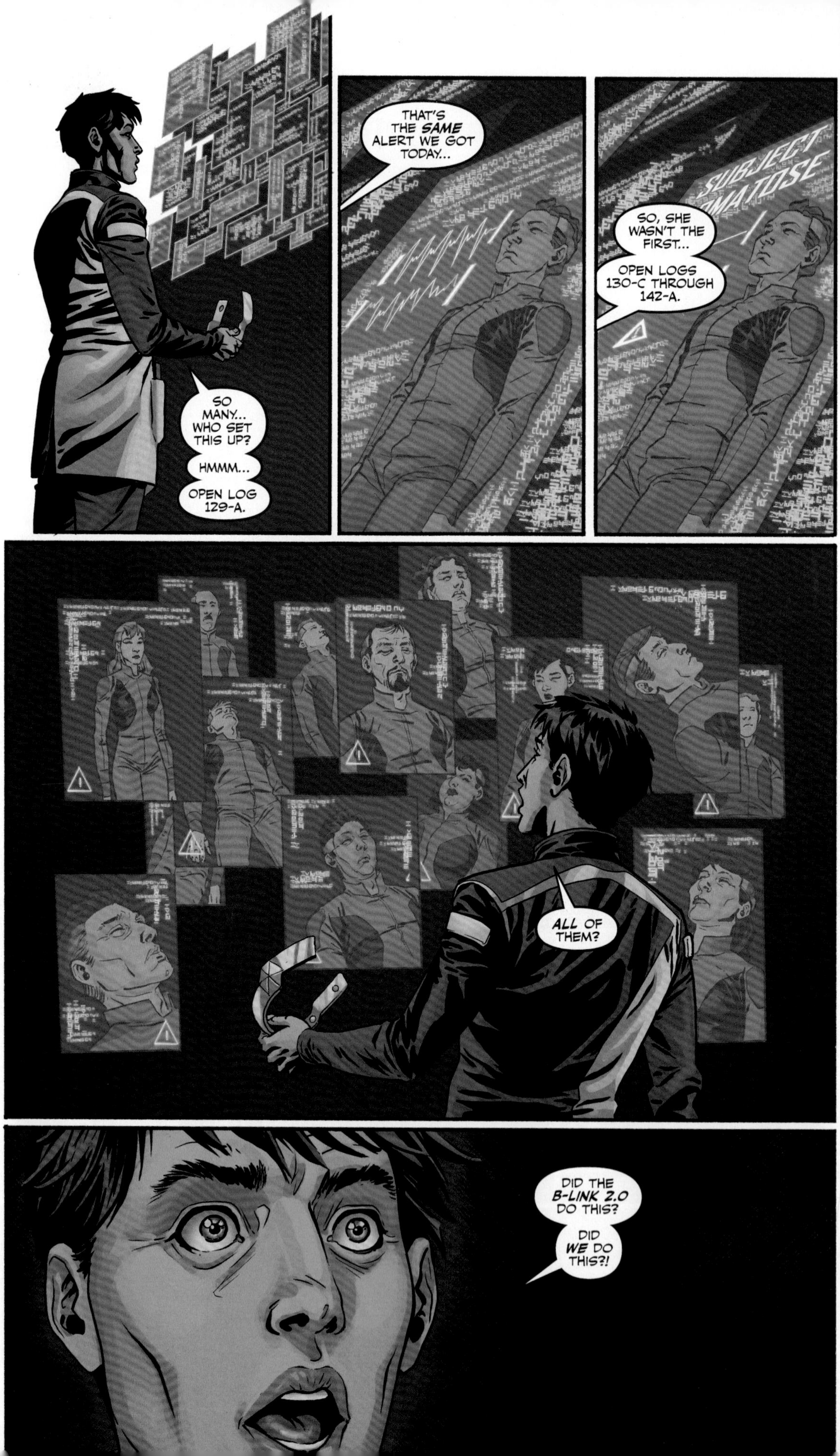
THAT'S THE SAME ALERT WE GOT TODAY...
SUBJECT COMATOSE
SO, SHE WASN'T THE FIRST...
OPEN LOGS 130-C THROUGH 142-A.
SO MANY... WHO SET THIS UP?
HMMM...
OPEN LOG 129-A.
ALL OF THEM?
DID THE B-LINK 2.0 DO THIS?
DID WE DO THIS?!

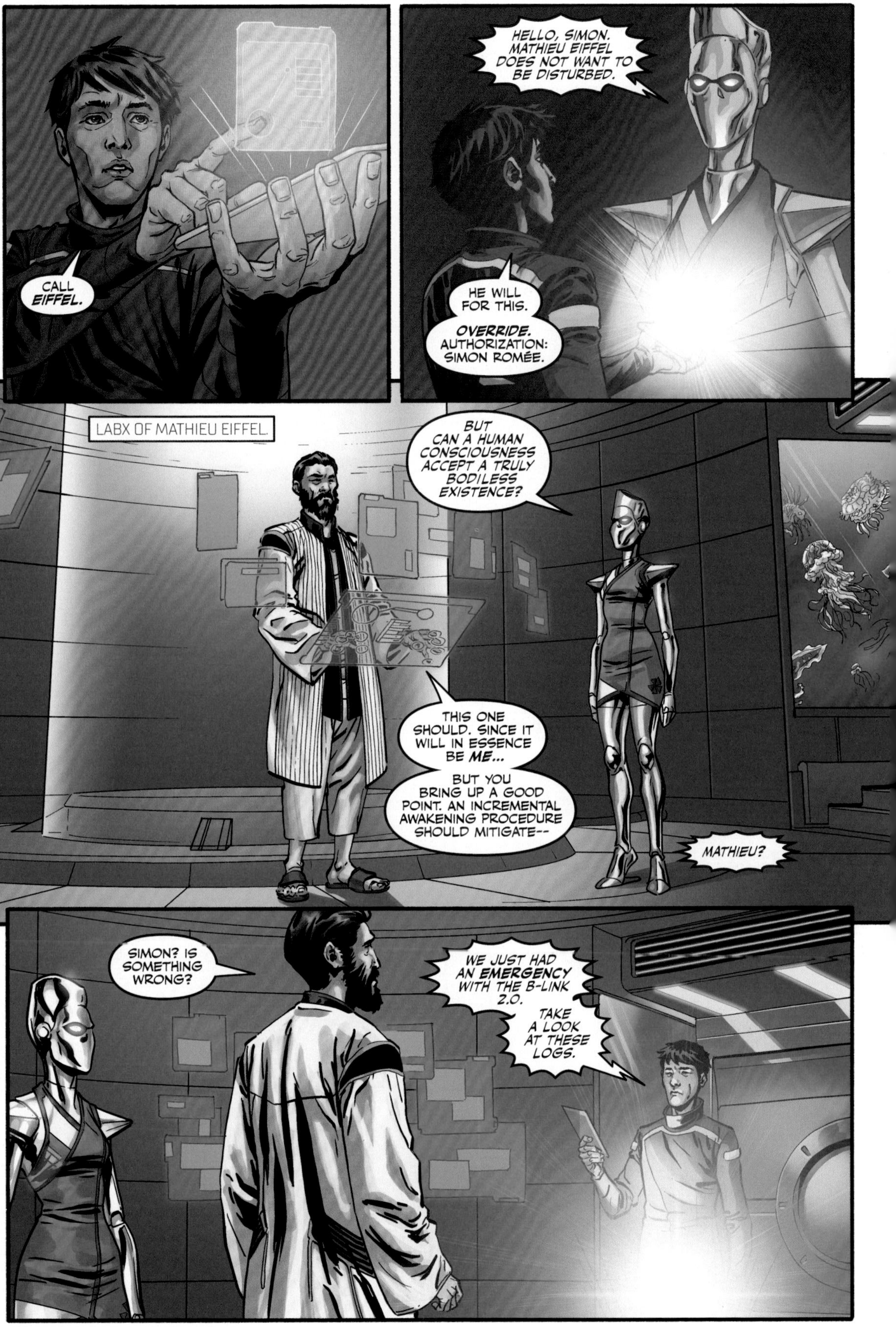
CALL EIFFEL.
HELLO, SIMON. MATHIEU EIFFEL DOES NOT WANT TO BE DISTURBED.
HE WILL FOR THIS.
OVERRIDE. AUTHORIZATION: SIMON ROMÉE.
LABX OF MATHIEU EIFFEL.
BUT CAN A HUMAN CONSCIOUSNESS ACCEPT A TRULY BODILESS EXISTENCE?
THIS ONE SHOULD. SINCE IT WILL IN ESSENCE BE ME...
BUT YOU BRING UP A GOOD POINT. AN INCREMENTAL AWAKENING PROCEDURE SHOULD MITIGATE--
MATHIEU?
SIMON? IS SOMETHING WRONG?
WE JUST HAD AN EMERGENCY WITH THE B-LINK 2.0.
TAKE A LOOK AT THESE LOGS.

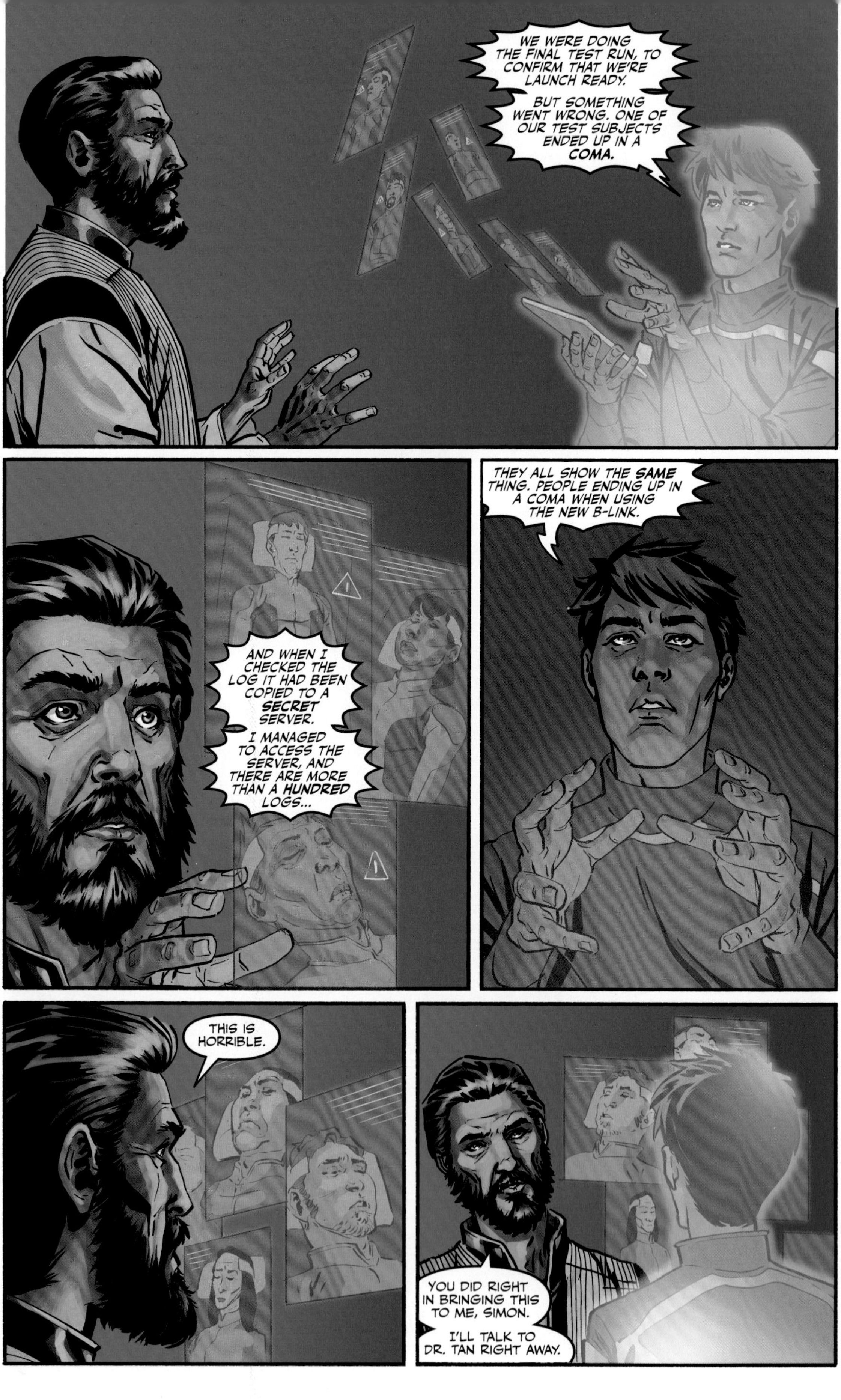
WE WERE DOING THE FINAL TEST RUN, TO CONFIRM THAT WE'RE LAUNCH READY.
BUT SOMETHING WENT WRONG. ONE OF OUR TEST SUBJECTS ENDED UP IN A COMA.
AND WHEN I CHECKED THE LOG IT HAD BEEN COPIED TO A SECRET SERVER.
I MANAGED TO ACCESS THE SERVER, AND THERE ARE MORE THAN A HUNDRED LOGS...
THEY ALL SHOW THE SAME THING. PEOPLE ENDING UP IN A COMA WHEN USING THE NEW B-LINK.
THIS IS HORRIBLE.
YOU DID RIGHT IN BRINGING THIS TO ME, SIMON.
I'LL TALK TO DR. TAN RIGHT AWAY.

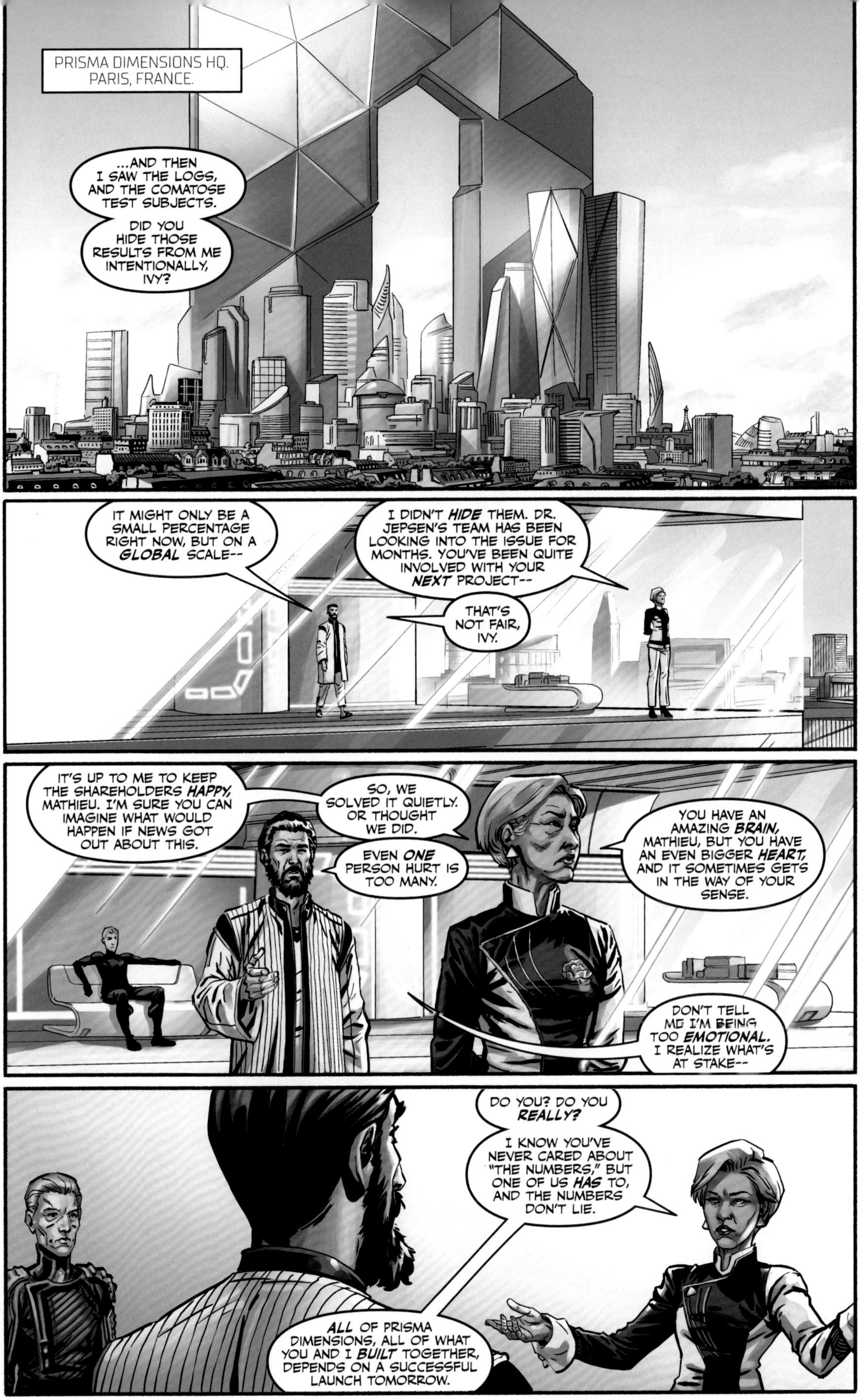
PRISMA DIMENSIONS HQ. PARIS, FRANCE.
...AND THEN I SAW THE LOGS, AND THE COMATOSE TEST SUBJECTS.
DID YOU HIDE THOSE RESULTS FROM ME INTENTIONALLY, IVY?
IT MIGHT ONLY BE A SMALL PERCENTAGE RIGHT NOW, BUT ON A GLOBAL SCALE--
I DIDN'T HIDE THEM. DR. JEPSEN'S TEAM HAS BEEN LOOKING INTO THE ISSUE FOR MONTHS. YOU'VE BEEN QUITE INVOLVED WITH YOUR NEXT PROJECT--
THAT'S NOT FAIR, IVY.
IT'S UP TO ME TO KEEP THE SHAREHOLDERS HAPPY, MATHIEU. I'M SURE YOU CAN IMAGINE WHAT WOULD HAPPEN IF NEWS GOT OUT ABOUT THIS.
SO, WE SOLVED IT QUIETLY. OR THOUGHT WE DID.
EVEN ONE PERSON HURT IS TOO MANY.
YOU HAVE AN AMAZING BRAIN, MATHIEU, BUT YOU HAVE AN EVEN BIGGER HEART, AND IT SOMETIMES GETS IN THE WAY OF YOUR SENSE.
DON'T TELL ME I'M BEING TOO EMOTIONAL. I REALIZE WHAT'S AT STAKE--
DO YOU? DO YOU REALLY?
I KNOW YOU'VE NEVER CARED ABOUT "THE NUMBERS," BUT ONE OF US HAS TO, AND THE NUMBERS DON'T LIE.
ALL OF PRISMA DIMENSIONS, ALL OF WHAT YOU AND I BUILT TOGETHER, DEPENDS ON A SUCCESSFUL LAUNCH TOMORROW.

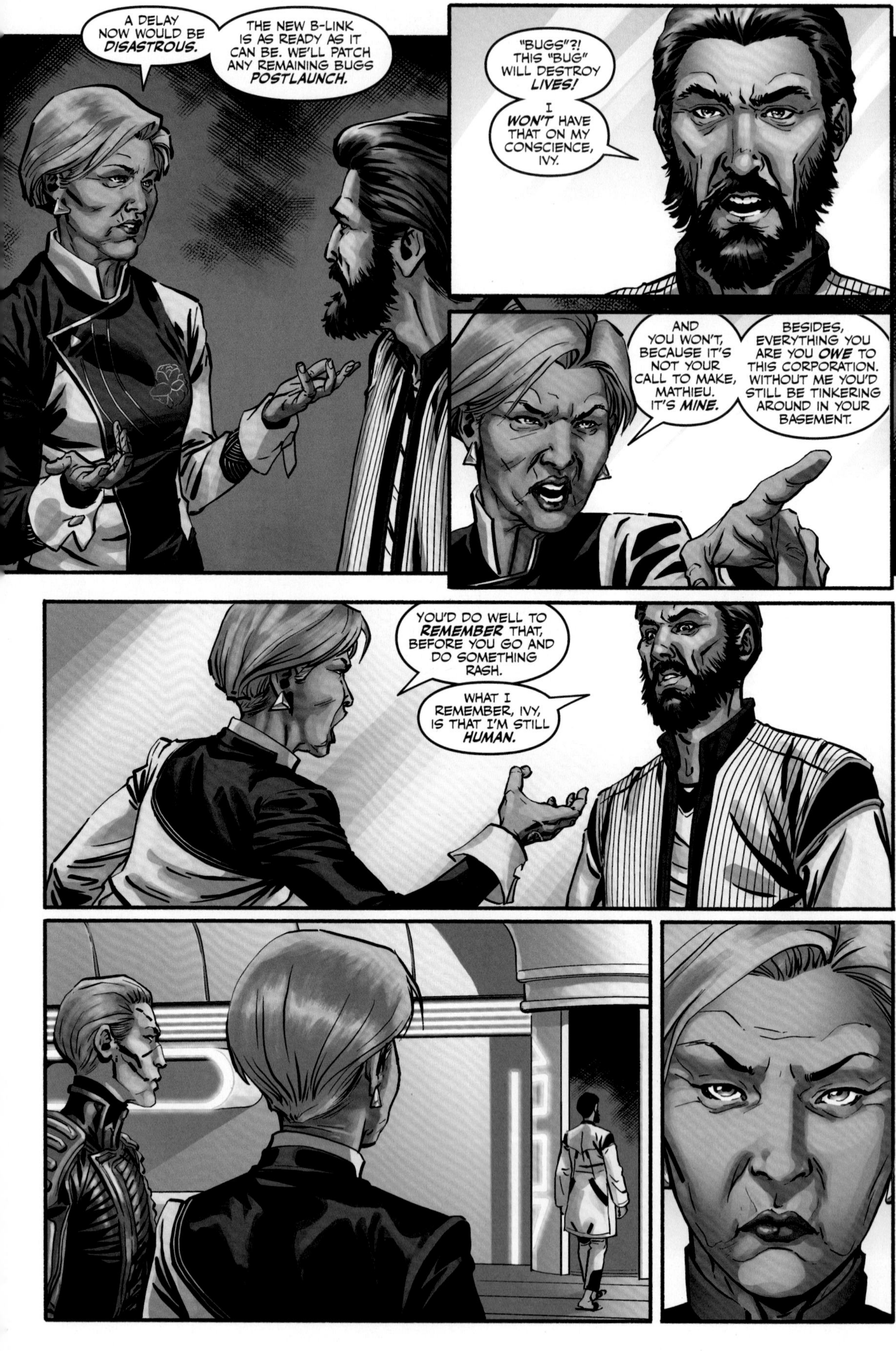
A DELAY NOW WOULD BE DISASTROUS.
THE NEW B-LINK IS AS READY AS IT CAN BE. WE'LL PATCH ANY REMAINING BUGS POSTLAUNCH.
"BUGS"?! THIS "BUG" WILL DESTROY LIVES!
I WON'T HAVE THAT ON MY CONSCIENCE, IVY.
AND YOU WON'T, BECAUSE IT'S NOT YOUR CALL TO MAKE, MATHIEU. IT'S MINE.
BESIDES, EVERYTHING YOU ARE YOU OWE TO THIS CORPORATION. WITHOUT ME YOU'D STILL BE TINKERING AROUND IN YOUR BASEMENT.
YOU'D DO WELL TO REMEMBER THAT, BEFORE YOU GO AND DO SOMETHING RASH.
WHAT I REMEMBER, IVY, IS THAT I'M STILL HUMAN.

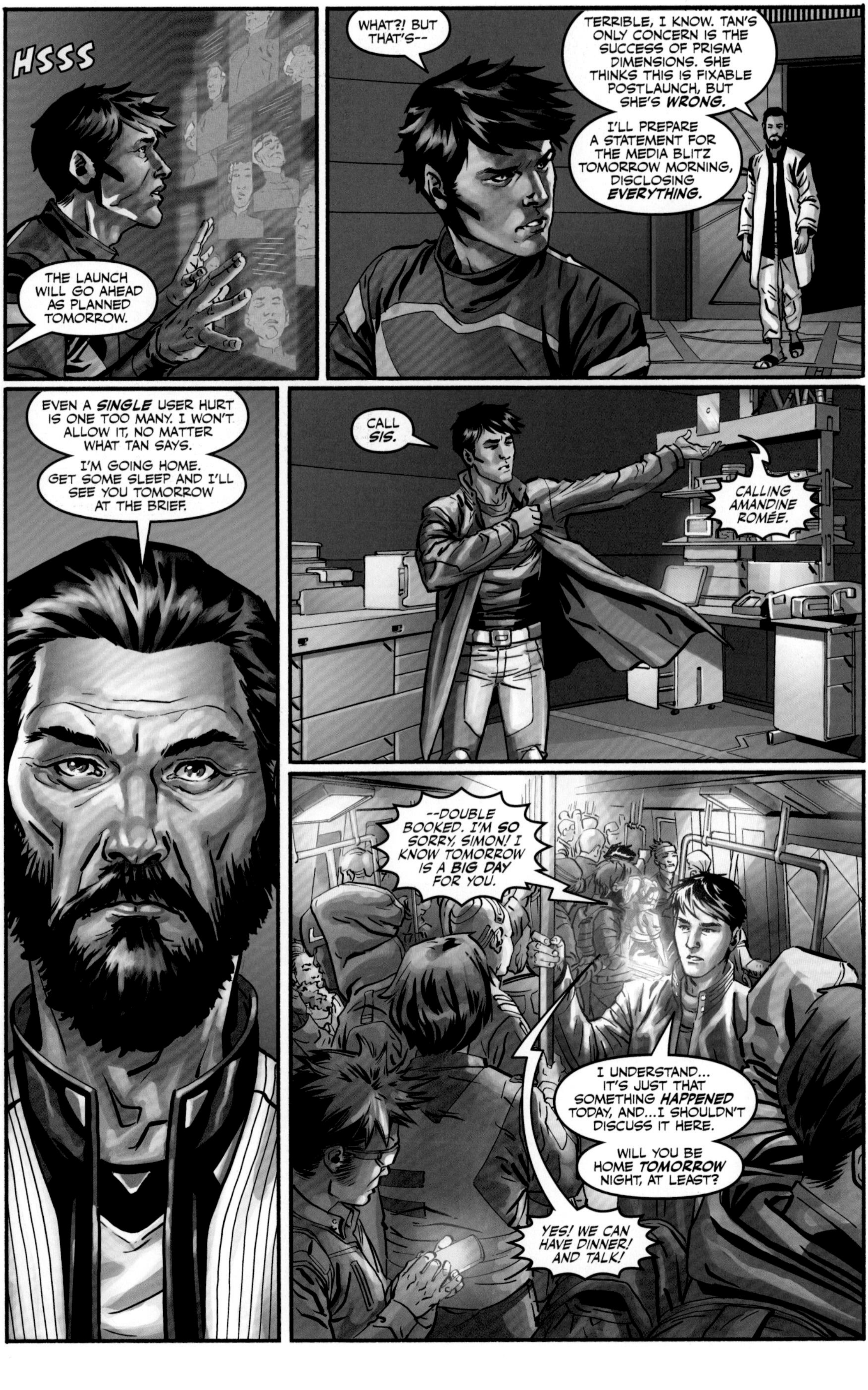
HSSS
THE LAUNCH WILL GO AHEAD AS PLANNED TOMORROW.
WHAT?! BUT THAT'S--
TERRIBLE, I KNOW. TAN'S ONLY CONCERN IS THE SUCCESS OF PRISMA DIMENSIONS. SHE THINKS THIS IS FIXABLE POSTLAUNCH, BUT SHE'S WRONG.
I'LL PREPARE A STATEMENT FOR THE MEDIA BLITZ TOMORROW MORNING, DISCLOSING EVERYTHING.
EVEN A SINGLE USER HURT IS ONE TOO MANY. I WON'T ALLOW IT, NO MATTER WHAT TAN SAYS.
I'M GOING HOME. GET SOME SLEEP AND I'LL SEE YOU TOMORROW AT THE BRIEF.
CALL SIS.
CALLING AMANDINE ROMÉE.
--DOUBLE BOOKED. I'M SO SORRY, SIMON! I KNOW TOMORROW IS A BIG DAY FOR YOU.
I UNDERSTAND... IT'S JUST THAT SOMETHING HAPPENED TODAY, AND...I SHOULDN'T DISCUSS IT HERE.
WILL YOU BE HOME TOMORROW NIGHT, AT LEAST?
YES! WE CAN HAVE DINNER! AND TALK!

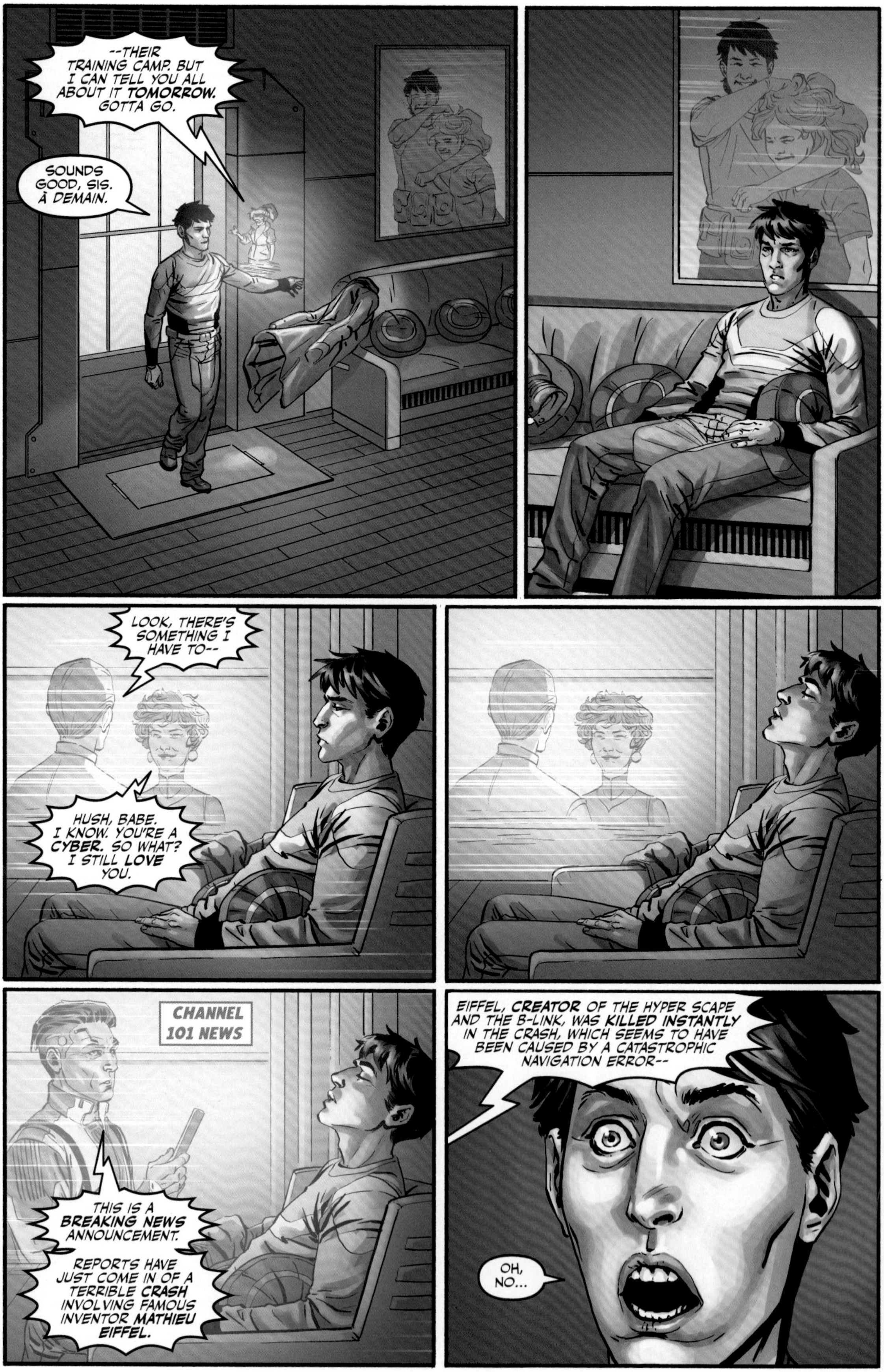
--THEIR TRAINING CAMP. BUT I CAN TELL YOU ALL ABOUT IT TOMORROW. GOTTA GO.
SOUNDS GOOD, SIS. À DEMAIN.
LOOK, THERE'S SOMETHING I HAVE TO--
HUSH, BABE. I KNOW. YOU'RE A CYBER. SO WHAT? I STILL LOVE YOU.
CHANNEL 101 NEWS
THIS IS A BREAKING NEWS ANNOUNCEMENT.
REPORTS HAVE JUST COME IN OF A TERRIBLE CRASH INVOLVING FAMOUS INVENTOR MATHIEU EIFFEL.
EIFFEL, CREATOR OF THE HYPER SCAPE AND THE B-LINK, WAS KILLED INSTANTLY IN THE CRASH, WHICH SEEMS TO HAVE BEEN CAUSED BY A CATASTROPHIC NAVIGATION ERROR--
OH, NO...

INVENTOR MATHIEU EIFFEL KILLED IN CRASH

...AND CONDOLENCES ARE COMING IN FROM ALL OVER THE WORLD AS PEOPLE WAKE UP TO THIS *TERRIBLE TRAGEDY.*

WE TURN SOON TO *PRISMA DIMENSIONS HQ* IN PARIS, WHERE CEO *DR. IVY TAN* IS ABOUT TO GIVE A MEDIA CONFERENCE.

PRISMA WAS SET TO ANNOUNCE THE RELEASE OF THE *B-LINK 2.0* TODAY, BUT WE CAN ASSUME DR. TAN WILL FOCUS ON THE TRAGIC LOSS OF MATHIEU EIFFEL.

THIS CAN'T BE REAL, MATHIEU...

WE NOW GO LIVE TO DR. TAN--

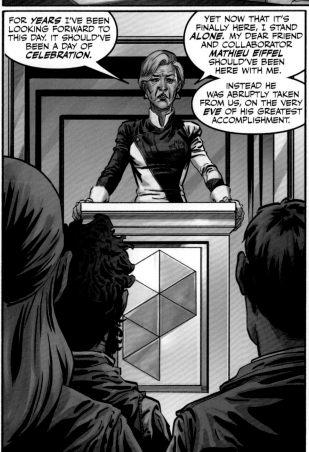

FOR *YEARS* I'VE BEEN LOOKING FORWARD TO THIS DAY. IT SHOULD'VE BEEN A DAY OF *CELEBRATION.*

YET NOW THAT IT'S FINALLY HERE, I STAND *ALONE.* MY DEAR FRIEND AND COLLABORATOR *MATHIEU EIFFEL* SHOULD'VE BEEN HERE WITH ME.

INSTEAD HE WAS ABRUPTLY TAKEN FROM US, ON THE VERY *EVE* OF HIS GREATEST ACCOMPLISHMENT.

TODAY IS A DAY TO *MOURN* HIS PASSING.

BUT WHAT BETTER WAY TO *HONOR* HIS MEMORY THAN TO ENSURE THAT HIS LAST LABOR OF LOVE IS RELEASED FOR *EVERYONE* TO ENJOY.

NO... SHE CAN'T DO THIS! IT'S NOT SAFE!

THEREFORE, I'M PLEASED TO ANNOUNCE THAT THE *B-LINK 2.0* IS *NOW AVAILABLE* WORLDWIDE.

ERASE THE BOUNDARY BETWEEN THE VIRTUAL AND THE REAL AND EXPERIENCE THE *HYPER SCAPE* LIKE *NEVER* BEFORE.

ENJOY MATHIEU'S LAST GIFT TO YOU. TO US *ALL.* THANK YOU.

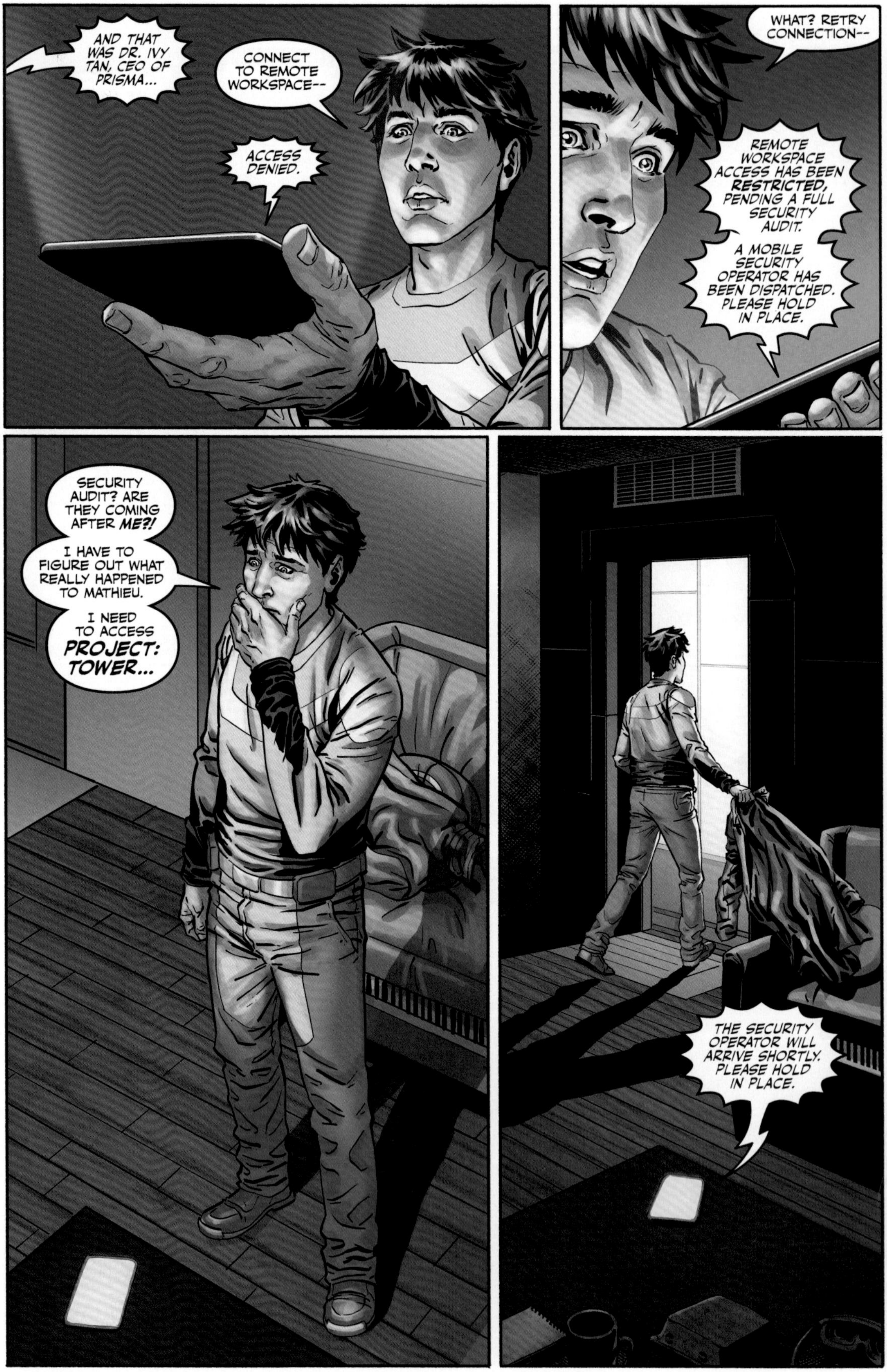
AND THAT WAS DR. IVY TAN, CEO OF PRISMA...
CONNECT TO REMOTE WORKSPACE--
ACCESS DENIED.
WHAT? RETRY CONNECTION--
REMOTE WORKSPACE ACCESS HAS BEEN RESTRICTED, PENDING A FULL SECURITY AUDIT.
A MOBILE SECURITY OPERATOR HAS BEEN DISPATCHED. PLEASE HOLD IN PLACE.
SECURITY AUDIT? ARE THEY COMING AFTER ME?!
I HAVE TO FIGURE OUT WHAT REALLY HAPPENED TO MATHIEU.
I NEED TO ACCESS PROJECT: TOWER...
THE SECURITY OPERATOR WILL ARRIVE SHORTLY. PLEASE HOLD IN PLACE.

NEW B-LINK

...full body immersion...

T-LOOP

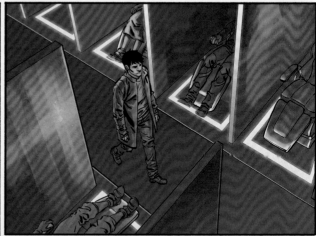

IF I CAN AVOID PRISMA SECURITY AND GET TO MATHIEU'S LABX...

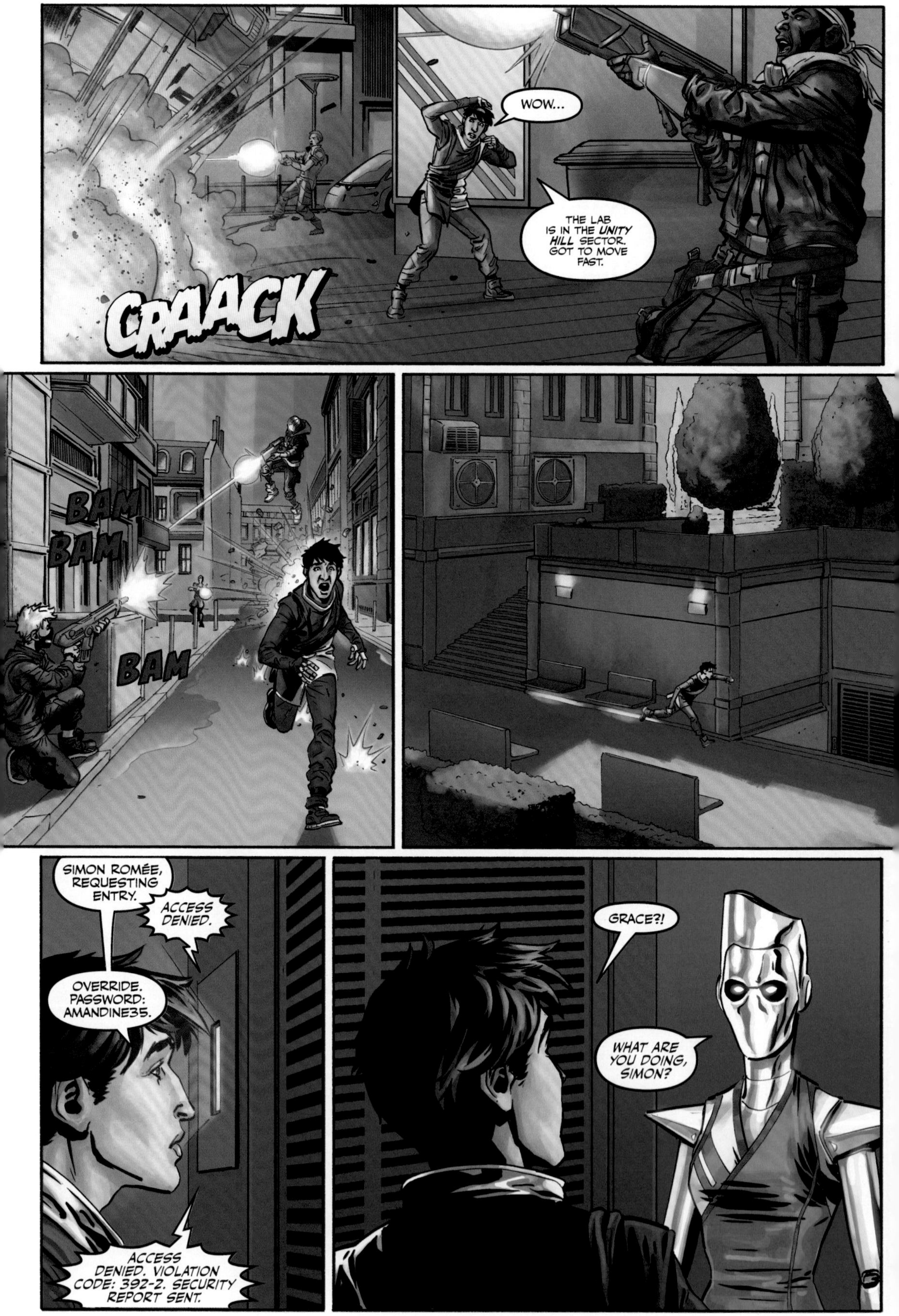
WOW...
THE LAB IS IN THE UNITY HILL SECTOR. GOT TO MOVE FAST.
CRAACK
BAM
BAM
BAM
SIMON ROMÉE, REQUESTING ENTRY.
ACCESS DENIED.
OVERRIDE. PASSWORD: AMANDINE35.
ACCESS DENIED. VIOLATION CODE: 392-2. SECURITY REPORT SENT.
GRACE?!
WHAT ARE YOU DOING, SIMON?

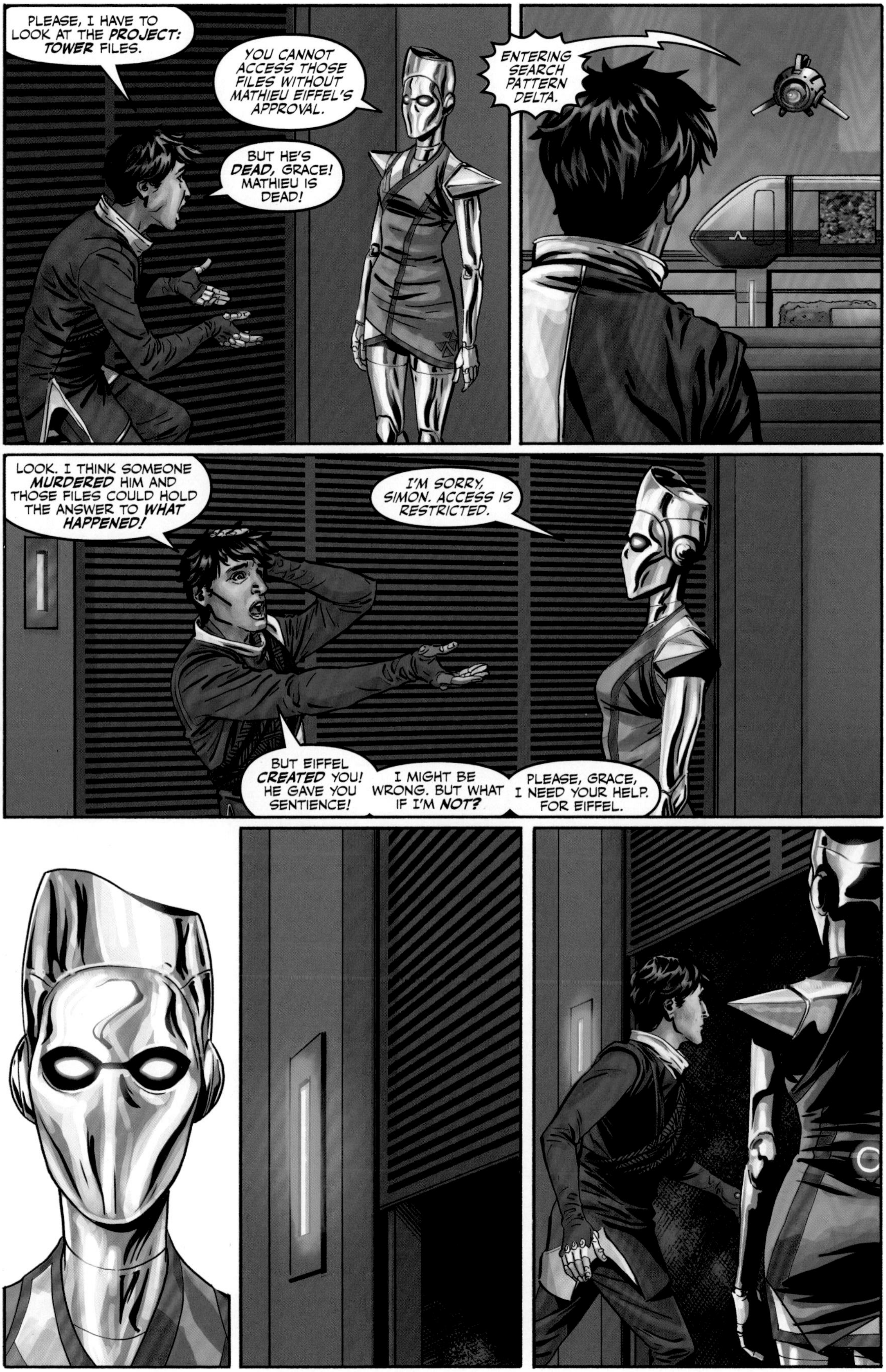
PLEASE, I HAVE TO LOOK AT THE *PROJECT: TOWER* FILES.
YOU CANNOT ACCESS THOSE FILES WITHOUT MATHIEU EIFFEL'S APPROVAL.
BUT HE'S *DEAD,* GRACE! MATHIEU IS DEAD!
ENTERING SEARCH PATTERN DELTA.
LOOK. I THINK SOMEONE *MURDERED* HIM AND THOSE FILES COULD HOLD THE ANSWER TO *WHAT HAPPENED!*
I'M SORRY, SIMON. ACCESS IS RESTRICTED.
BUT EIFFEL *CREATED* YOU! HE GAVE YOU SENTIENCE!
I MIGHT BE WRONG. BUT WHAT IF I'M *NOT?*
PLEASE, GRACE, I NEED YOUR HELP. FOR EIFFEL.

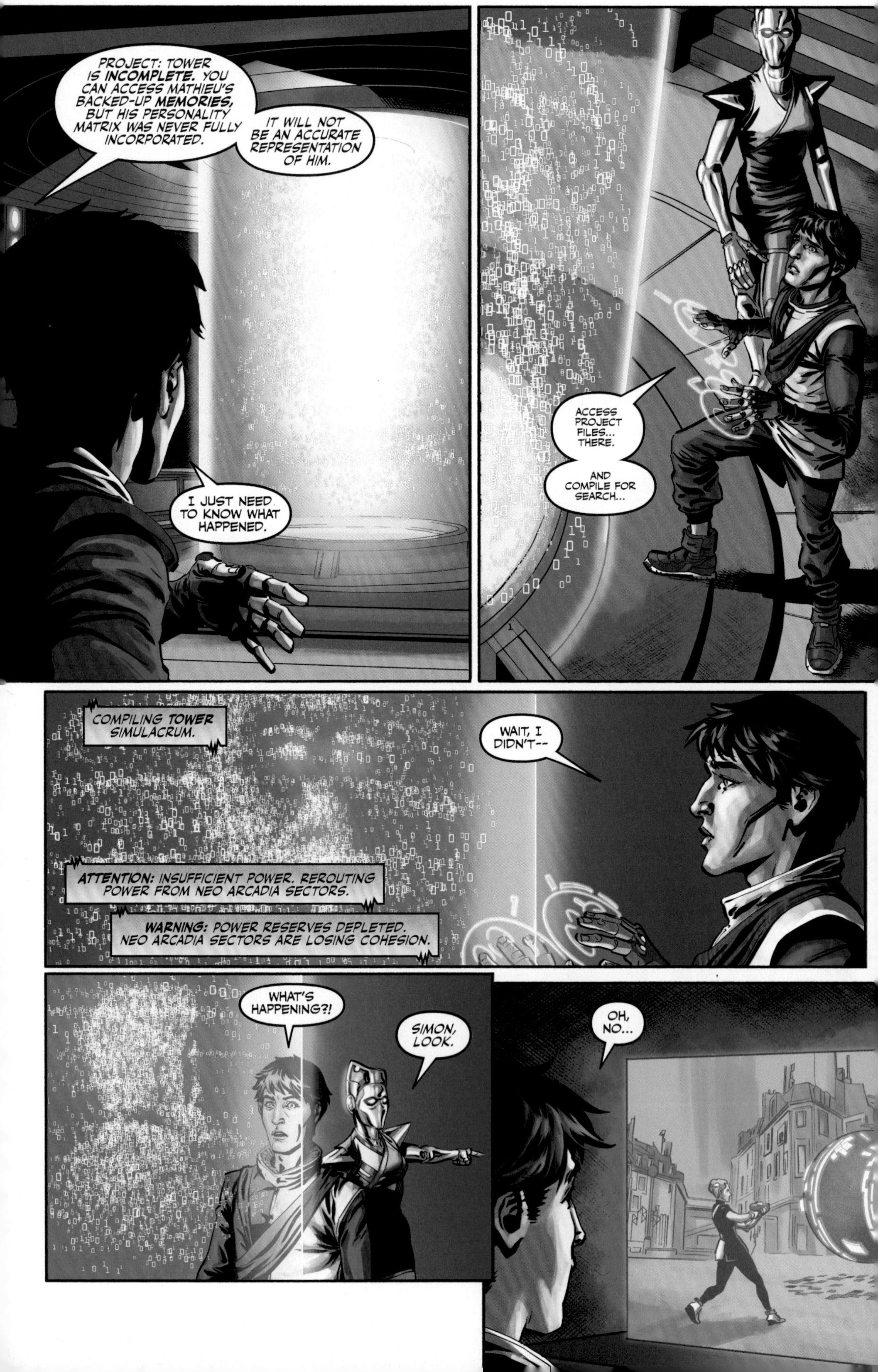
PROJECT: TOWER IS INCOMPLETE. YOU CAN ACCESS MATHIEU'S BACKED-UP MEMORIES, BUT HIS PERSONALITY MATRIX WAS NEVER FULLY INCORPORATED.
IT WILL NOT BE AN ACCURATE REPRESENTATION OF HIM.
I JUST NEED TO KNOW WHAT HAPPENED.
ACCESS PROJECT FILES... THERE.
AND COMPILE FOR SEARCH...
COMPILING TOWER SIMULACRUM.
WAIT, I DIDN'T--
ATTENTION: INSUFFICIENT POWER. REROUTING POWER FROM NEO ARCADIA SECTORS.
WARNING: POWER RESERVES DEPLETED. NEO ARCADIA SECTORS ARE LOSING COHESION.
WHAT'S HAPPENING?!
SIMON, LOOK.
OH, NO...

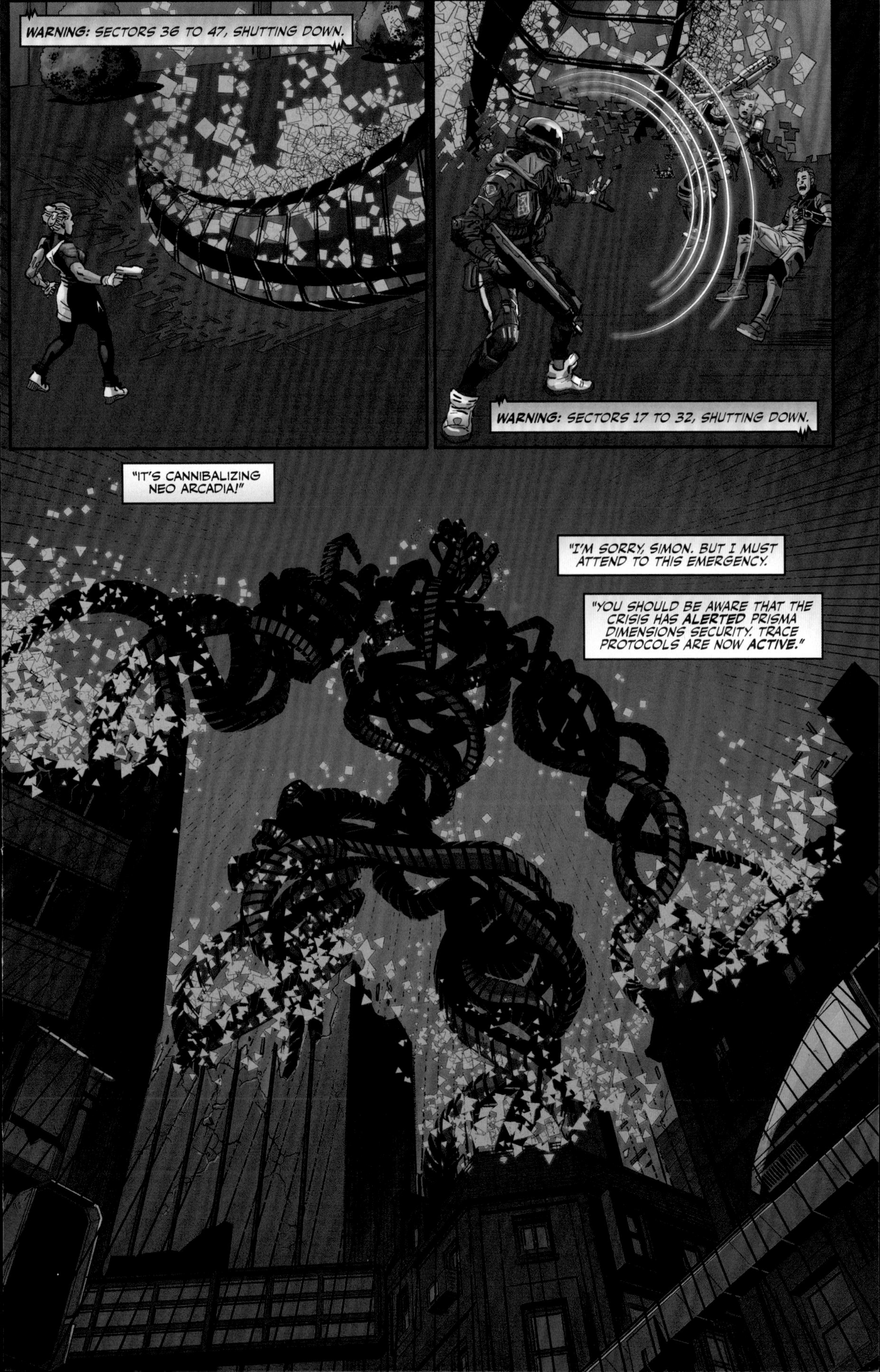
WARNING: SECTORS 36 TO 47, SHUTTING DOWN.
WARNING: SECTORS 17 TO 32, SHUTTING DOWN.
"IT'S CANNIBALIZING NEO ARCADIA!"
"I'M SORRY, SIMON. BUT I MUST ATTEND TO THIS EMERGENCY.
"YOU SHOULD BE AWARE THAT THE CRISIS HAS ALERTED PRISMA DIMENSIONS SECURITY. TRACE PROTOCOLS ARE NOW ACTIVE."

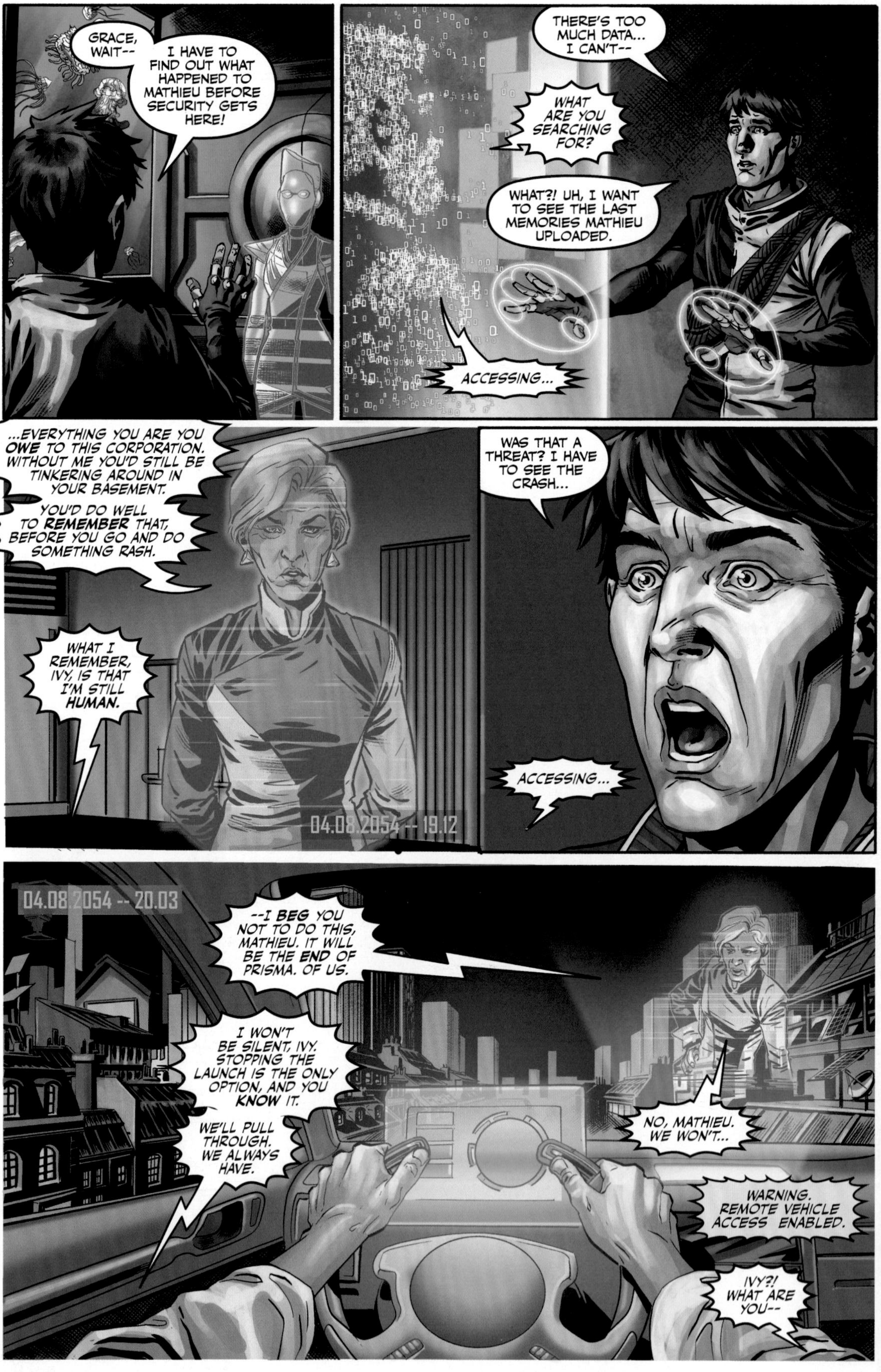
GRACE, WAIT--
I HAVE TO FIND OUT WHAT HAPPENED TO MATHIEU BEFORE SECURITY GETS HERE!
THERE'S TOO MUCH DATA... I CAN'T--
WHAT ARE YOU SEARCHING FOR?
WHAT?! UH, I WANT TO SEE THE LAST MEMORIES MATHIEU UPLOADED.
ACCESSING...
...EVERYTHING YOU ARE YOU OWE TO THIS CORPORATION. WITHOUT ME YOU'D STILL BE TINKERING AROUND IN YOUR BASEMENT.
YOU'D DO WELL TO REMEMBER THAT, BEFORE YOU GO AND DO SOMETHING RASH.
WHAT I REMEMBER, IVY, IS THAT I'M STILL HUMAN.
04.08.2054 -- 19.12
WAS THAT A THREAT? I HAVE TO SEE THE CRASH...
ACCESSING...
04.08.2054 -- 20.03
--I BEG YOU NOT TO DO THIS, MATHIEU. IT WILL BE THE END OF PRISMA. OF US.
I WON'T BE SILENT, IVY. STOPPING THE LAUNCH IS THE ONLY OPTION, AND YOU KNOW IT.
WE'LL PULL THROUGH. WE ALWAYS HAVE.
NO, MATHIEU. WE WON'T...
WARNING. REMOTE VEHICLE ACCESS ENABLED.
IVY?! WHAT ARE YOU--

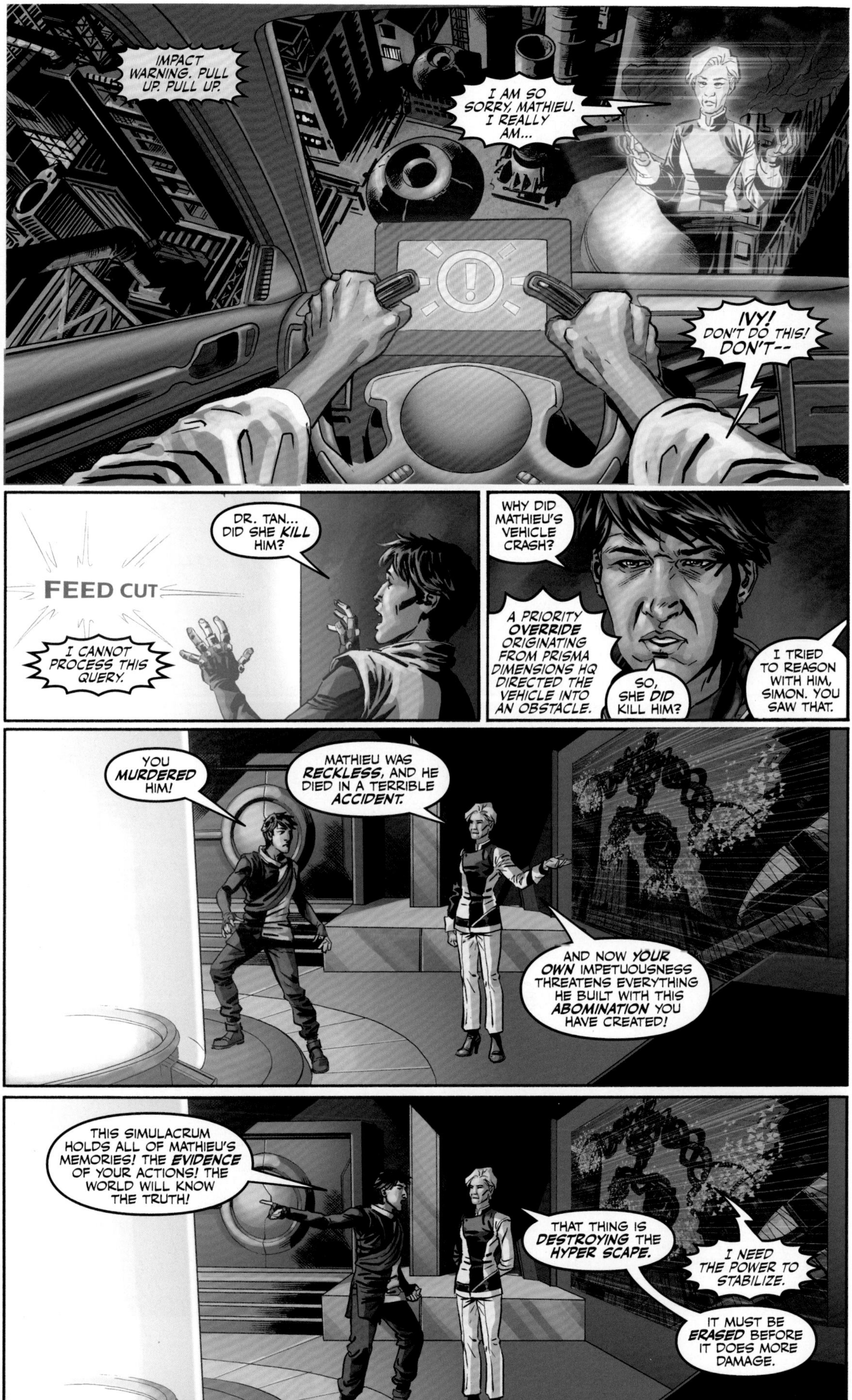
IMPACT WARNING. PULL UP. PULL UP.
I AM SO SORRY, MATHIEU. I REALLY AM...
IVY! DON'T DO THIS! DON'T--
FEED CUT
DR. TAN... DID SHE KILL HIM?
I CANNOT PROCESS THIS QUERY.
WHY DID MATHIEU'S VEHICLE CRASH?
A PRIORITY OVERRIDE ORIGINATING FROM PRISMA DIMENSIONS HQ DIRECTED THE VEHICLE INTO AN OBSTACLE.
SO, SHE DID KILL HIM?
I TRIED TO REASON WITH HIM, SIMON. YOU SAW THAT.
YOU MURDERED HIM!
MATHIEU WAS RECKLESS, AND HE DIED IN A TERRIBLE ACCIDENT.
AND NOW YOUR OWN IMPETUOUSNESS THREATENS EVERYTHING HE BUILT WITH THIS ABOMINATION YOU HAVE CREATED!
THIS SIMULACRUM HOLDS ALL OF MATHIEU'S MEMORIES! THE EVIDENCE OF YOUR ACTIONS! THE WORLD WILL KNOW THE TRUTH!
THAT THING IS DESTROYING THE HYPER SCAPE.
I NEED THE POWER TO STABILIZE.
IT MUST BE ERASED BEFORE IT DOES MORE DAMAGE.

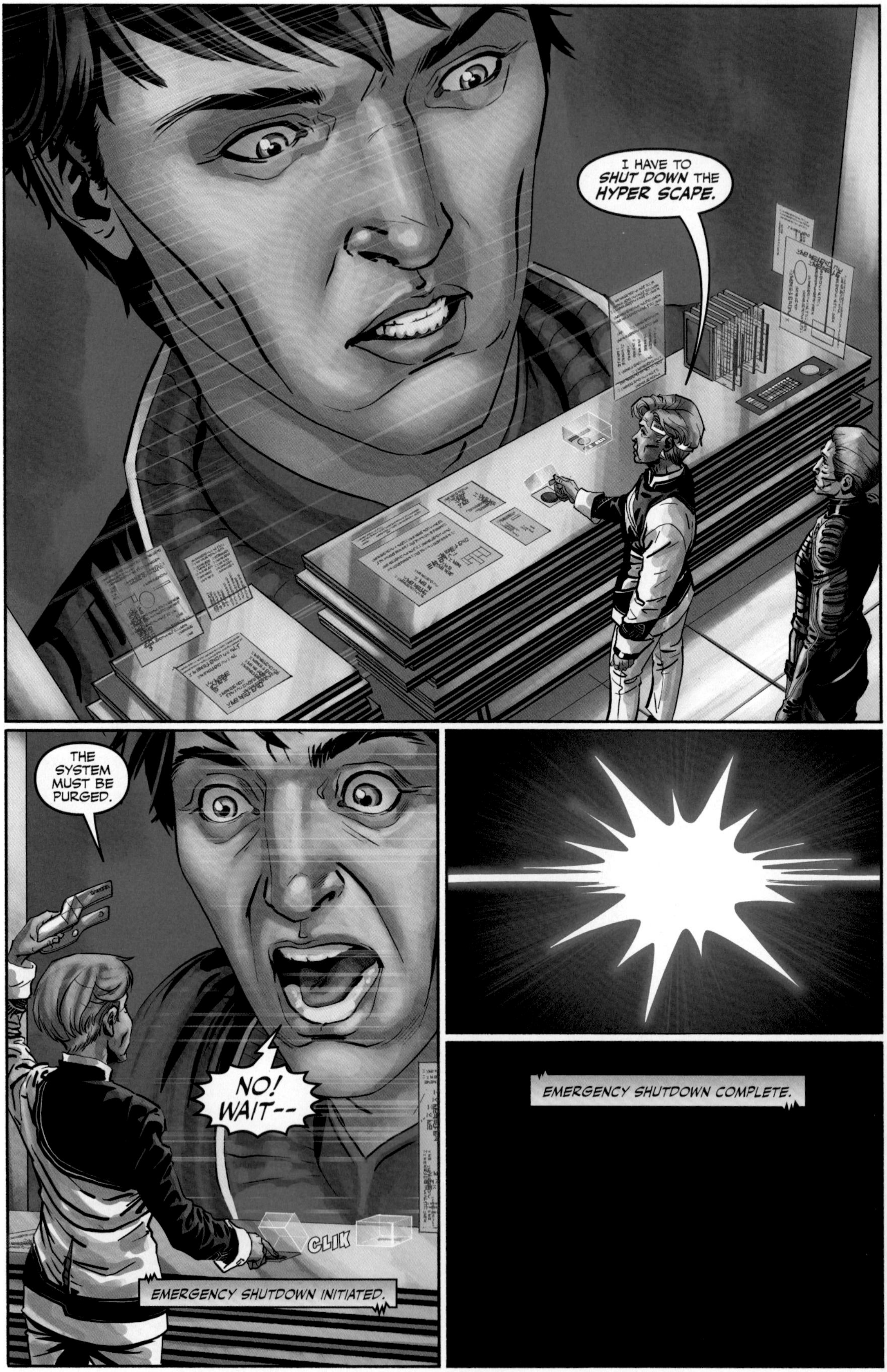
I HAVE TO SHUT DOWN THE HYPER SCAPE.
THE SYSTEM MUST BE PURGED.
NO! WAIT--
CLIK
EMERGENCY SHUTDOWN INITIATED.
EMERGENCY SHUTDOWN COMPLETE.

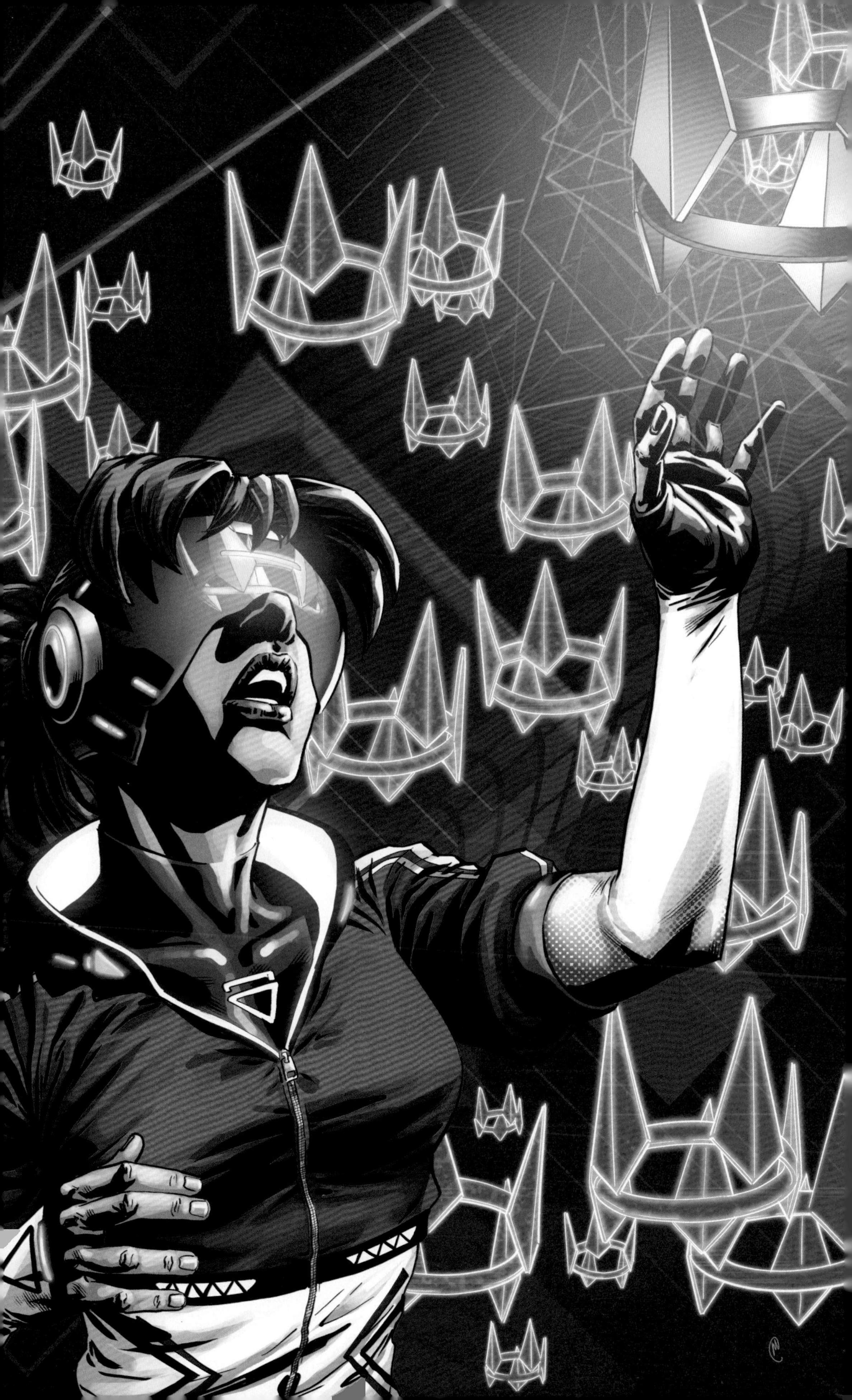

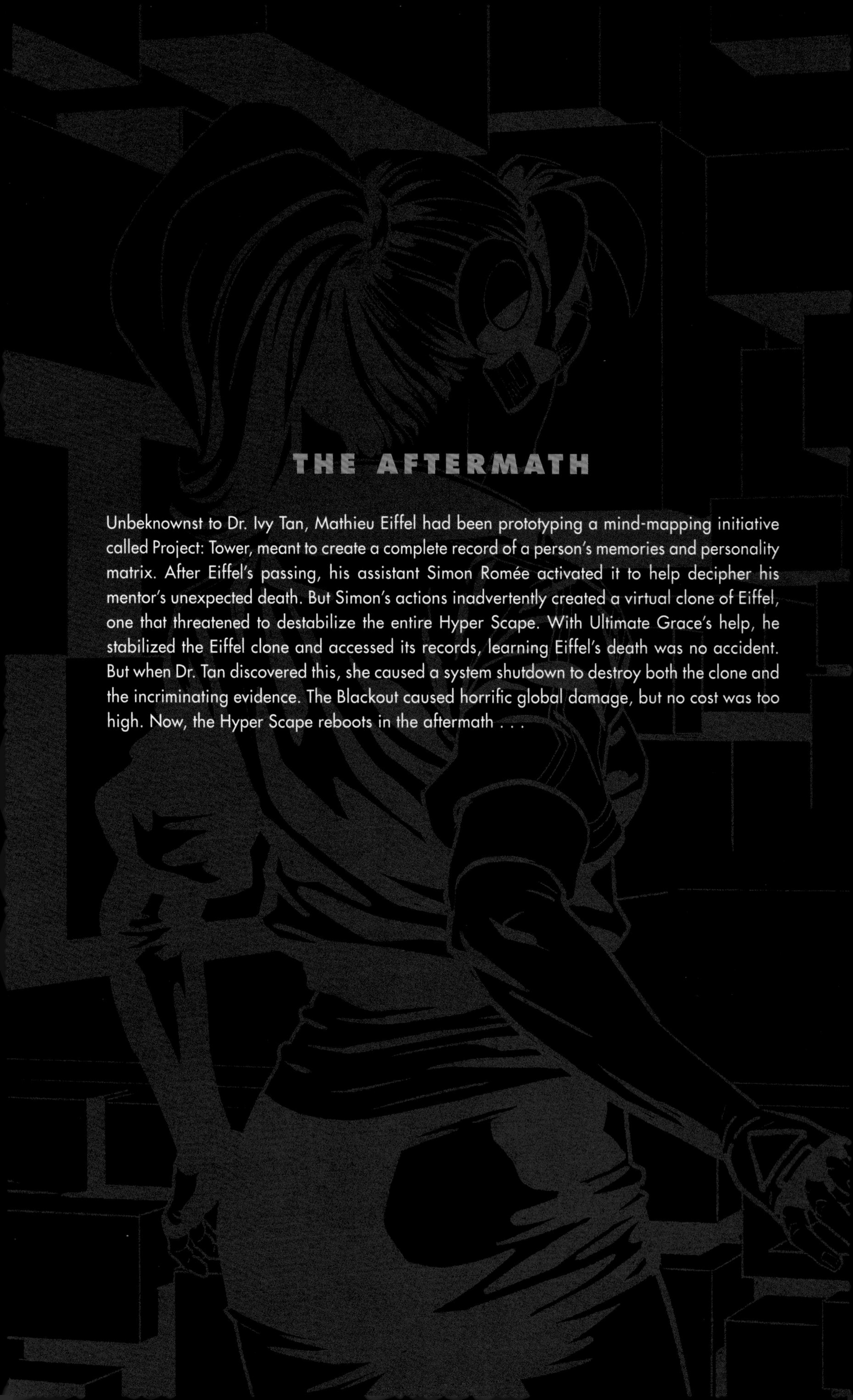

THE AFTERMATH

Unbeknownst to Dr. Ivy Tan, Mathieu Eiffel had been prototyping a mind-mapping initiative called Project: Tower, meant to create a complete record of a person's memories and personality matrix. After Eiffel's passing, his assistant Simon Romée activated it to help decipher his mentor's unexpected death. But Simon's actions inadvertently created a virtual clone of Eiffel, one that threatened to destabilize the entire Hyper Scape. With Ultimate Grace's help, he stabilized the Eiffel clone and accessed its records, learning Eiffel's death was no accident. But when Dr. Tan discovered this, she caused a system shutdown to destroy both the clone and the incriminating evidence. The Blackout caused horrific global damage, but no cost was too high. Now, the Hyper Scape reboots in the aftermath . . .

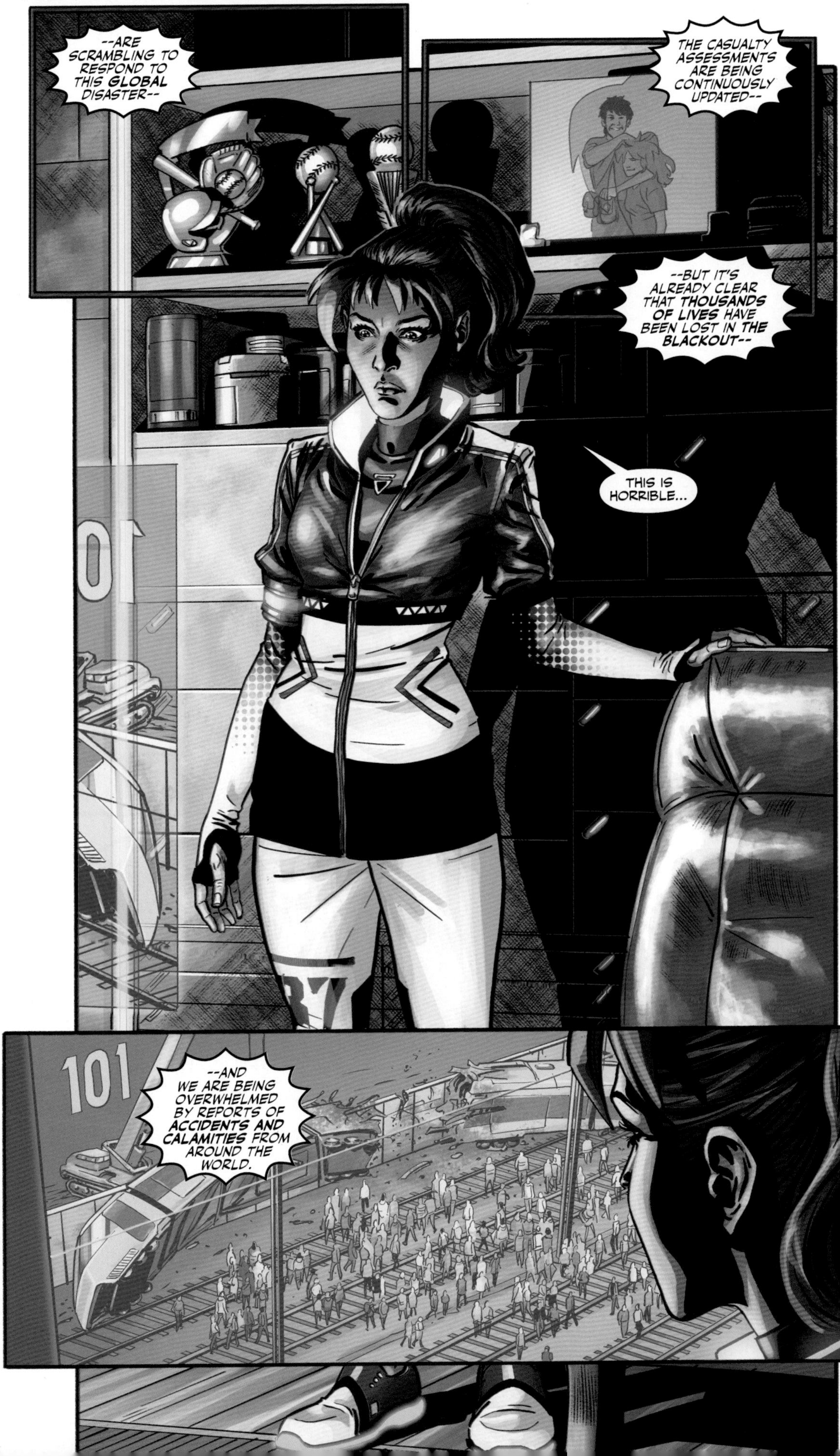
--ARE SCRAMBLING TO RESPOND TO THIS GLOBAL DISASTER--
THE CASUALTY ASSESSMENTS ARE BEING CONTINUOUSLY UPDATED--
--BUT IT'S ALREADY CLEAR THAT THOUSANDS OF LIVES HAVE BEEN LOST IN THE BLACKOUT--
THIS IS HORRIBLE...
101
--AND WE ARE BEING OVERWHELMED BY REPORTS OF ACCIDENTS AND CALAMITIES FROM AROUND THE WORLD.

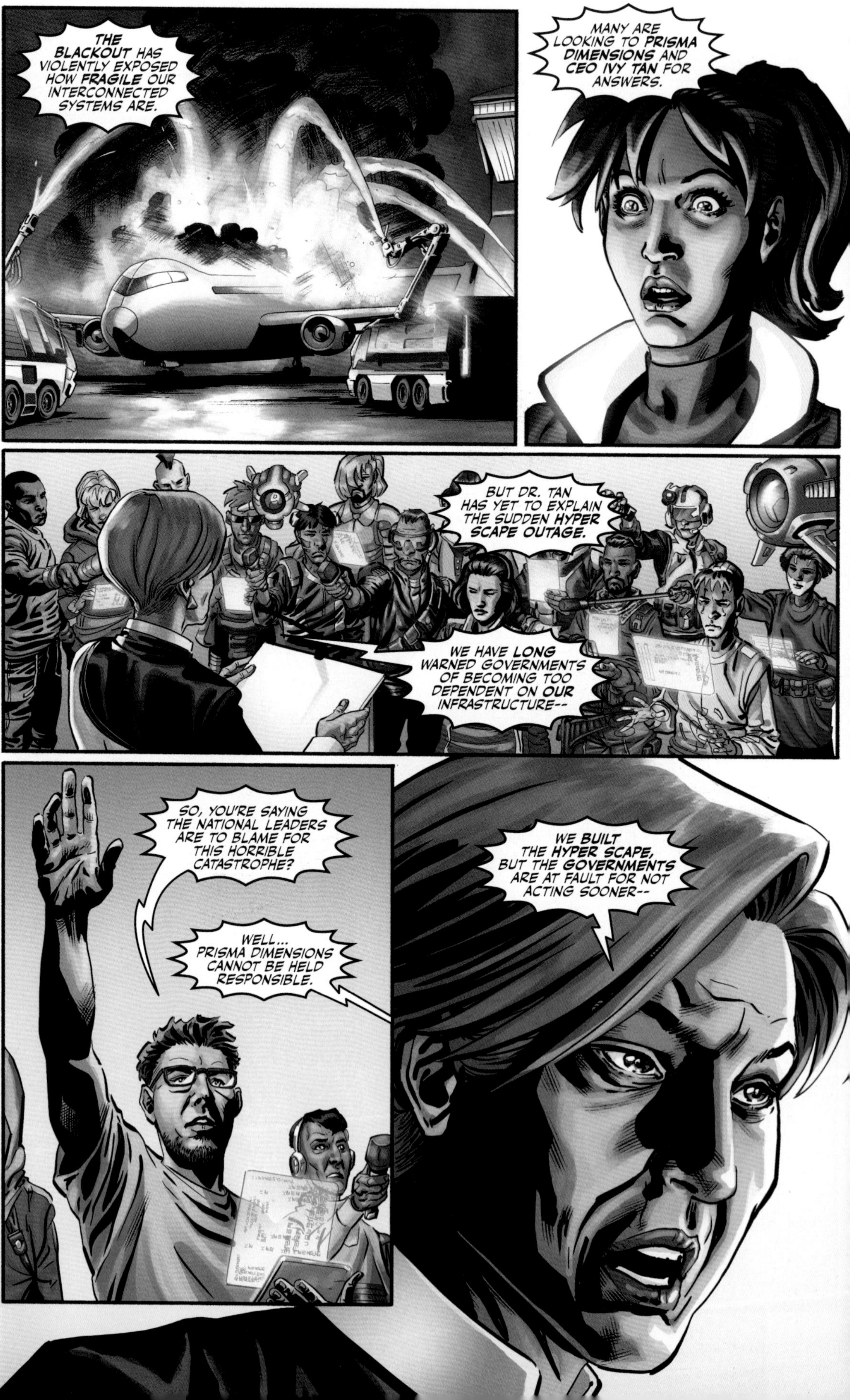

THE BLACKOUT HAS VIOLENTLY EXPOSED HOW FRAGILE OUR INTERCONNECTED SYSTEMS ARE.
MANY ARE LOOKING TO PRISMA DIMENSIONS AND CEO IVY TAN FOR ANSWERS.
BUT DR. TAN HAS YET TO EXPLAIN THE SUDDEN HYPER SCAPE OUTAGE.
WE HAVE LONG WARNED GOVERNMENTS OF BECOMING TOO DEPENDENT ON OUR INFRASTRUCTURE--
SO, YOU'RE SAYING THE NATIONAL LEADERS ARE TO BLAME FOR THIS HORRIBLE CATASTROPHE?
WE BUILT THE HYPER SCAPE, BUT THE GOVERNMENTS ARE AT FAULT FOR NOT ACTING SOONER--
WELL... PRISMA DIMENSIONS CANNOT BE HELD RESPONSIBLE.

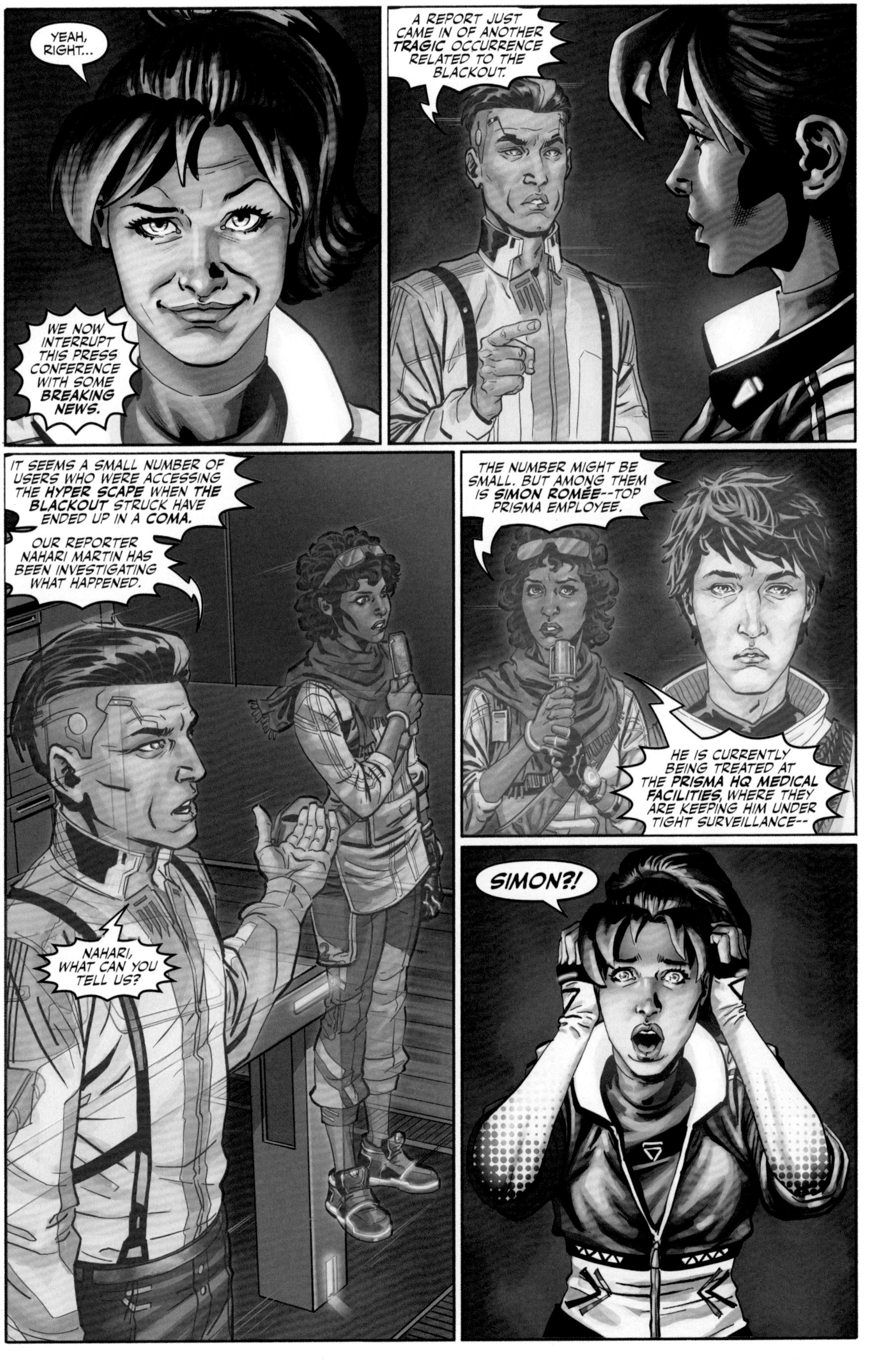
YEAH, RIGHT...
WE NOW INTERRUPT THIS PRESS CONFERENCE WITH SOME BREAKING NEWS.
A REPORT JUST CAME IN OF ANOTHER TRAGIC OCCURRENCE RELATED TO THE BLACKOUT.
IT SEEMS A SMALL NUMBER OF USERS WHO WERE ACCESSING THE HYPER SCAPE WHEN THE BLACKOUT STRUCK HAVE ENDED UP IN A COMA.
OUR REPORTER NAHARI MARTIN HAS BEEN INVESTIGATING WHAT HAPPENED.
NAHARI, WHAT CAN YOU TELL US?
THE NUMBER MIGHT BE SMALL. BUT AMONG THEM IS SIMON ROMÉE--TOP PRISMA EMPLOYEE.
HE IS CURRENTLY BEING TREATED AT THE PRISMA HQ MEDICAL FACILITIES, WHERE THEY ARE KEEPING HIM UNDER TIGHT SURVEILLANCE--
SIMON?!

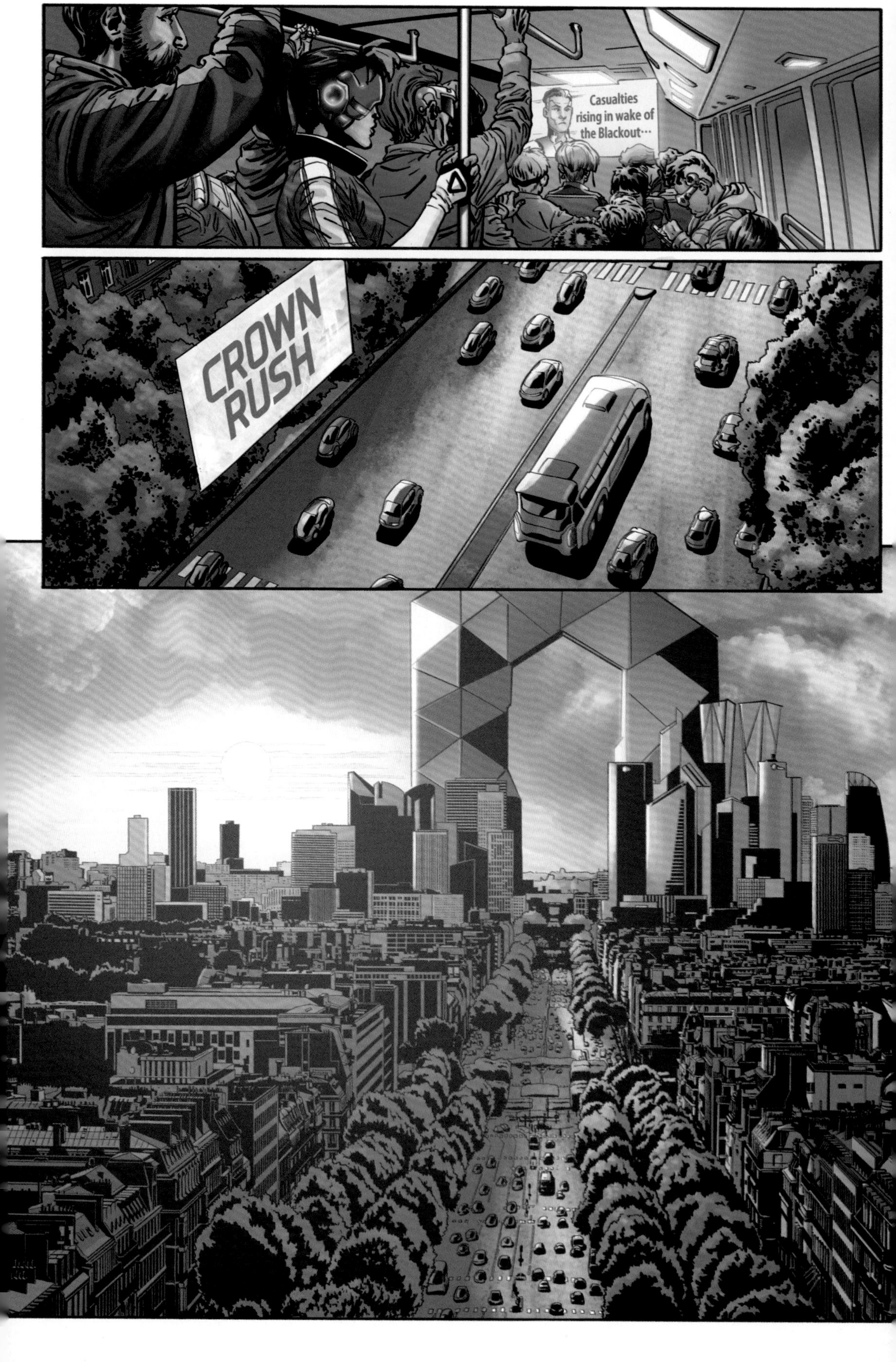
Casualties rising in wake of the Blackout…
CROWN RUSH

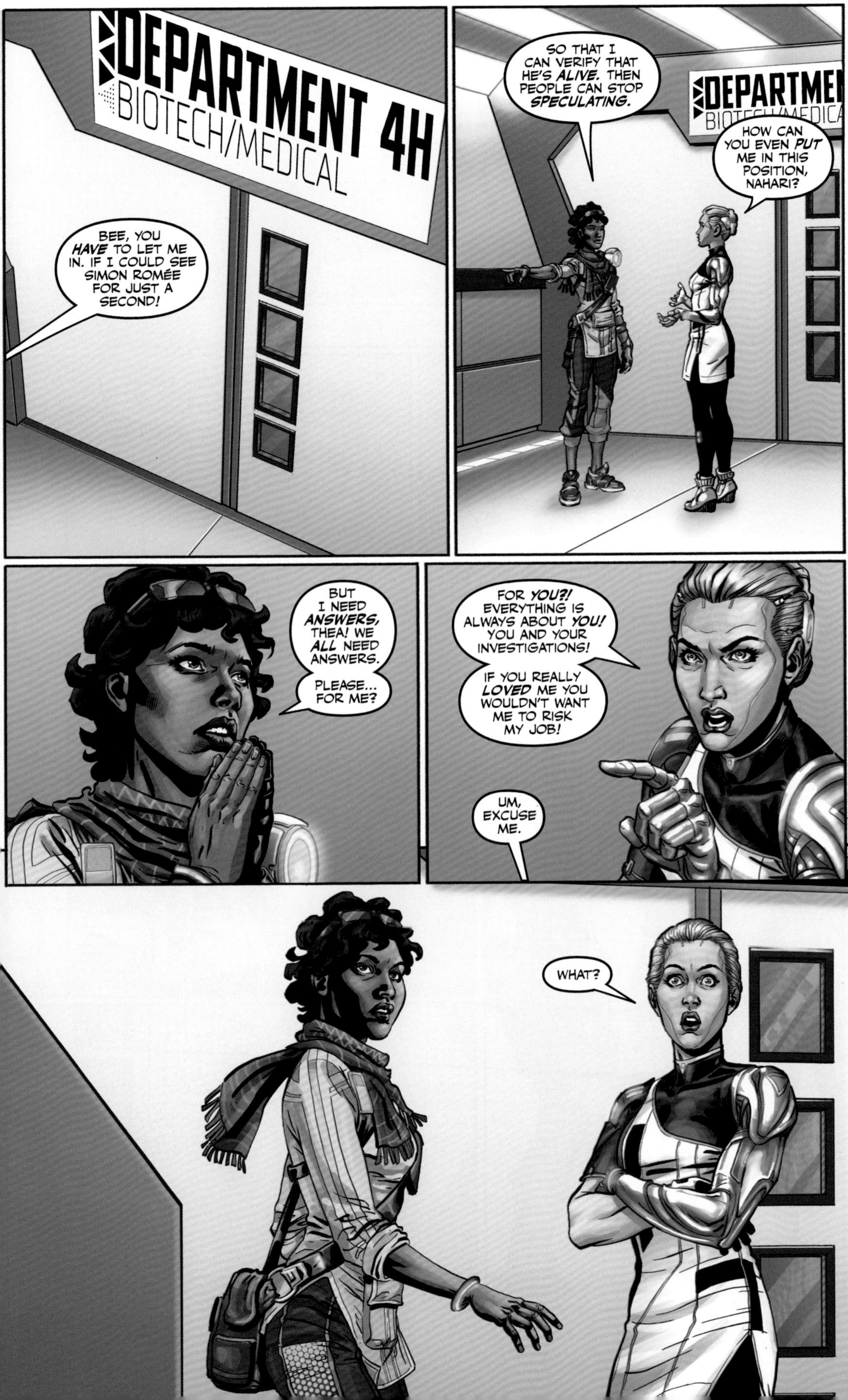
DEPARTMENT 4H
BIOTECH/MEDICAL
BEE, YOU HAVE TO LET ME IN. IF I COULD SEE SIMON ROMÉE FOR JUST A SECOND!
SO THAT I CAN VERIFY THAT HE'S ALIVE. THEN PEOPLE CAN STOP SPECULATING.
HOW CAN YOU EVEN PUT ME IN THIS POSITION, NAHARI?
BUT I NEED ANSWERS, THEA! WE ALL NEED ANSWERS.
PLEASE... FOR ME?
FOR YOU?! EVERYTHING IS ALWAYS ABOUT YOU! YOU AND YOUR INVESTIGATIONS!
IF YOU REALLY LOVED ME YOU WOULDN'T WANT ME TO RISK MY JOB!
UM, EXCUSE ME.
WHAT?

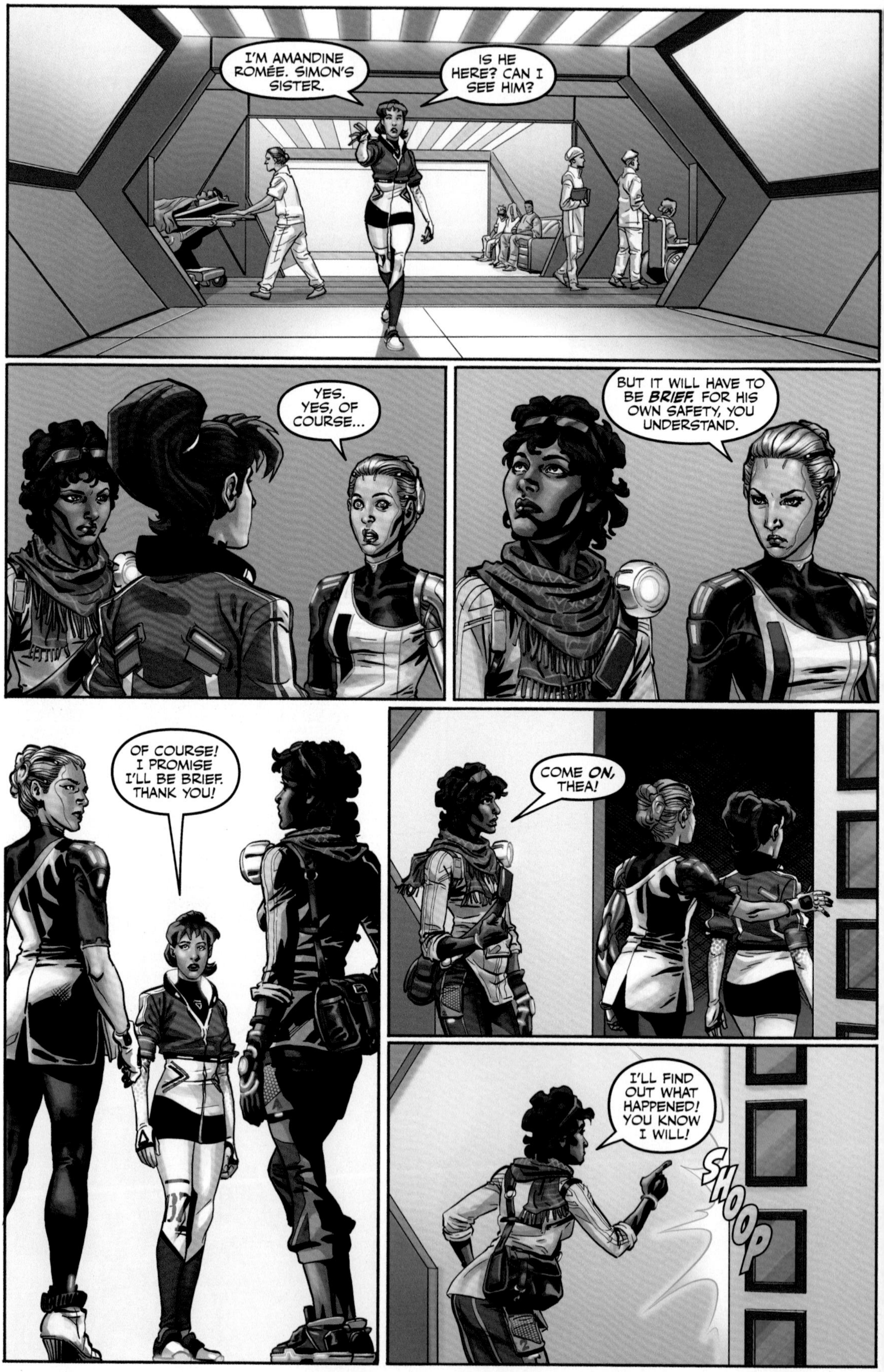
I'M AMANDINE ROMÉE. SIMON'S SISTER.
IS HE HERE? CAN I SEE HIM?
YES. YES, OF COURSE...
BUT IT WILL HAVE TO BE BRIEF. FOR HIS OWN SAFETY, YOU UNDERSTAND.
OF COURSE! I PROMISE I'LL BE BRIEF. THANK YOU!
COME ON, THEA!
I'LL FIND OUT WHAT HAPPENED! YOU KNOW I WILL!
SHOOP

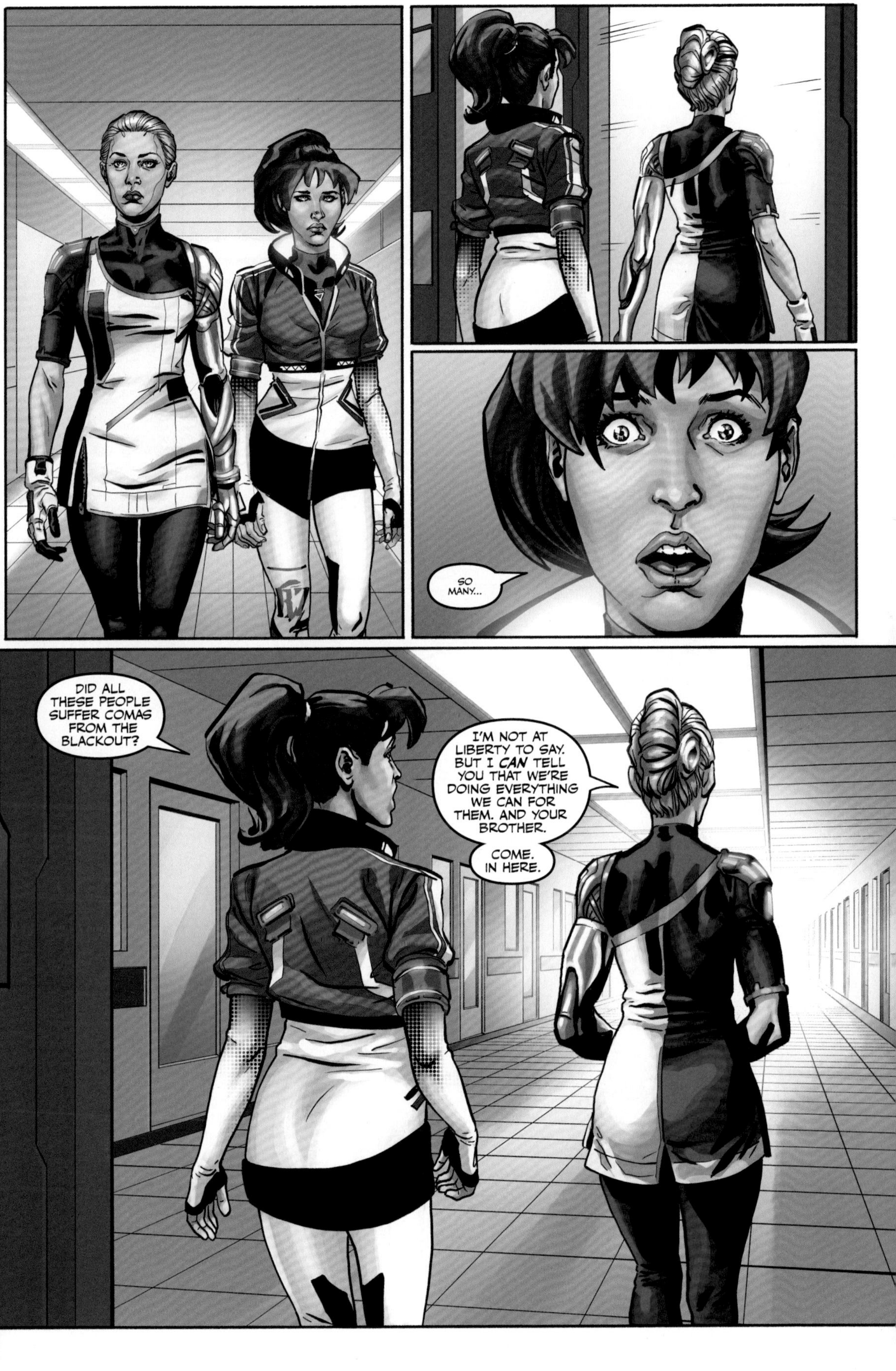
SO MANY...
DID ALL THESE PEOPLE SUFFER COMAS FROM THE BLACKOUT?
I'M NOT AT LIBERTY TO SAY. BUT I *CAN* TELL YOU THAT WE'RE DOING EVERYTHING WE CAN FOR THEM. AND YOUR BROTHER.
COME. IN HERE.

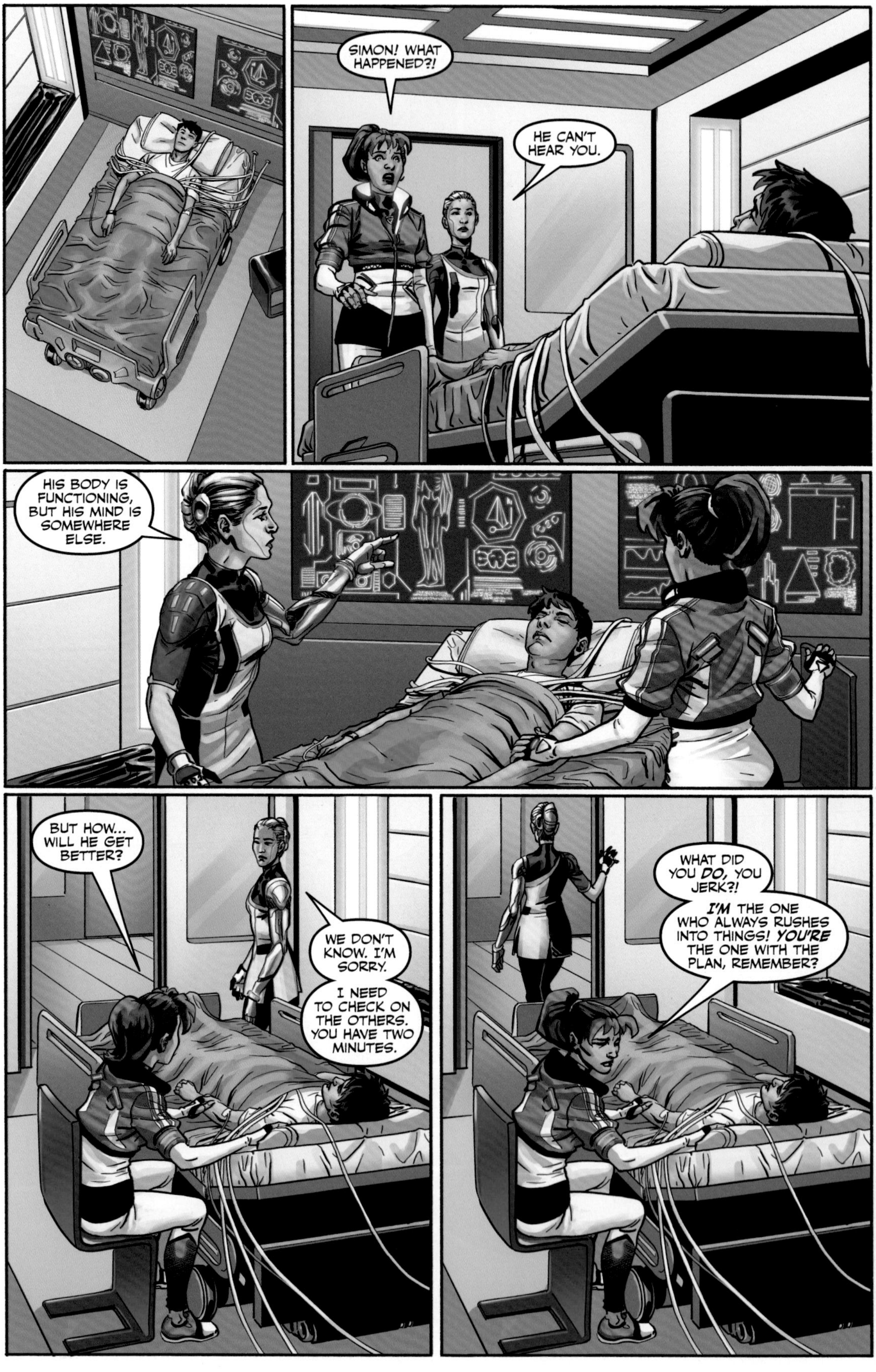
SIMON! WHAT HAPPENED?!
HE CAN'T HEAR YOU.
HIS BODY IS FUNCTIONING, BUT HIS MIND IS SOMEWHERE ELSE.
BUT HOW... WILL HE GET BETTER?
WE DON'T KNOW. I'M SORRY.
I NEED TO CHECK ON THE OTHERS. YOU HAVE TWO MINUTES.
WHAT DID YOU *DO*, YOU JERK?!
I'M THE ONE WHO ALWAYS RUSHES INTO THINGS! ***YOU'RE*** THE ONE WITH THE PLAN, REMEMBER?

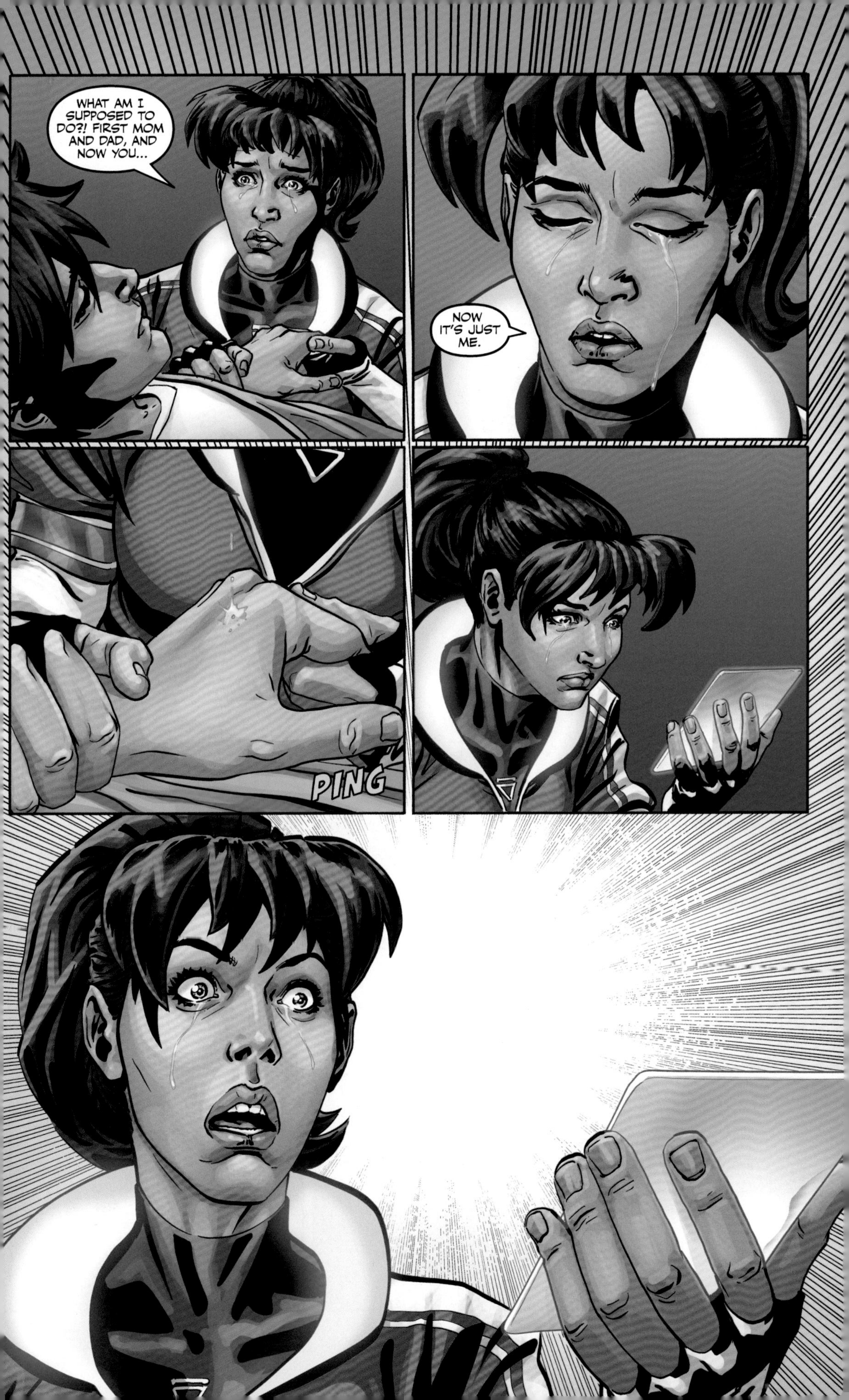
WHAT AM I SUPPOSED TO DO?! FIRST MOM AND DAD, AND NOW YOU...
NOW IT'S JUST ME.
PING

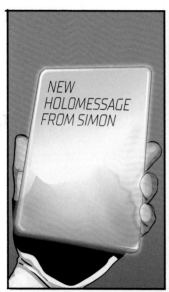

NEW
HOLOMESSAGE
FROM SIMON

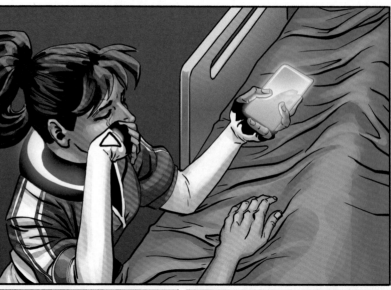

SIMON...?

WHAT'S
GOING
ON?!

COMA...THE BLACKOUT...

SEARCH: COMA, THE BLACKOUT, HYPER SCAPE, PRISMA.

-Coma - A coma is a deep state of...

-My blackout led to a coma...

-Mathieu Eiffel, creator of the HYPER SCAPE, dies in accident...

-'Who cares about the Lost? -- The comatose victims no one will speak of,' by Nahari Martin

NAHARI? SHE WAS AT PRISMA TOO...

--THE HACKS THAT ARE AFFECTING NEO ARCADIA IN DIFFERENT WAYS. PRISMA DIMENSIONS WON'T EVEN DISCUSS THEIR EXISTENCE.

t the Lost? -- The comatose ill speak of,' Nahari Martin

HACKS?

NOR WILL THEY ACKNOWLEDGE THE LOST, THOSE POOR USERS WHO ENDED UP IN A COMA DURING THE BLACKOUT.

ARE THESE MYSTERIOUS HACKS AND THE LOST CONNECTED SOMEHOW?

I HAVE TO TALK TO HER...

AND HOW DO THEY RELATE TO THE BLACKOUT?

CALL: NAHARI MARTIN.

CALLING...

WE WILL KEEP ASKING THESE QUESTIONS UNTIL--

BRRRR BRRRR

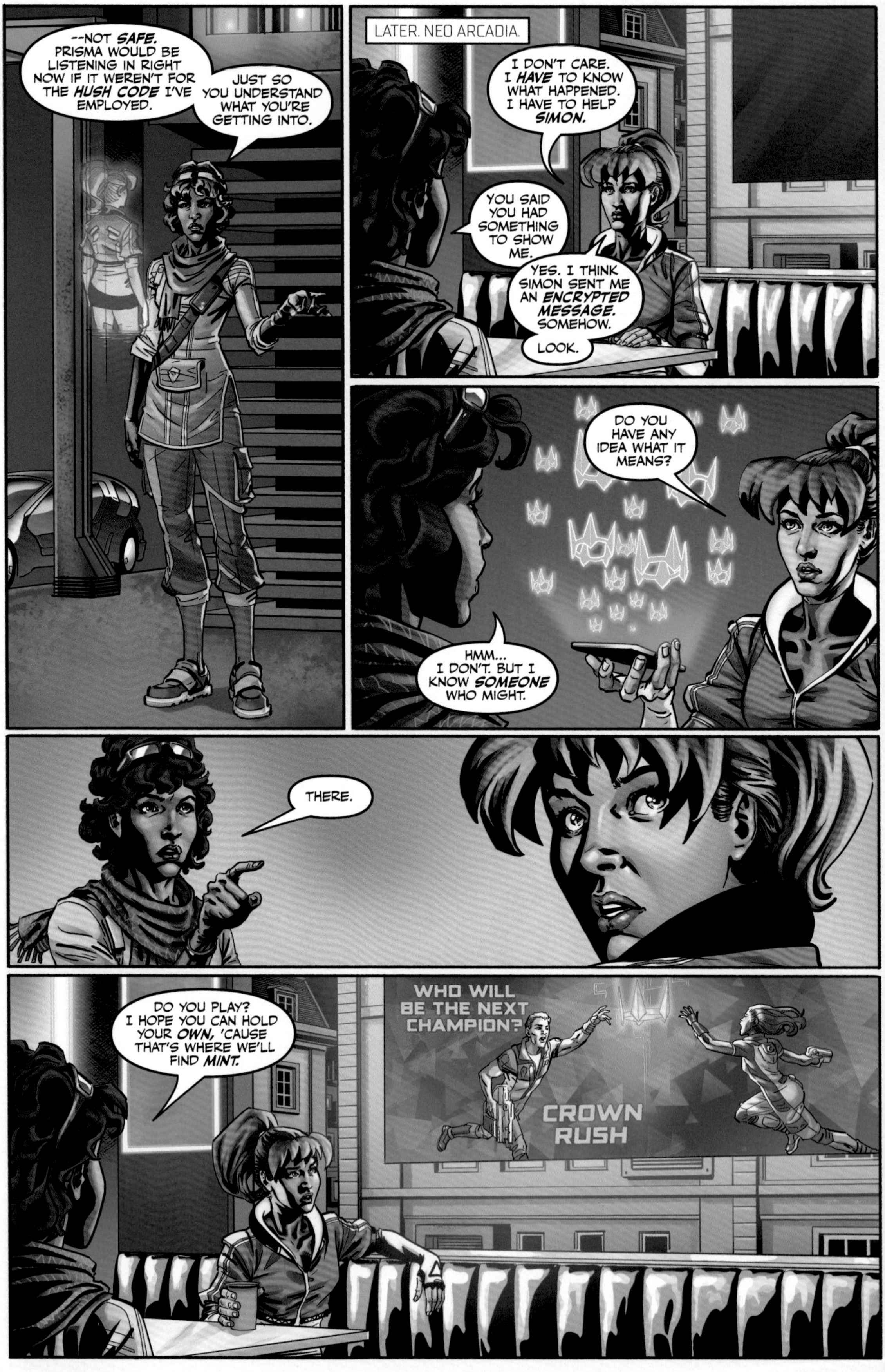
--NOT SAFE. PRISMA WOULD BE LISTENING IN RIGHT NOW IF IT WEREN'T FOR THE HUSH CODE I'VE EMPLOYED.
JUST SO YOU UNDERSTAND WHAT YOU'RE GETTING INTO.
LATER. NEO ARCADIA.
I DON'T CARE. I HAVE TO KNOW WHAT HAPPENED. I HAVE TO HELP SIMON.
YOU SAID YOU HAD SOMETHING TO SHOW ME.
YES. I THINK SIMON SENT ME AN ENCRYPTED MESSAGE. SOMEHOW.
LOOK.
DO YOU HAVE ANY IDEA WHAT IT MEANS?
HMM... I DON'T. BUT I KNOW SOMEONE WHO MIGHT.
THERE.
DO YOU PLAY? I HOPE YOU CAN HOLD YOUR OWN, 'CAUSE THAT'S WHERE WE'LL FIND MINT.
WHO WILL BE THE NEXT CHAMPION?
CROWN RUSH

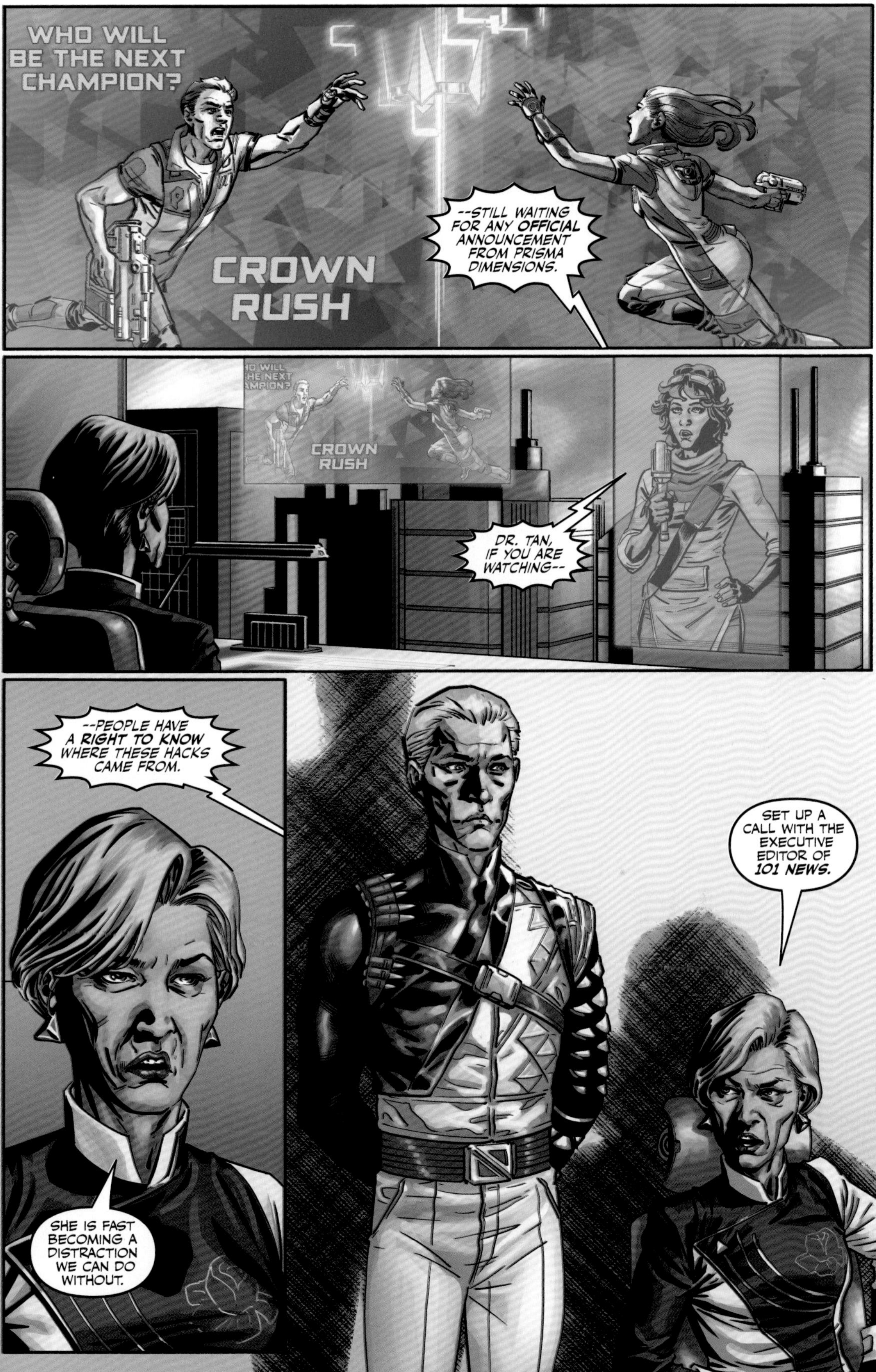
WHO WILL BE THE NEXT CHAMPION?
CROWN RUSH
--STILL WAITING FOR ANY OFFICIAL ANNOUNCEMENT FROM PRISMA DIMENSIONS.
DR. TAN, IF YOU ARE WATCHING--
--PEOPLE HAVE A RIGHT TO KNOW WHERE THESE HACKS CAME FROM.
SHE IS FAST BECOMING A DISTRACTION WE CAN DO WITHOUT.
SET UP A CALL WITH THE EXECUTIVE EDITOR OF 101 NEWS.

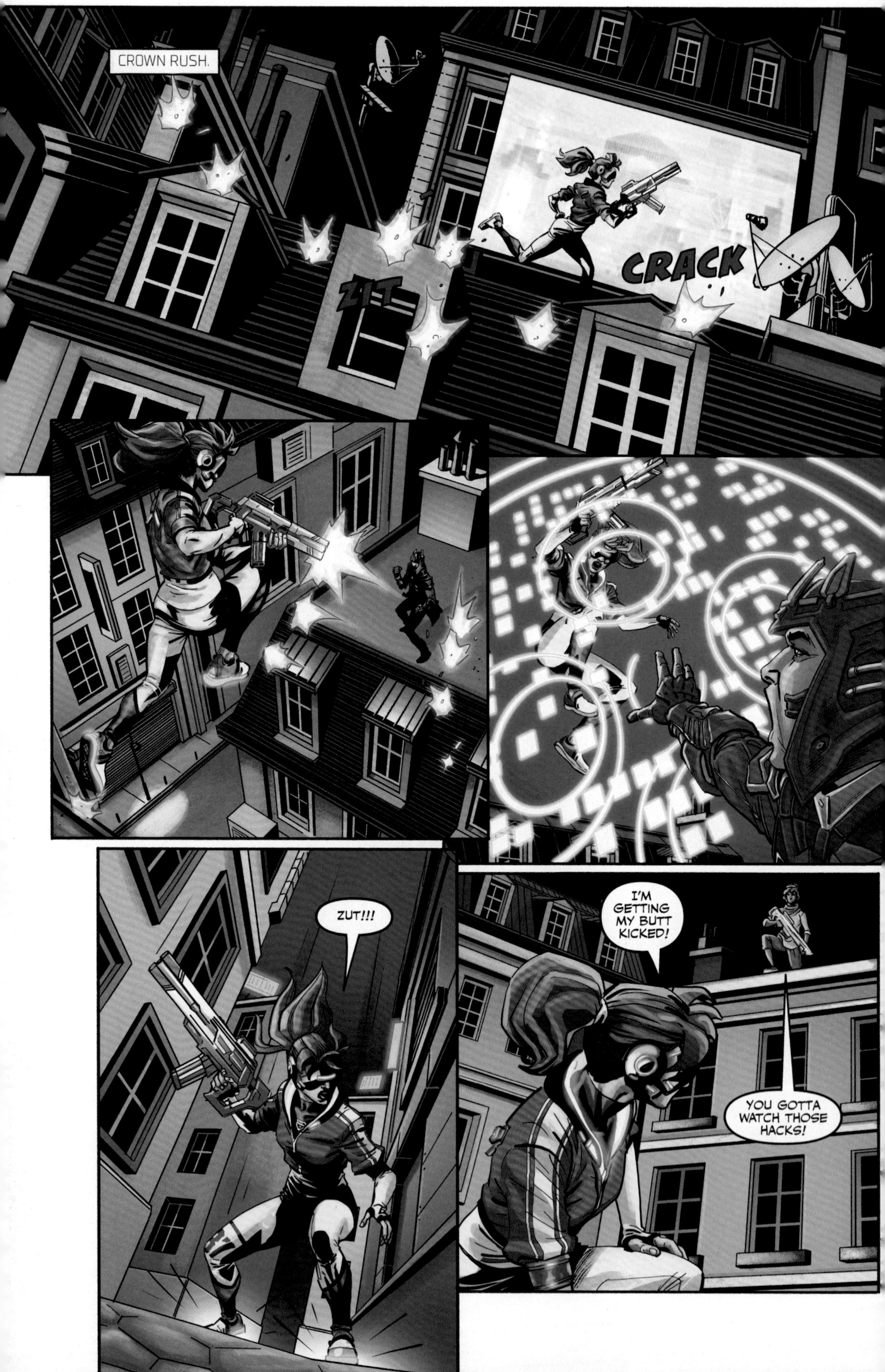
CROWN RUSH.
ZIT
CRACK
ZUT!!!
I'M GETTING MY BUTT KICKED!
YOU GOTTA WATCH THOSE HACKS!

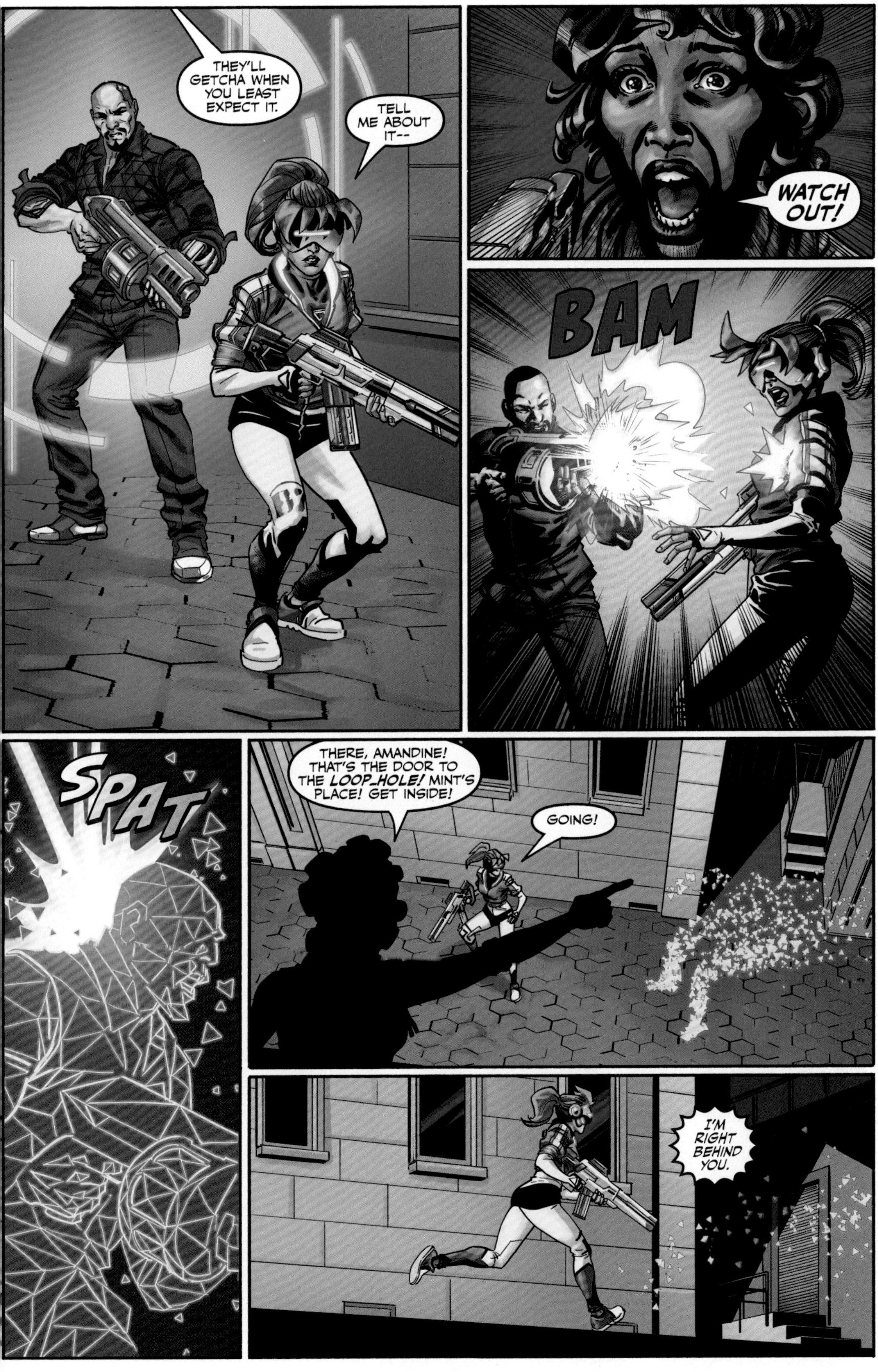
THEY'LL GETCHA WHEN YOU LEAST EXPECT IT.
TELL ME ABOUT IT--
WATCH OUT!
BAM
SPAT
THERE, AMANDINE! THAT'S THE DOOR TO THE LOOP-HOLE! MINT'S PLACE! GET INSIDE!
GOING!
I'M RIGHT BEHIND YOU.

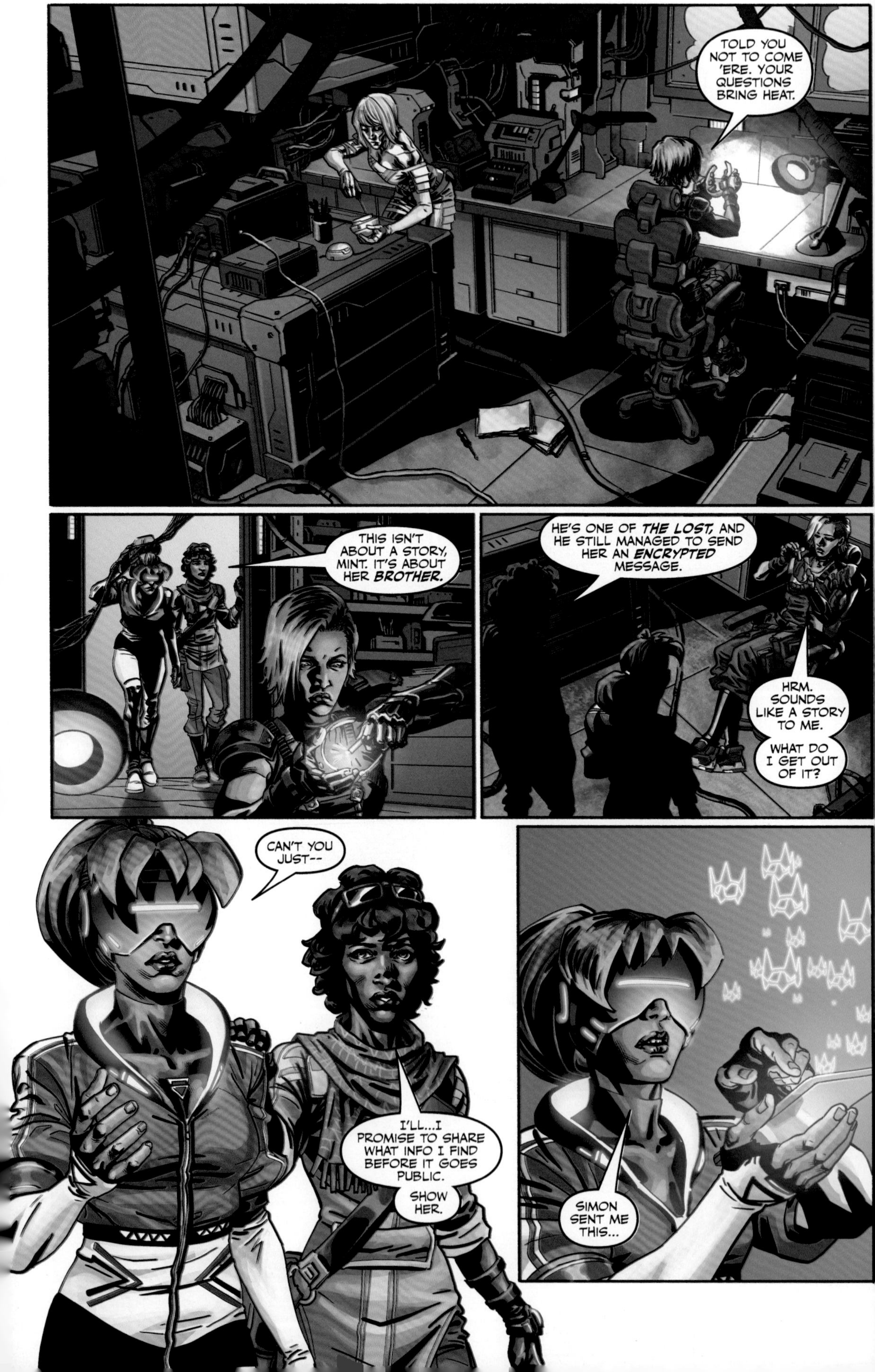
TOLD YOU NOT TO COME 'ERE. YOUR QUESTIONS BRING HEAT.
THIS ISN'T ABOUT A STORY, MINT. IT'S ABOUT HER BROTHER.
HE'S ONE OF THE LOST, AND HE STILL MANAGED TO SEND HER AN ENCRYPTED MESSAGE.
HRM. SOUNDS LIKE A STORY TO ME.
WHAT DO I GET OUT OF IT?
CAN'T YOU JUST--
I'LL...I PROMISE TO SHARE WHAT INFO I FIND BEFORE IT GOES PUBLIC.
SHOW HER.
SIMON SENT ME THIS...

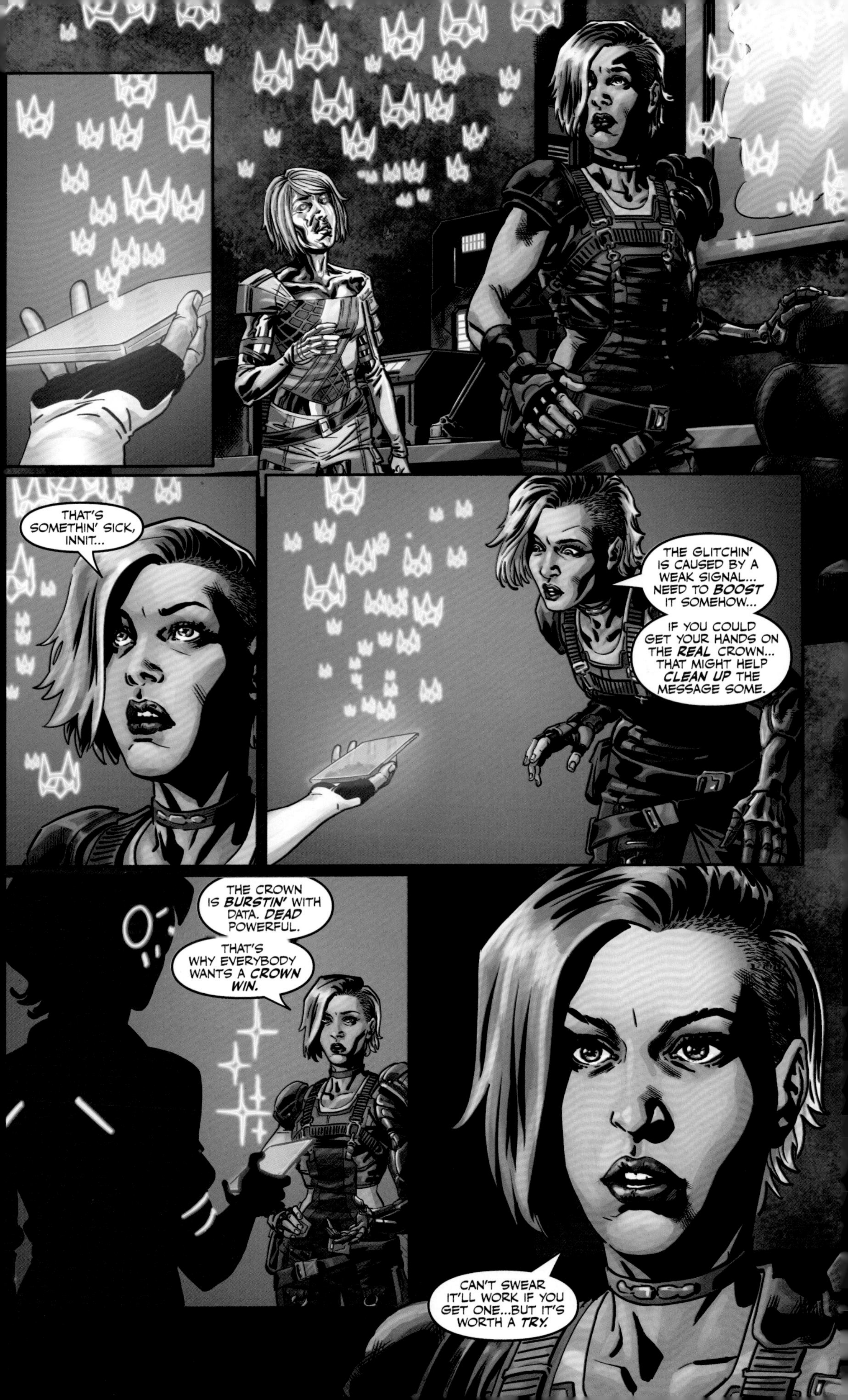
THAT'S SOMETHIN' SICK, INNIT...
THE GLITCHIN' IS CAUSED BY A WEAK SIGNAL... NEED TO BOOST IT SOMEHOW...
IF YOU COULD GET YOUR HANDS ON THE REAL CROWN... THAT MIGHT HELP CLEAN UP THE MESSAGE SOME.
THE CROWN IS BURSTIN' WITH DATA. DEAD POWERFUL.
THAT'S WHY EVERYBODY WANTS A CROWN WIN.
CAN'T SWEAR IT'LL WORK IF YOU GET ONE...BUT IT'S WORTH A TRY.

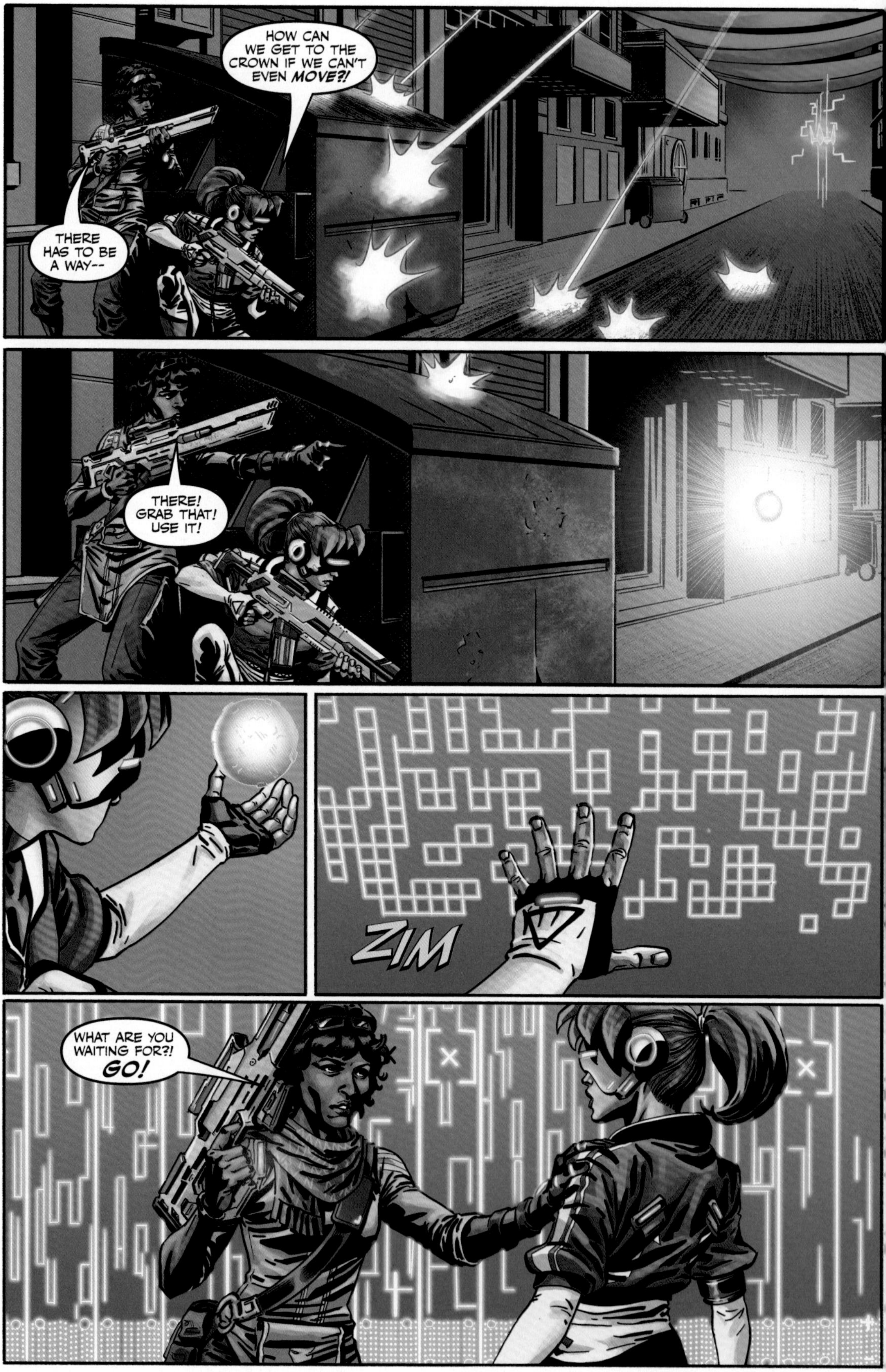
HOW CAN WE GET TO THE CROWN IF WE CAN'T EVEN *MOVE?!*
THERE HAS TO BE A WAY--
THERE! GRAB THAT! USE IT!
ZIM
WHAT ARE YOU WAITING FOR?! **GO!**

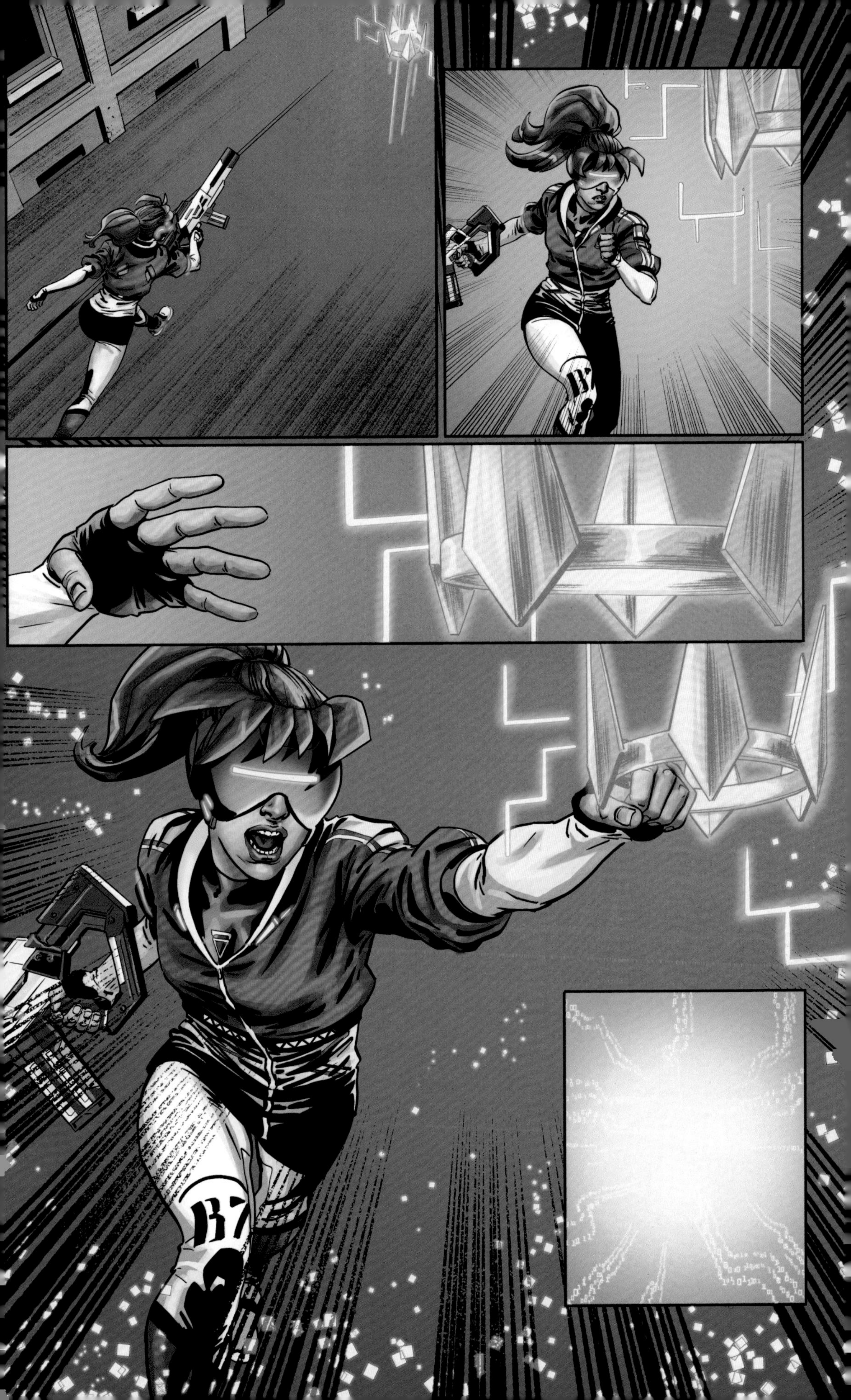
B7

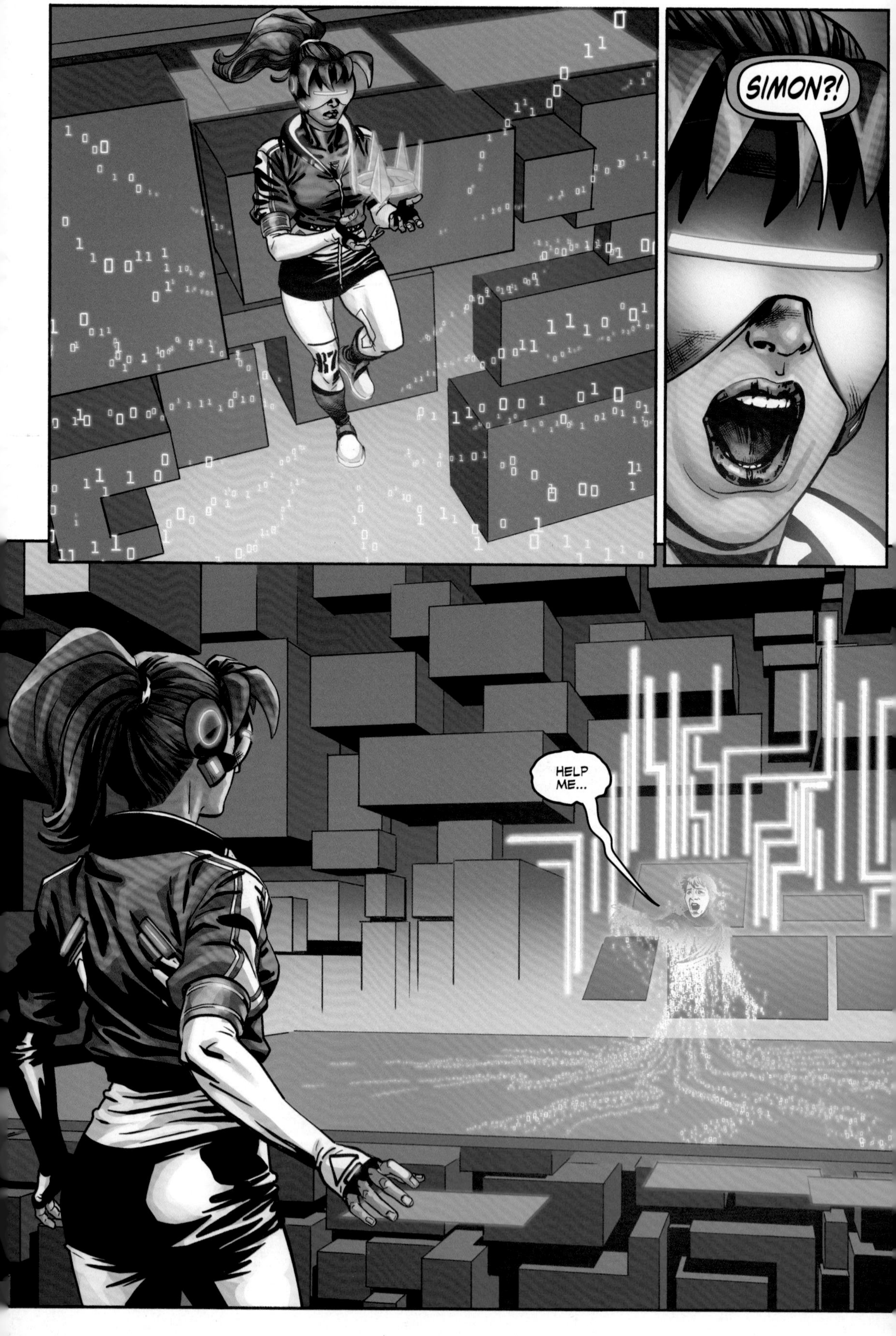
SIMON?!
HELP ME...

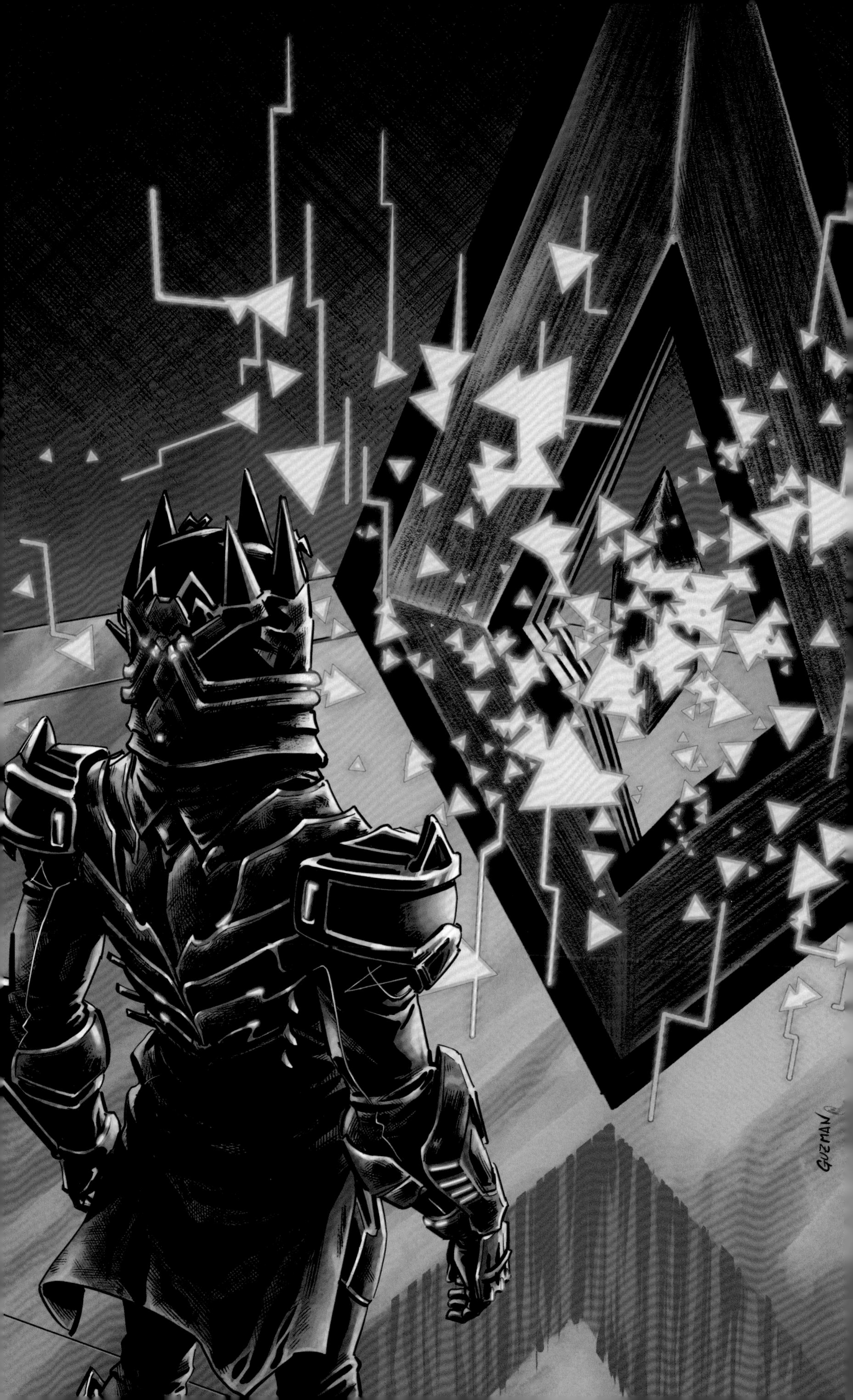
GUZMAN

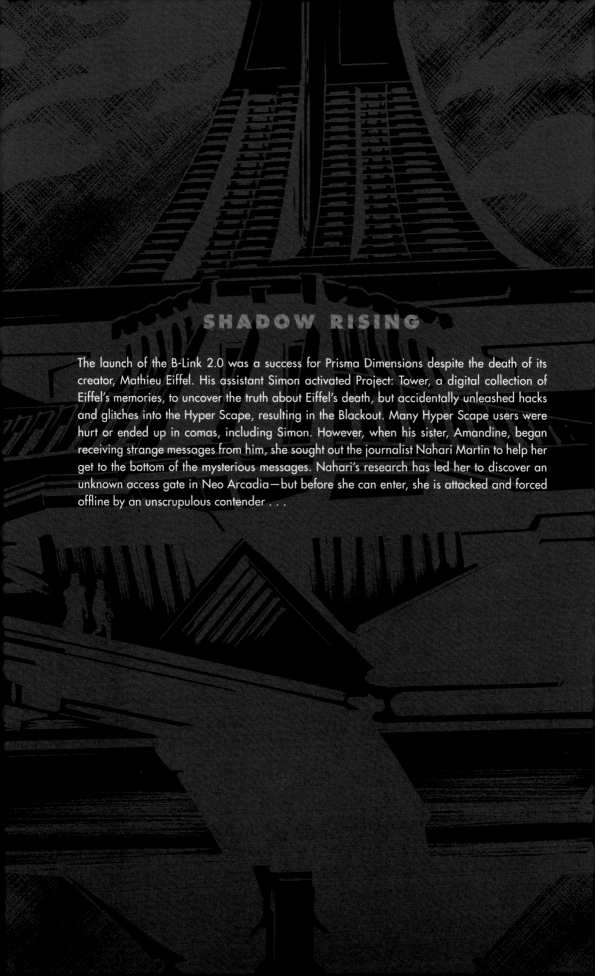

SHADOW RISING

The launch of the B-Link 2.0 was a success for Prisma Dimensions despite the death of its creator, Mathieu Eiffel. His assistant Simon activated Project: Tower, a digital collection of Eiffel's memories, to uncover the truth about Eiffel's death, but accidentally unleashed hacks and glitches into the Hyper Scape, resulting in the Blackout. Many Hyper Scape users were hurt or ended up in comas, including Simon. However, when his sister, Amandine, began receiving strange messages from him, she sought out the journalist Nahari Martin to help her get to the bottom of the mysterious messages. Nahari's research has led her to discover an unknown access gate in Neo Arcadia—but before she can enter, she is attacked and forced offline by an unscrupulous contender . . .

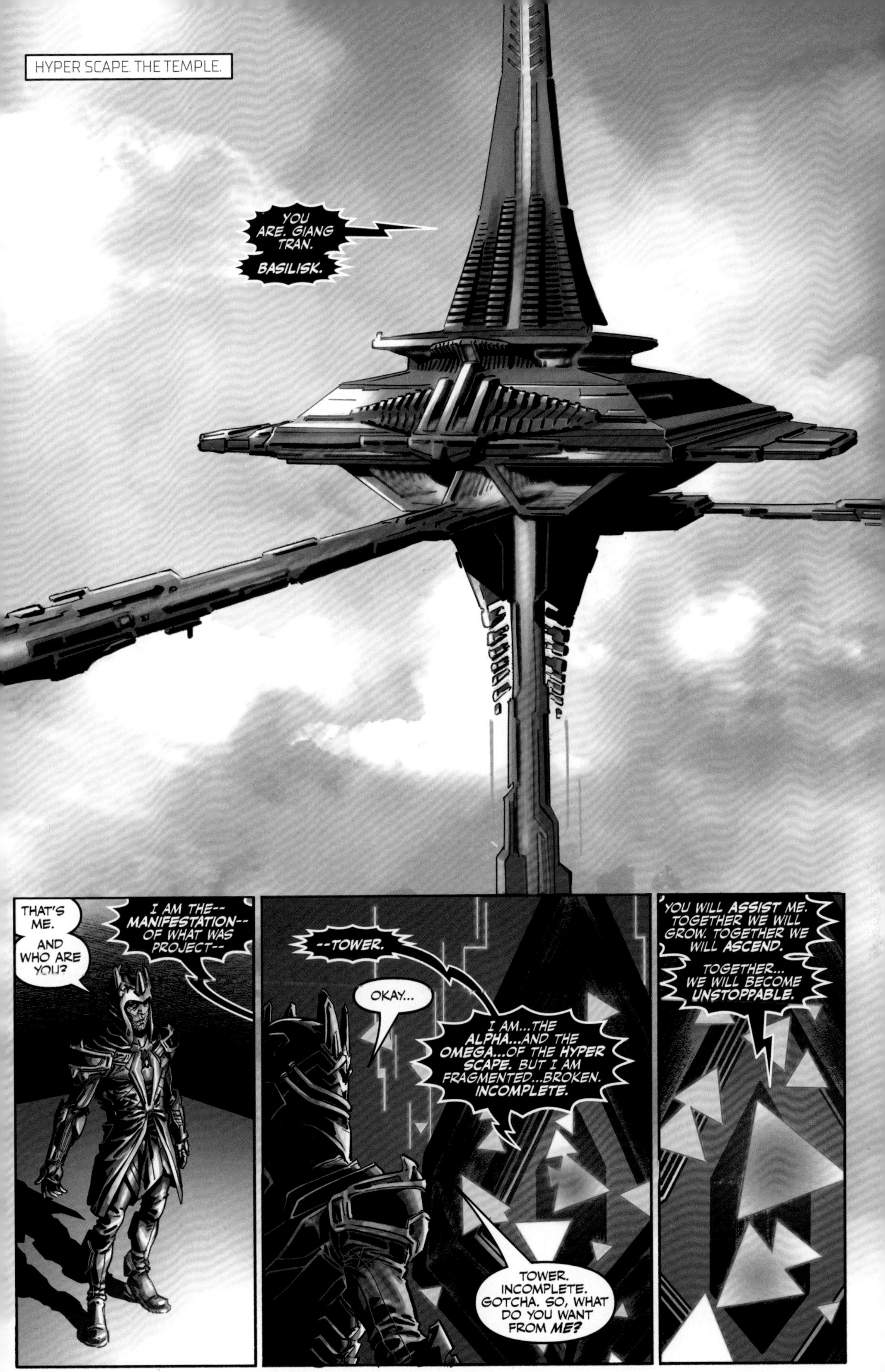
HYPER SCAPE. THE TEMPLE.
YOU ARE. GIANG TRAN.
BASILISK.
THAT'S ME.
AND WHO ARE YOU?
I AM THE-- MANIFESTATION-- OF WHAT WAS PROJECT--
--TOWER.
OKAY...
I AM...THE ALPHA...AND THE OMEGA...OF THE HYPER SCAPE. BUT I AM FRAGMENTED...BROKEN. INCOMPLETE.
TOWER. INCOMPLETE. GOTCHA. SO, WHAT DO YOU WANT FROM ME?
YOU WILL ASSIST ME. TOGETHER WE WILL GROW. TOGETHER WE WILL ASCEND.
TOGETHER... WE WILL BECOME UNSTOPPABLE.

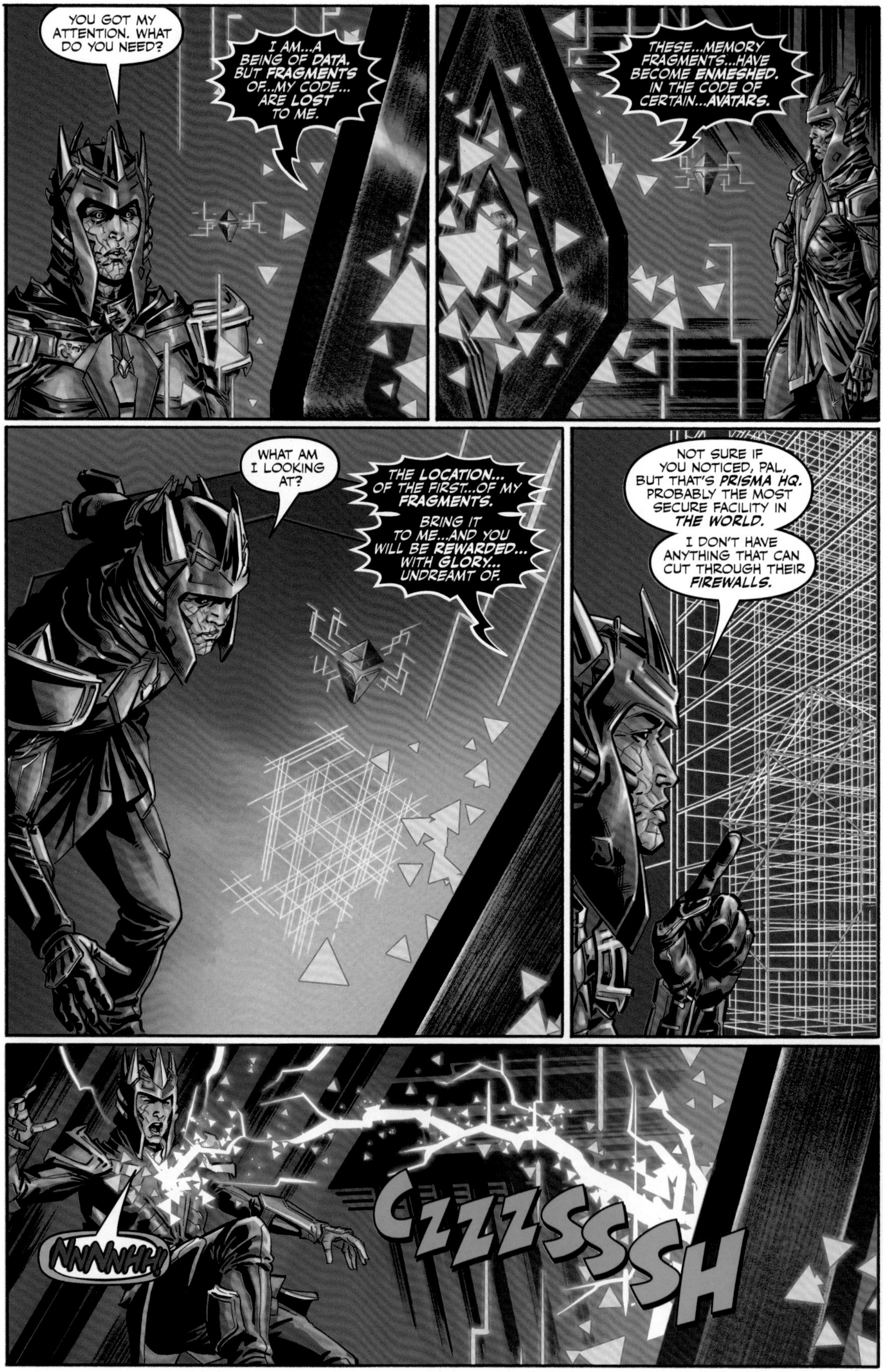
YOU GOT MY ATTENTION. WHAT DO YOU NEED?
I AM...A BEING OF DATA. BUT FRAGMENTS OF...MY CODE... ARE LOST TO ME.
THESE...MEMORY FRAGMENTS...HAVE BECOME ENMESHED. IN THE CODE OF CERTAIN...AVATARS.
WHAT AM I LOOKING AT?
THE LOCATION... OF THE FIRST...OF MY FRAGMENTS.
BRING IT TO ME...AND YOU WILL BE REWARDED... WITH GLORY.. UNDREAMT OF.
NOT SURE IF YOU NOTICED, PAL, BUT THAT'S PRISMA HQ. PROBABLY THE MOST SECURE FACILITY IN THE WORLD.
I DON'T HAVE ANYTHING THAT CAN CUT THROUGH THEIR FIREWALLS.
NNNNHH!
CZZZSSSSH

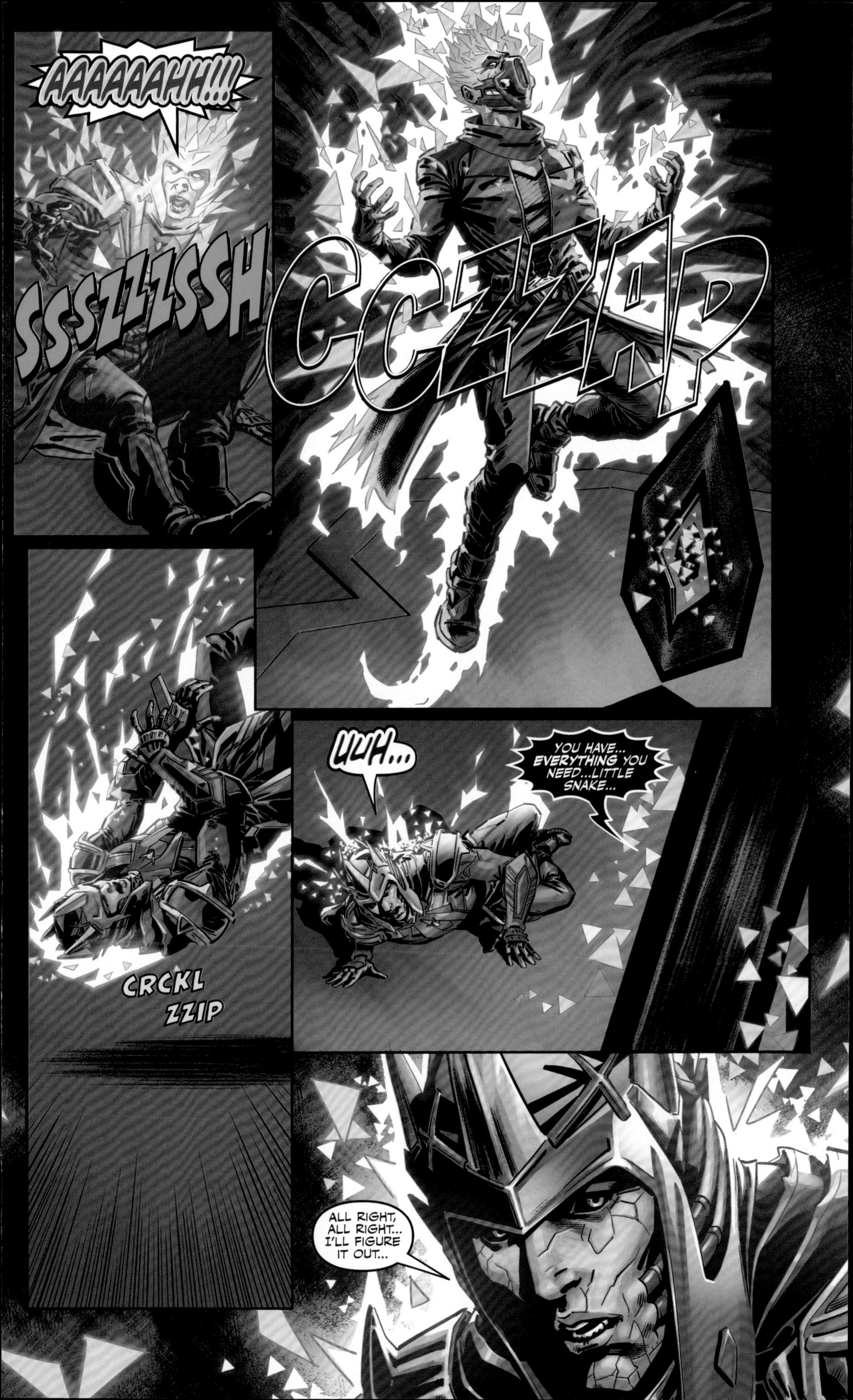
AAAAAAHH!!!
SSSZZZSSH
CCZZZAP
CRCKL
ZZIP
UUH...
YOU HAVE... EVERYTHING YOU NEED...LITTLE SNAKE...
ALL RIGHT, ALL RIGHT... I'LL FIGURE IT OUT...

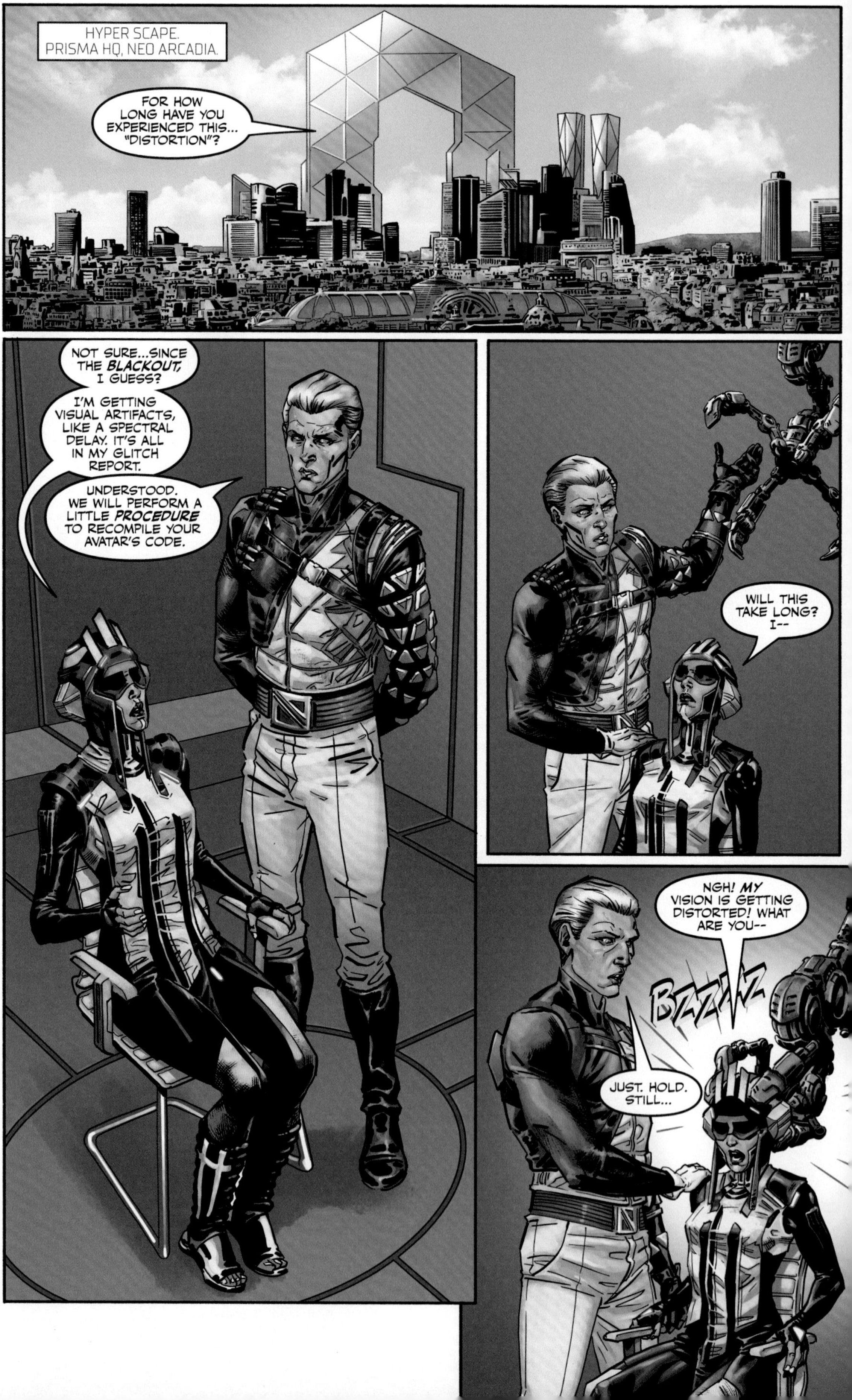
HYPER SCAPE.
PRISMA HQ, NEO ARCADIA.
FOR HOW LONG HAVE YOU EXPERIENCED THIS... "DISTORTION"?
NOT SURE...SINCE THE *BLACKOUT,* I GUESS?
I'M GETTING VISUAL ARTIFACTS, LIKE A SPECTRAL DELAY. IT'S ALL IN MY GLITCH REPORT.
UNDERSTOOD. WE WILL PERFORM A LITTLE *PROCEDURE* TO RECOMPILE YOUR AVATAR'S CODE.
WILL THIS TAKE LONG? I--
NGH! *MY* VISION IS GETTING DISTORTED! WHAT ARE YOU--
BZZZZT
JUST. HOLD. STILL...

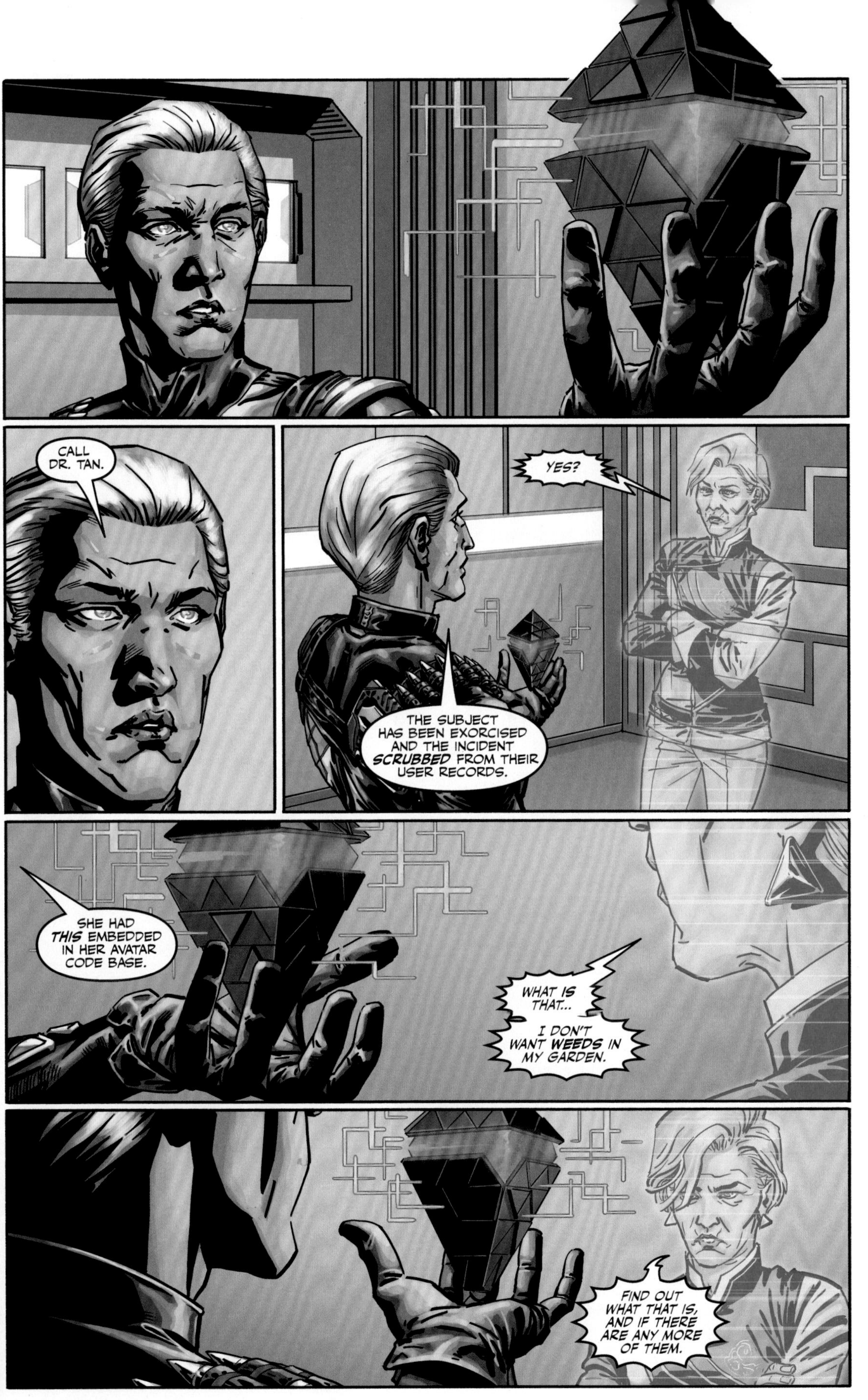
CALL DR. TAN.
YES?
THE SUBJECT HAS BEEN EXORCISED AND THE INCIDENT SCRUBBED FROM THEIR USER RECORDS.
SHE HAD THIS EMBEDDED IN HER AVATAR CODE BASE.
WHAT IS THAT...
I DON'T WANT WEEDS IN MY GARDEN.
FIND OUT WHAT THAT IS, AND IF THERE ARE ANY MORE OF THEM.

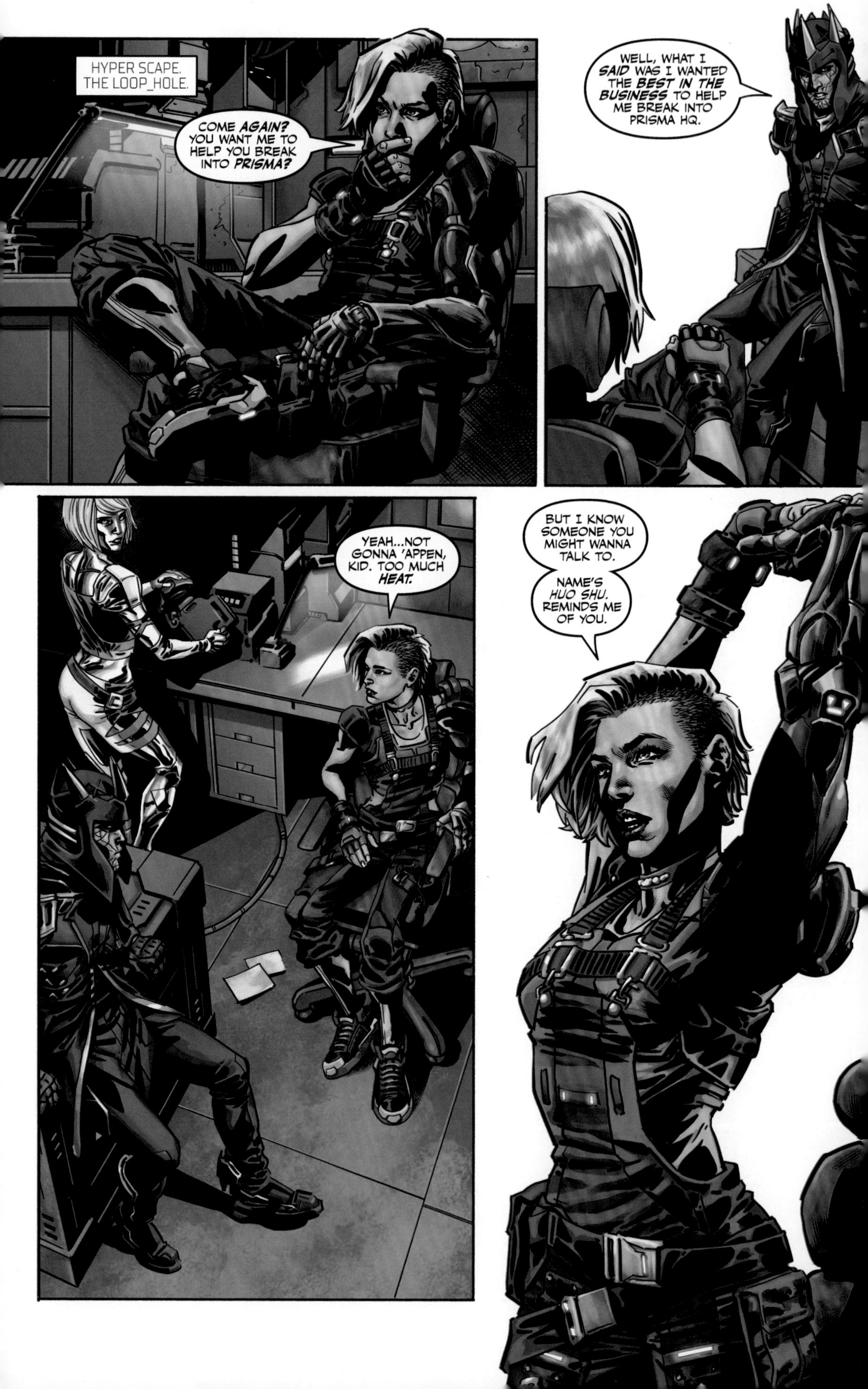
HYPER SCAPE.
THE LOOP_HOLE.
COME AGAIN? YOU WANT ME TO HELP YOU BREAK INTO PRISMA?
WELL, WHAT I SAID WAS I WANTED THE BEST IN THE BUSINESS TO HELP ME BREAK INTO PRISMA HQ.
YEAH...NOT GONNA 'APPEN, KID. TOO MUCH HEAT.
BUT I KNOW SOMEONE YOU MIGHT WANNA TALK TO.
NAME'S HUO SHU. REMINDS ME OF YOU.

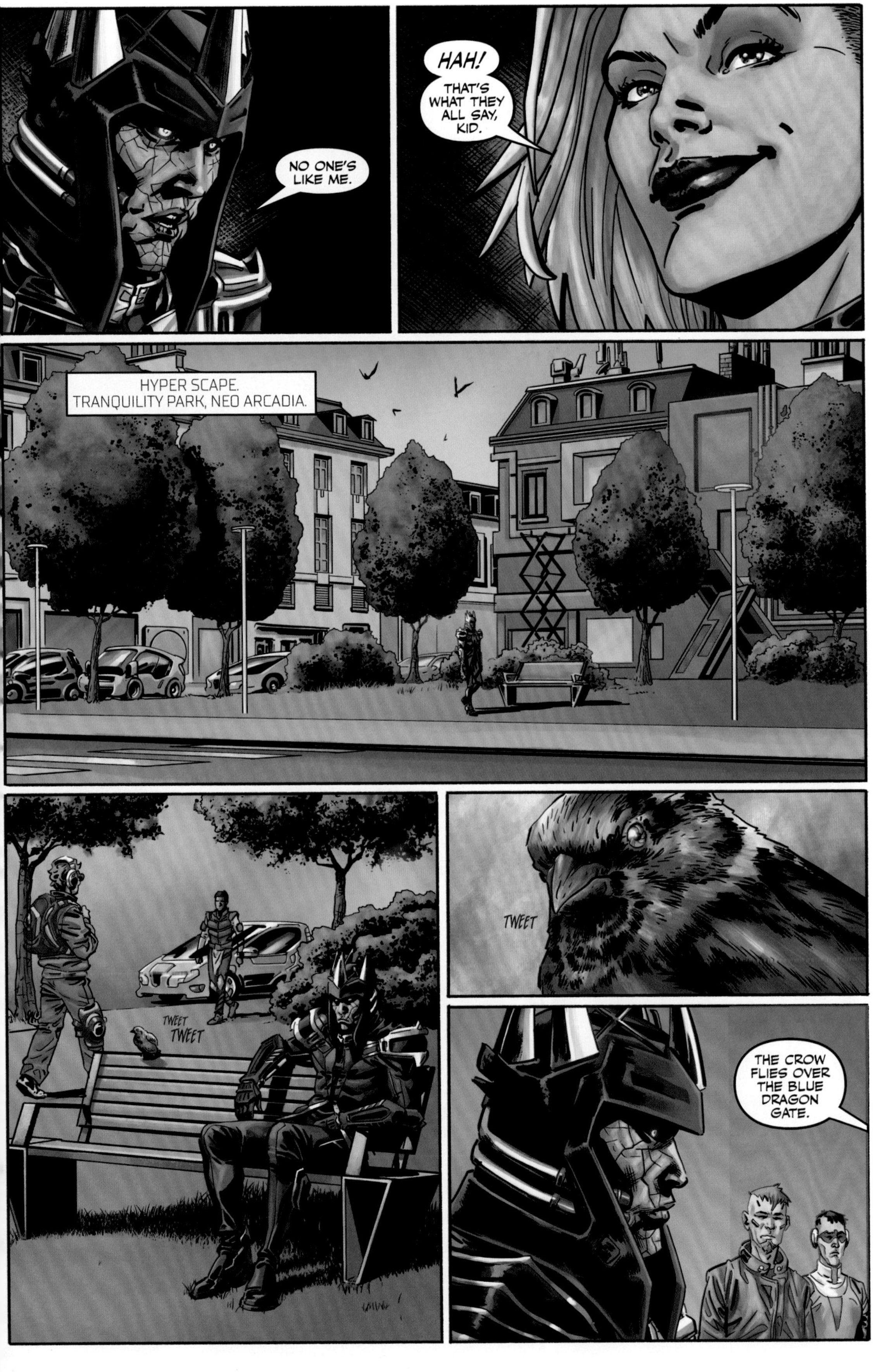
NO ONE'S LIKE ME.
HAH!
THAT'S WHAT THEY ALL SAY, KID.
HYPER SCAPE.
TRANQUILITY PARK, NEO ARCADIA.
TWEET
TWEET
TWEET
THE CROW FLIES OVER THE BLUE DRAGON GATE.

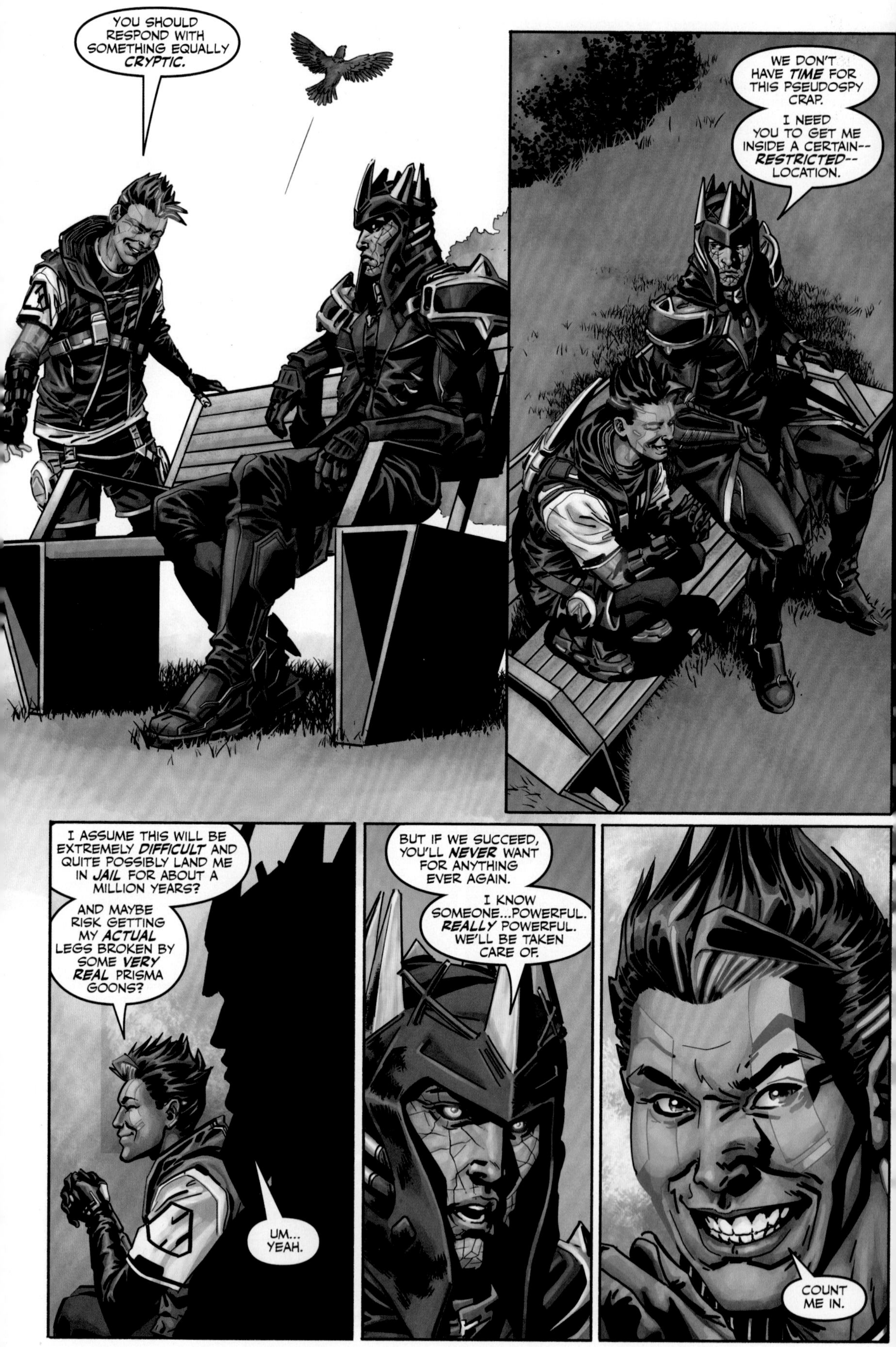

YOU SHOULD RESPOND WITH SOMETHING EQUALLY CRYPTIC.
WE DON'T HAVE TIME FOR THIS PSEUDOSPY CRAP.
I NEED YOU TO GET ME INSIDE A CERTAIN-- RESTRICTED-- LOCATION.
I ASSUME THIS WILL BE EXTREMELY DIFFICULT AND QUITE POSSIBLY LAND ME IN JAIL FOR ABOUT A MILLION YEARS?
AND MAYBE RISK GETTING MY ACTUAL LEGS BROKEN BY SOME VERY REAL PRISMA GOONS?
UM... YEAH.
BUT IF WE SUCCEED, YOU'LL NEVER WANT FOR ANYTHING EVER AGAIN.
I KNOW SOMEONE...POWERFUL. REALLY POWERFUL. WE'LL BE TAKEN CARE OF.
COUNT ME IN.

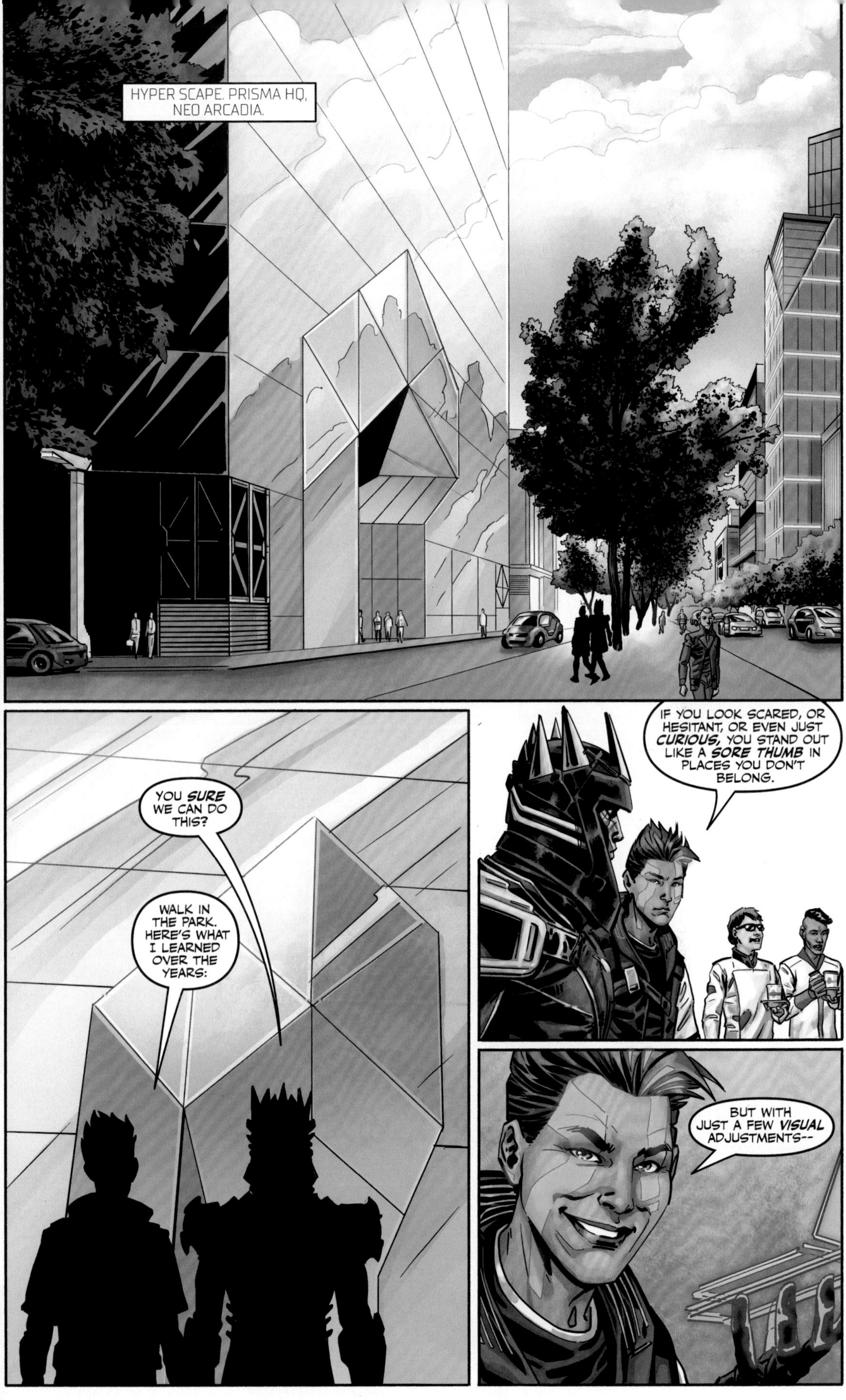
HYPER SCAPE. PRISMA HQ, NEO ARCADIA.
YOU SURE WE CAN DO THIS?
WALK IN THE PARK. HERE'S WHAT I LEARNED OVER THE YEARS:
IF YOU LOOK SCARED, OR HESITANT, OR EVEN JUST CURIOUS, YOU STAND OUT LIKE A SORE THUMB IN PLACES YOU DON'T BELONG.
BUT WITH JUST A FEW VISUAL ADJUSTMENTS--

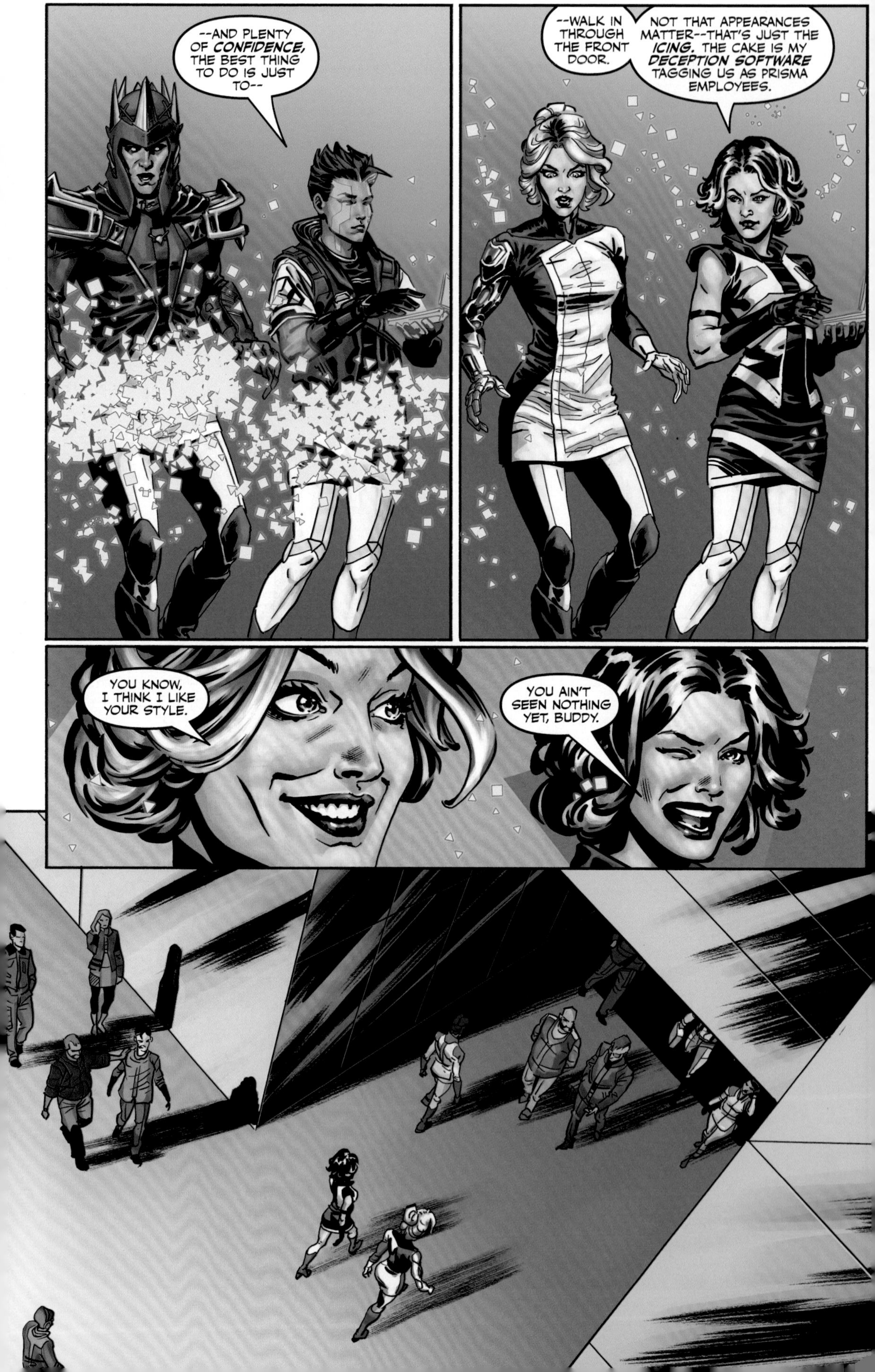
--AND PLENTY OF CONFIDENCE, THE BEST THING TO DO IS JUST TO--
--WALK IN THROUGH THE FRONT DOOR.
NOT THAT APPEARANCES MATTER--THAT'S JUST THE ICING. THE CAKE IS MY DECEPTION SOFTWARE TAGGING US AS PRISMA EMPLOYEES.
YOU KNOW, I THINK I LIKE YOUR STYLE.
YOU AIN'T SEEN NOTHING YET, BUDDY.

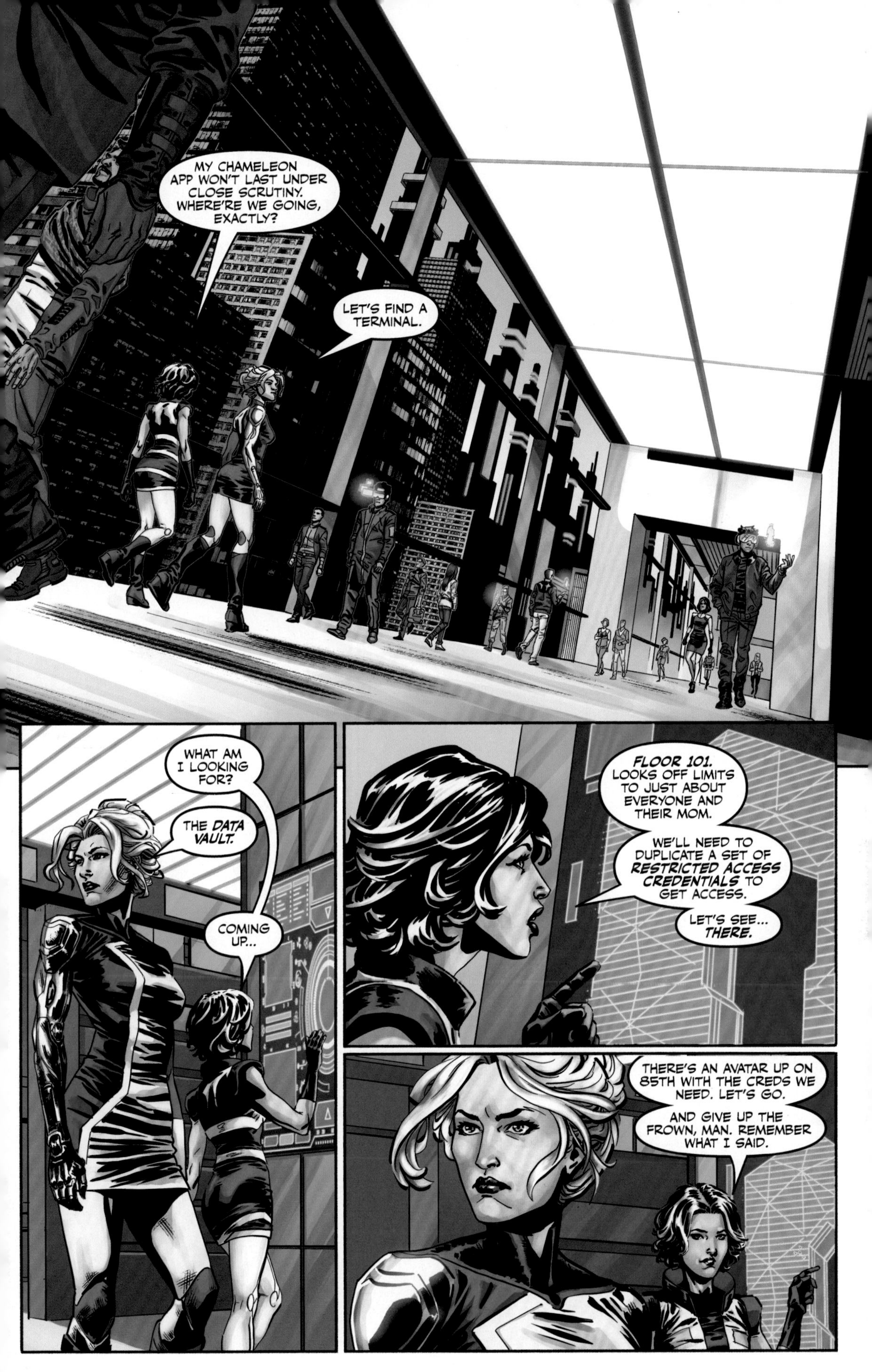
MY CHAMELEON APP WON'T LAST UNDER CLOSE SCRUTINY. WHERE'RE WE GOING, EXACTLY?
LET'S FIND A TERMINAL.
WHAT AM I LOOKING FOR?
THE *DATA VAULT.*
COMING UP...
FLOOR 101. LOOKS OFF LIMITS TO JUST ABOUT EVERYONE AND THEIR MOM.
WE'LL NEED TO DUPLICATE A SET OF ***RESTRICTED ACCESS CREDENTIALS*** TO GET ACCESS.
LET'S SEE... ***THERE.***
THERE'S AN AVATAR UP ON 85TH WITH THE CREDS WE NEED. LET'S GO.
AND GIVE UP THE FROWN, MAN. REMEMBER WHAT I SAID.

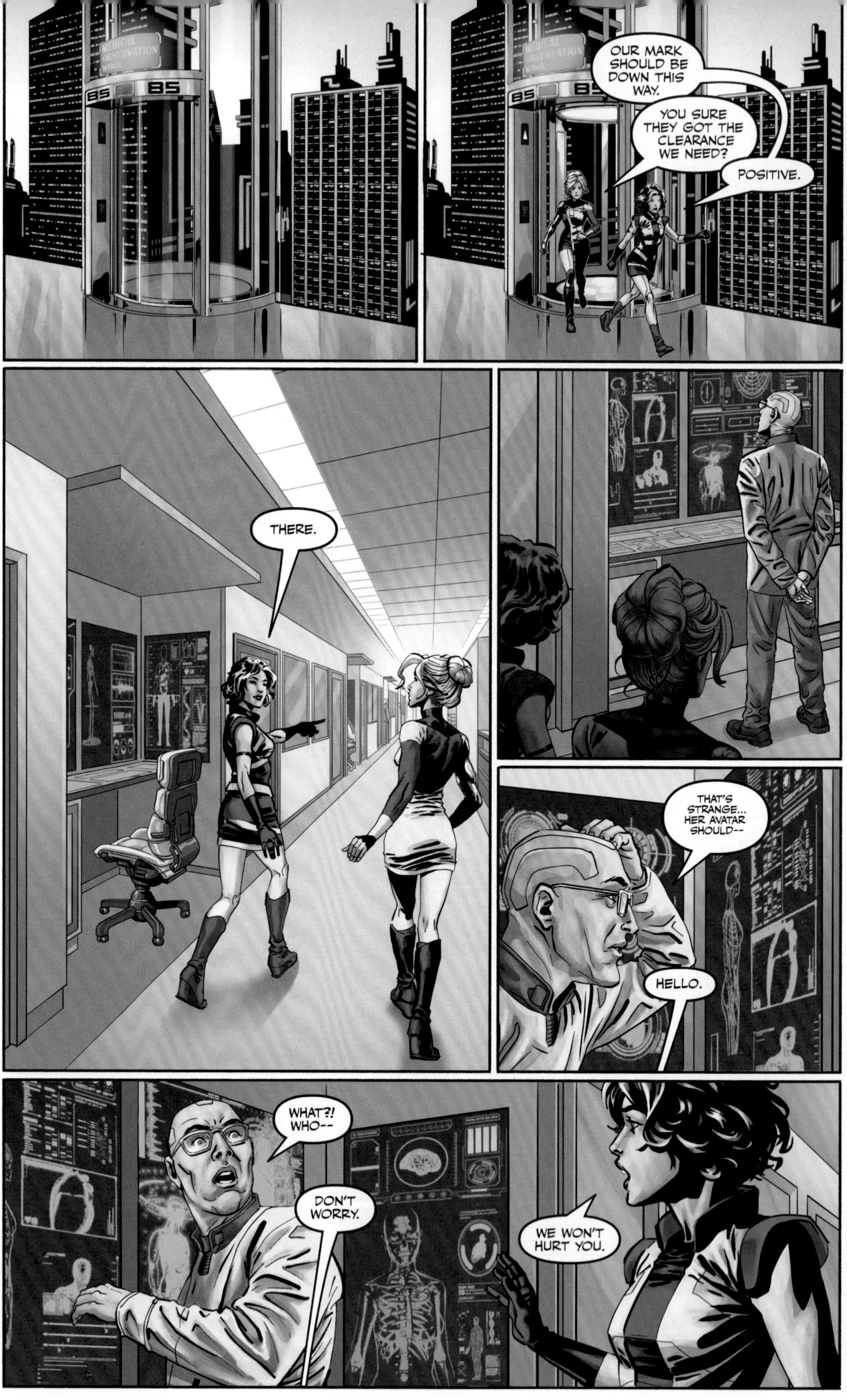
MEDICAL OBSERVATION WING
85
85
OUR MARK SHOULD BE DOWN THIS WAY.
YOU SURE THEY GOT THE CLEARANCE WE NEED?
POSITIVE.
THERE.
THAT'S STRANGE... HER AVATAR SHOULD--
HELLO.
WHAT?! WHO--
DON'T WORRY.
WE WON'T HURT YOU.

IN FACT, YOU WON'T FEEL A THING.

WAIT! I--

GOT THE *CREDS*, BUT MY STASIS HACK ISN'T HOLDING. WE SHOULD MOVE.

YOU SEE A *GHOST* OR SOMETHING?

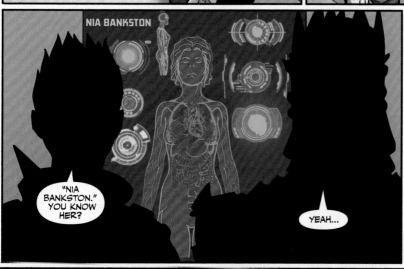

NIA BANKSTON

"NIA BANKSTON." YOU KNOW HER?

YEAH...

THAT'S *PALADIN'S MOM.* WHAT'S GOING ON HERE?

NIA BANKSTON

NO *TIME*, PAL. WE GOTTA GET UP TO 101.

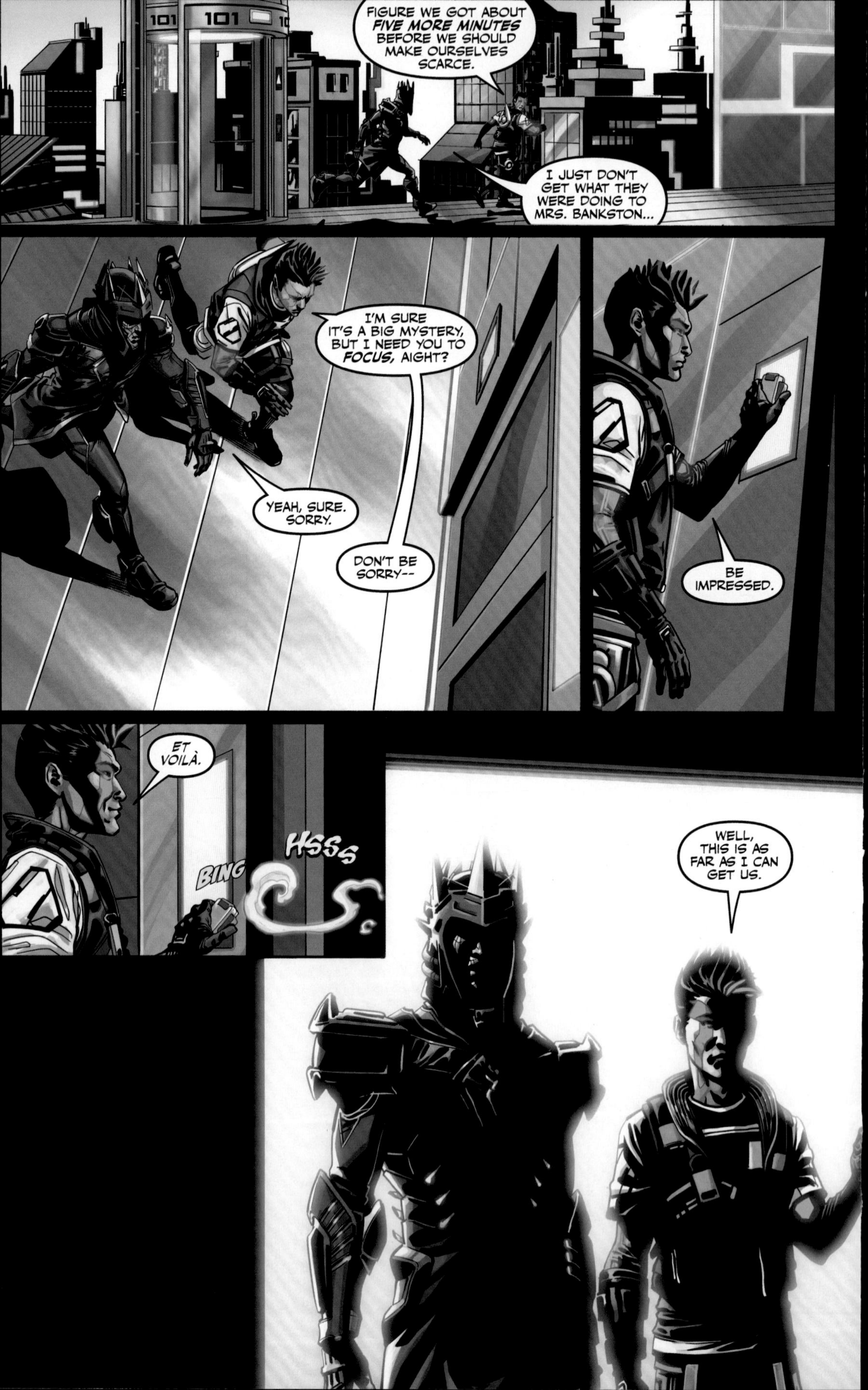
101
101
FIGURE WE GOT ABOUT *FIVE MORE MINUTES* BEFORE WE SHOULD MAKE OURSELVES SCARCE.
I JUST DON'T GET WHAT THEY WERE DOING TO MRS. BANKSTON...
I'M SURE IT'S A BIG MYSTERY, BUT I NEED YOU TO *FOCUS,* AIGHT?
YEAH, SURE. SORRY.
DON'T BE SORRY--
BE IMPRESSED.
ET VOILÀ.
BING
HSSS
WELL, THIS IS AS FAR AS I CAN GET US.

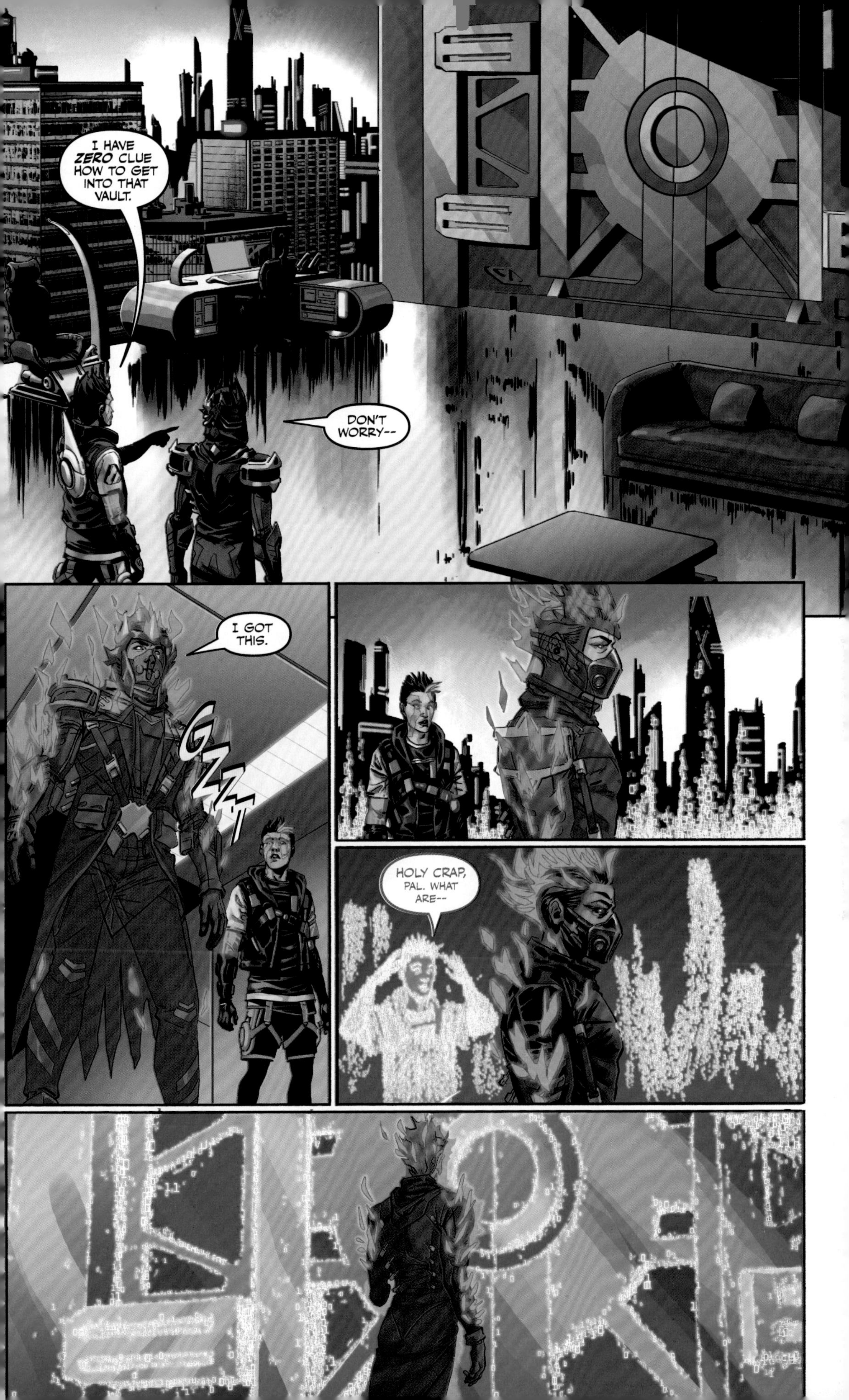
I HAVE ZERO CLUE HOW TO GET INTO THAT VAULT.
DON'T WORRY--
I GOT THIS.
GZZZT
HOLY CRAP, PAL. WHAT ARE--

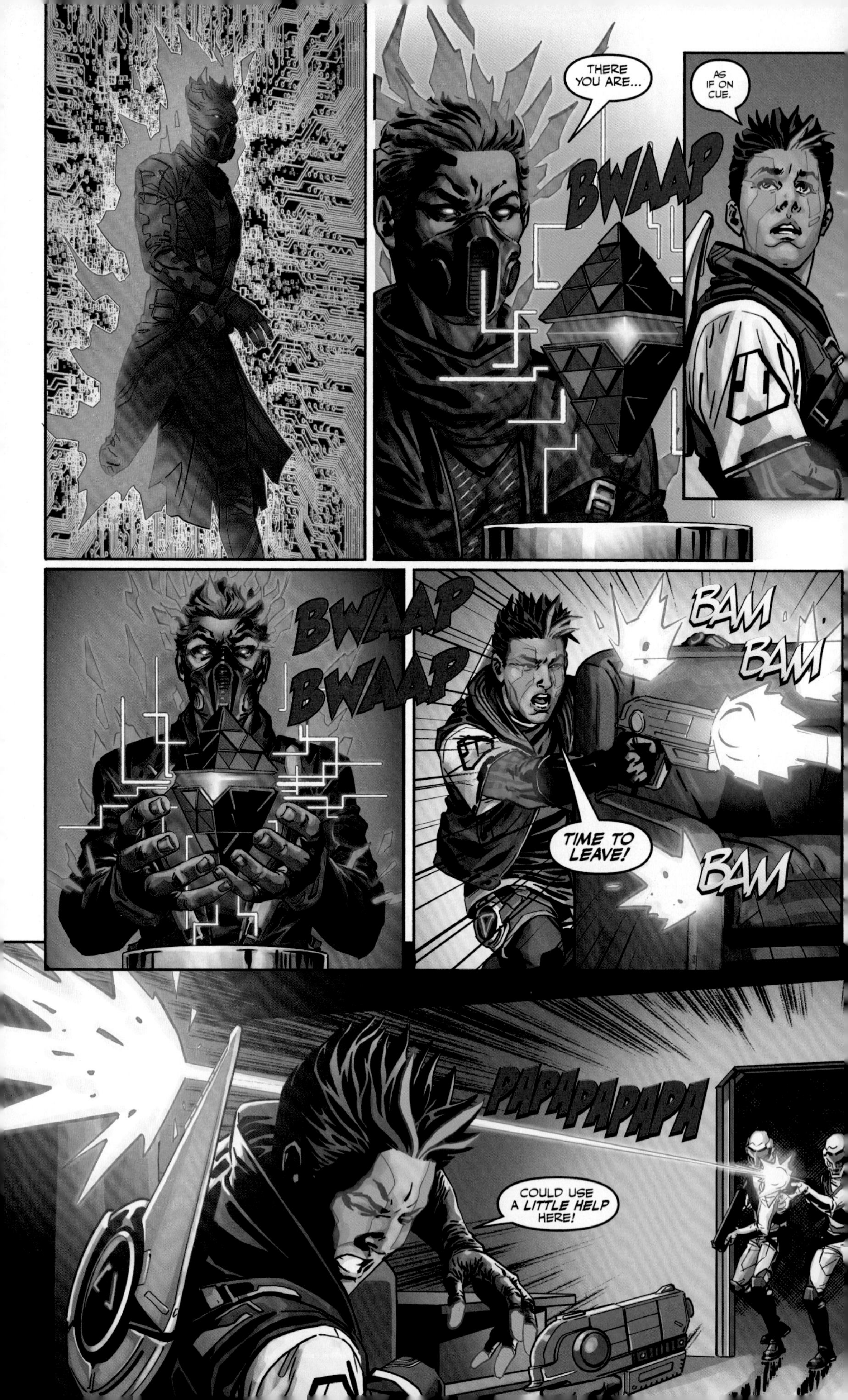
THERE YOU ARE...
AS IF ON CUE.
BWAAP
BWAAP
BWAAP
BAM
BAM
TIME TO LEAVE!
BAM
PAPAPAPAPAPA
COULD USE A LITTLE HELP HERE!

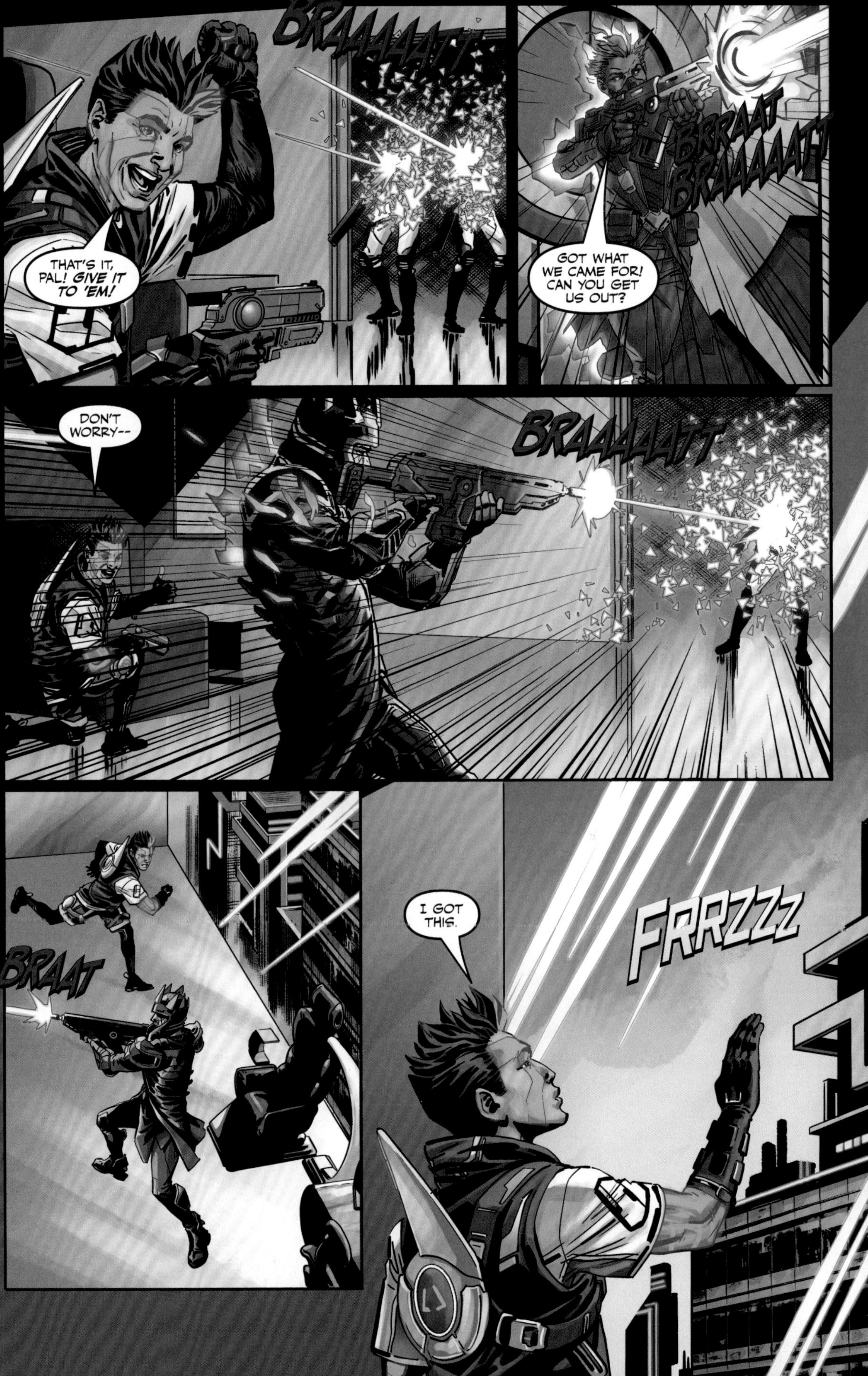
BRAAAAATT
THAT'S IT, PAL! GIVE IT TO 'EM!
BRRAAT BRAAAAATT
GOT WHAT WE CAME FOR! CAN YOU GET US OUT?
DON'T WORRY--
BRAAAAATT
BRAAT
I GOT THIS.
FRRZZZ

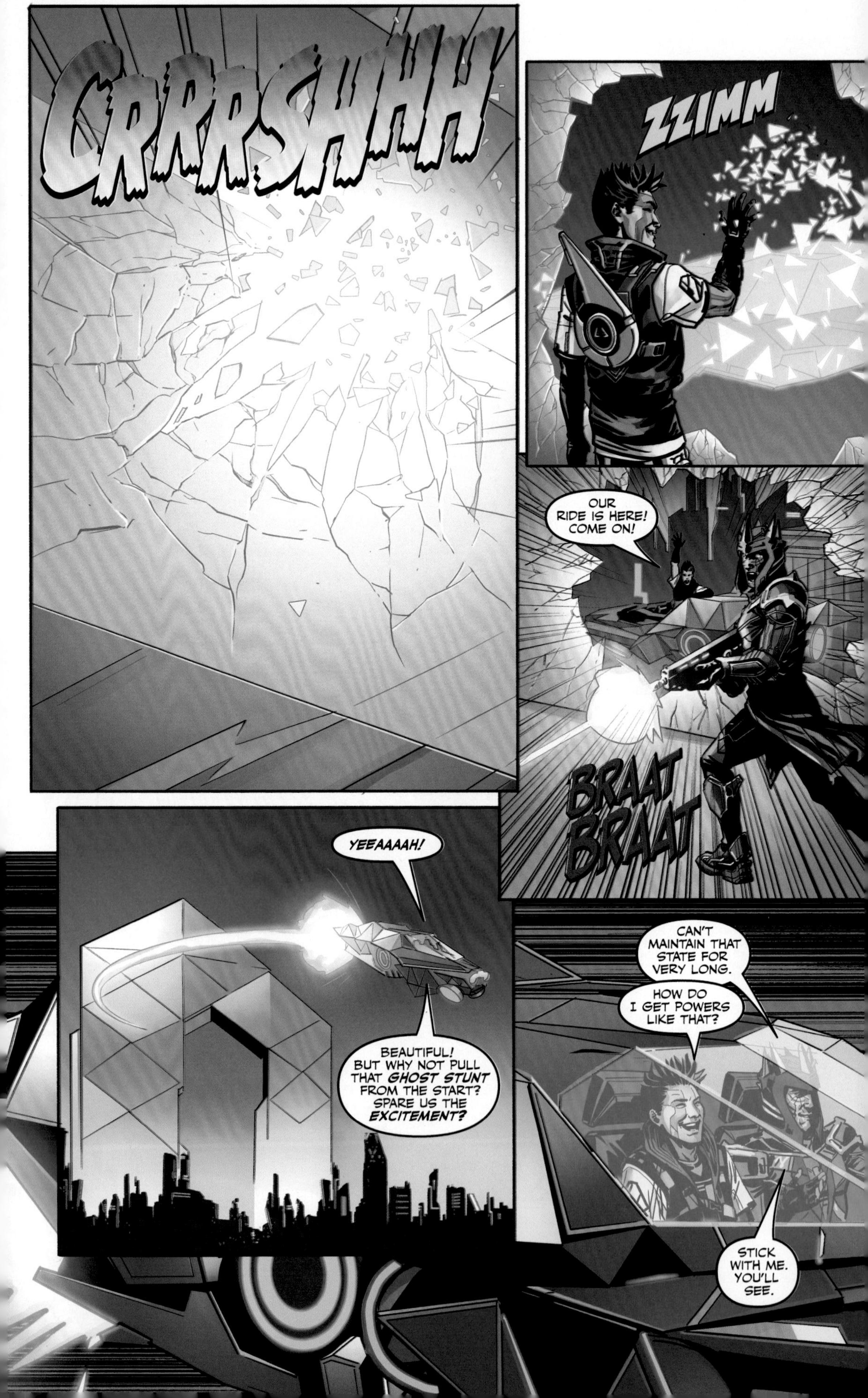
CRRRSHHH
ZZIMM
OUR RIDE IS HERE! COME ON!
BRAAT BRAAT
YEEAAAAH!
BEAUTIFUL! BUT WHY NOT PULL THAT GHOST STUNT FROM THE START? SPARE US THE EXCITEMENT?
CAN'T MAINTAIN THAT STATE FOR VERY LONG.
HOW DO I GET POWERS LIKE THAT?
STICK WITH ME. YOU'LL SEE.

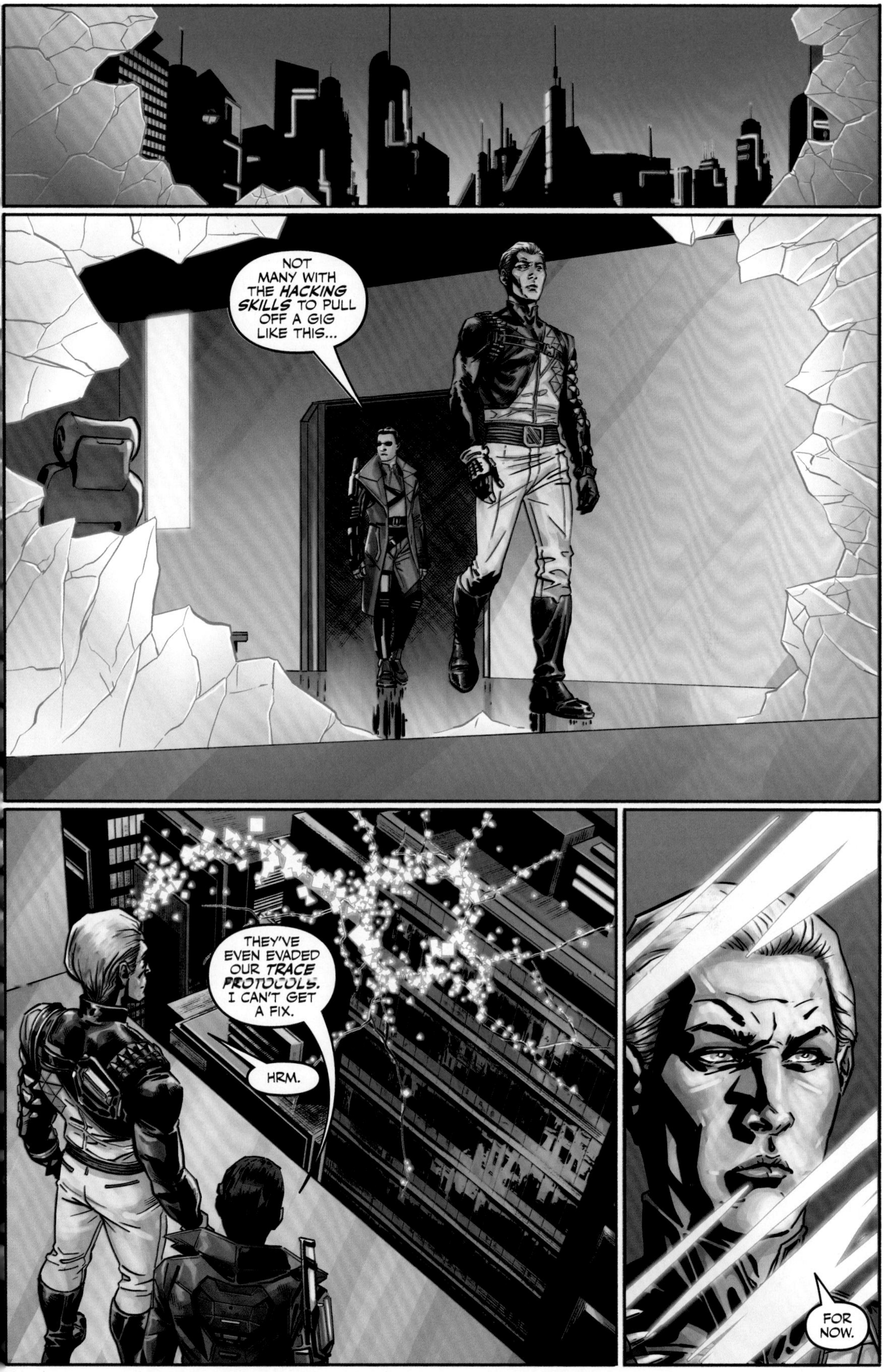
NOT MANY WITH THE HACKING SKILLS TO PULL OFF A GIG LIKE THIS...
THEY'VE EVEN EVADED OUR TRACE PROTOCOLS. I CAN'T GET A FIX.
HRM.
FOR NOW.

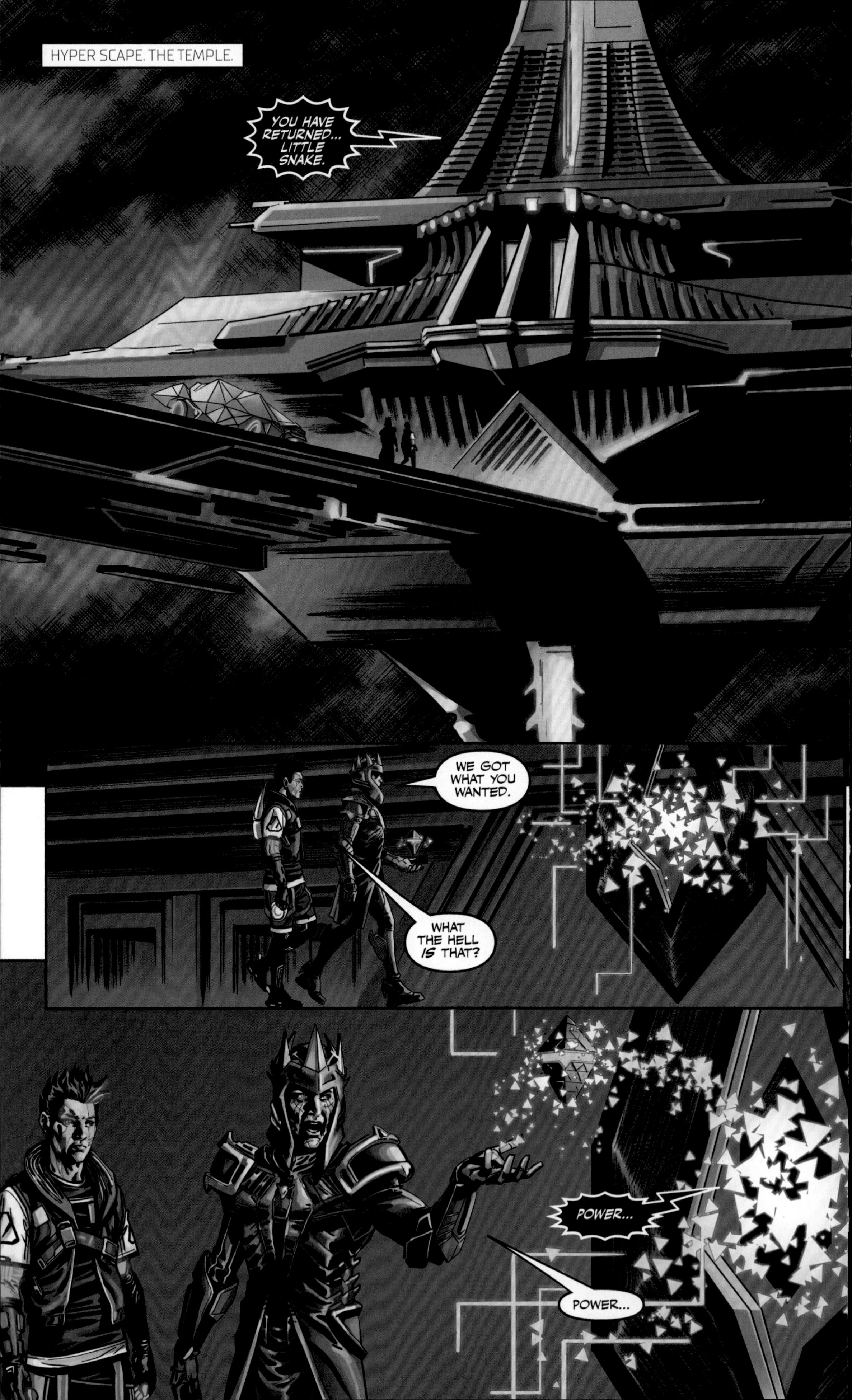
HYPER SCAPE. THE TEMPLE.
YOU HAVE RETURNED... LITTLE SNAKE.
WE GOT WHAT YOU WANTED.
WHAT THE HELL IS THAT?
POWER...
POWER...

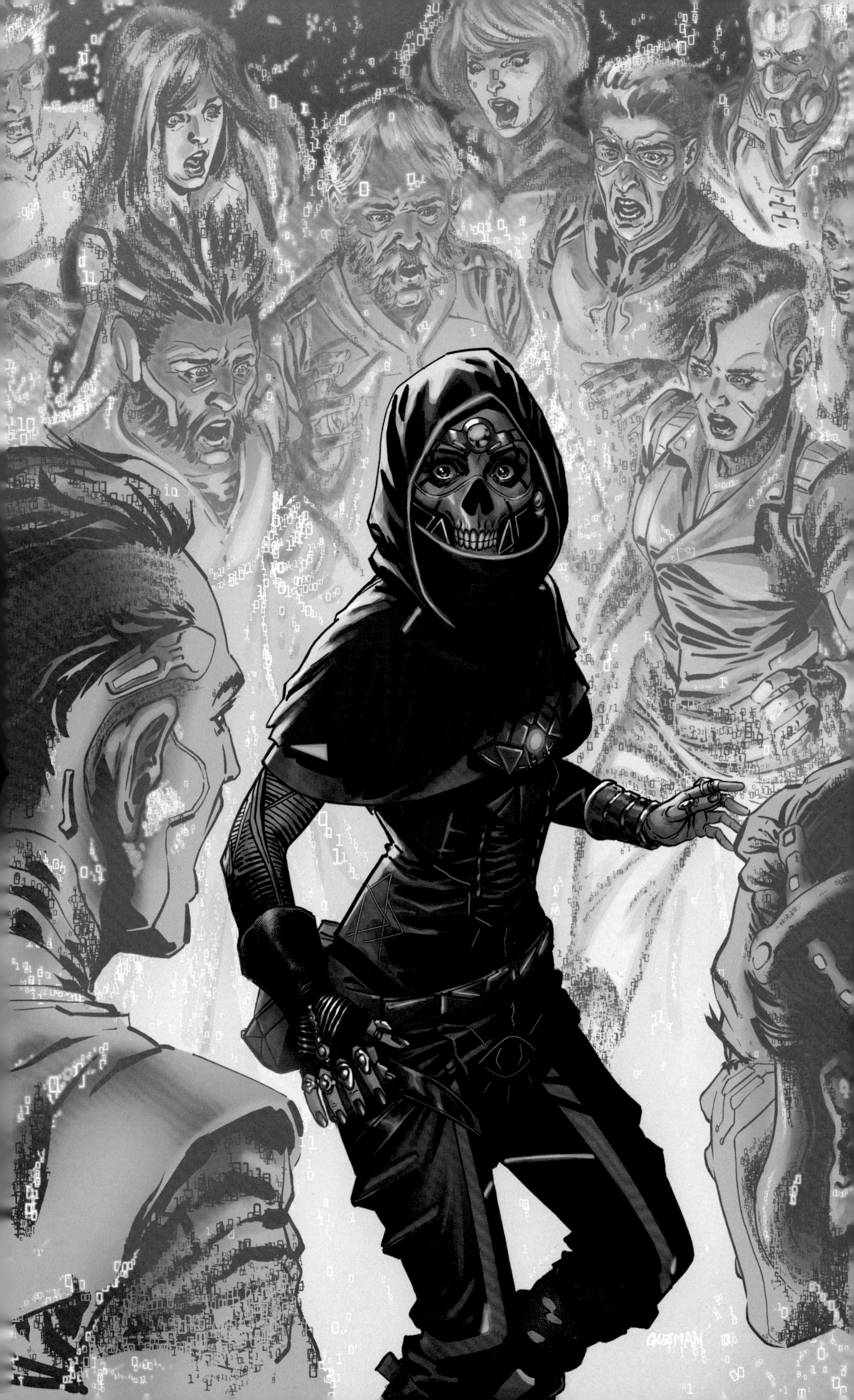
GUZMAN

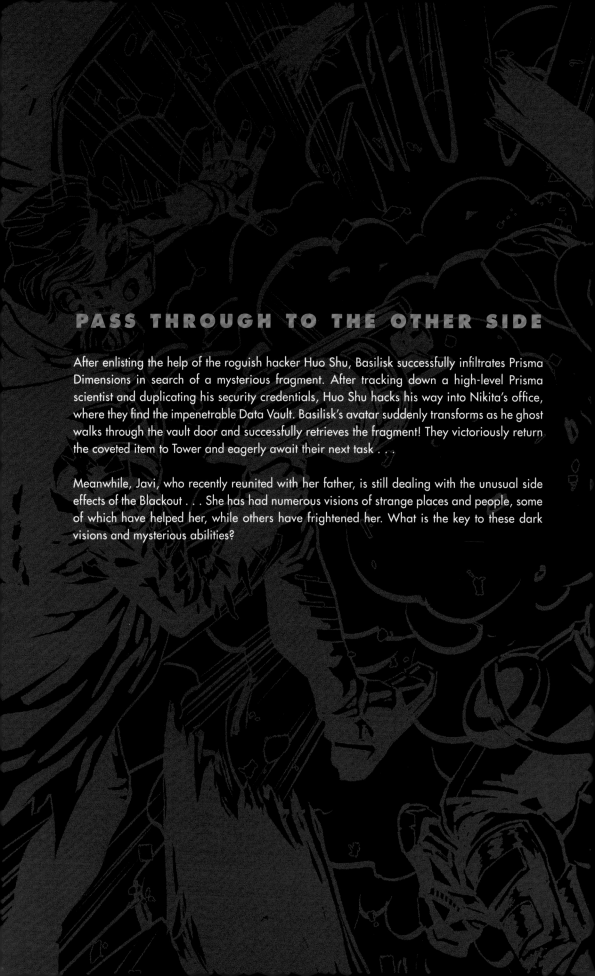

PASS THROUGH TO THE OTHER SIDE

After enlisting the help of the roguish hacker Huo Shu, Basilisk successfully infiltrates Prisma Dimensions in search of a mysterious fragment. After tracking down a high-level Prisma scientist and duplicating his security credentials, Huo Shu hacks his way into Nikita's office, where they find the impenetrable Data Vault. Basilisk's avatar suddenly transforms as he ghost walks through the vault door and successfully retrieves the fragment! They victoriously return the coveted item to Tower and eagerly await their next task . . .

Meanwhile, Javi, who recently reunited with her father, is still dealing with the unusual side effects of the Blackout . . . She has had numerous visions of strange places and people, some of which have helped her, while others have frightened her. What is the key to these dark visions and mysterious abilities?

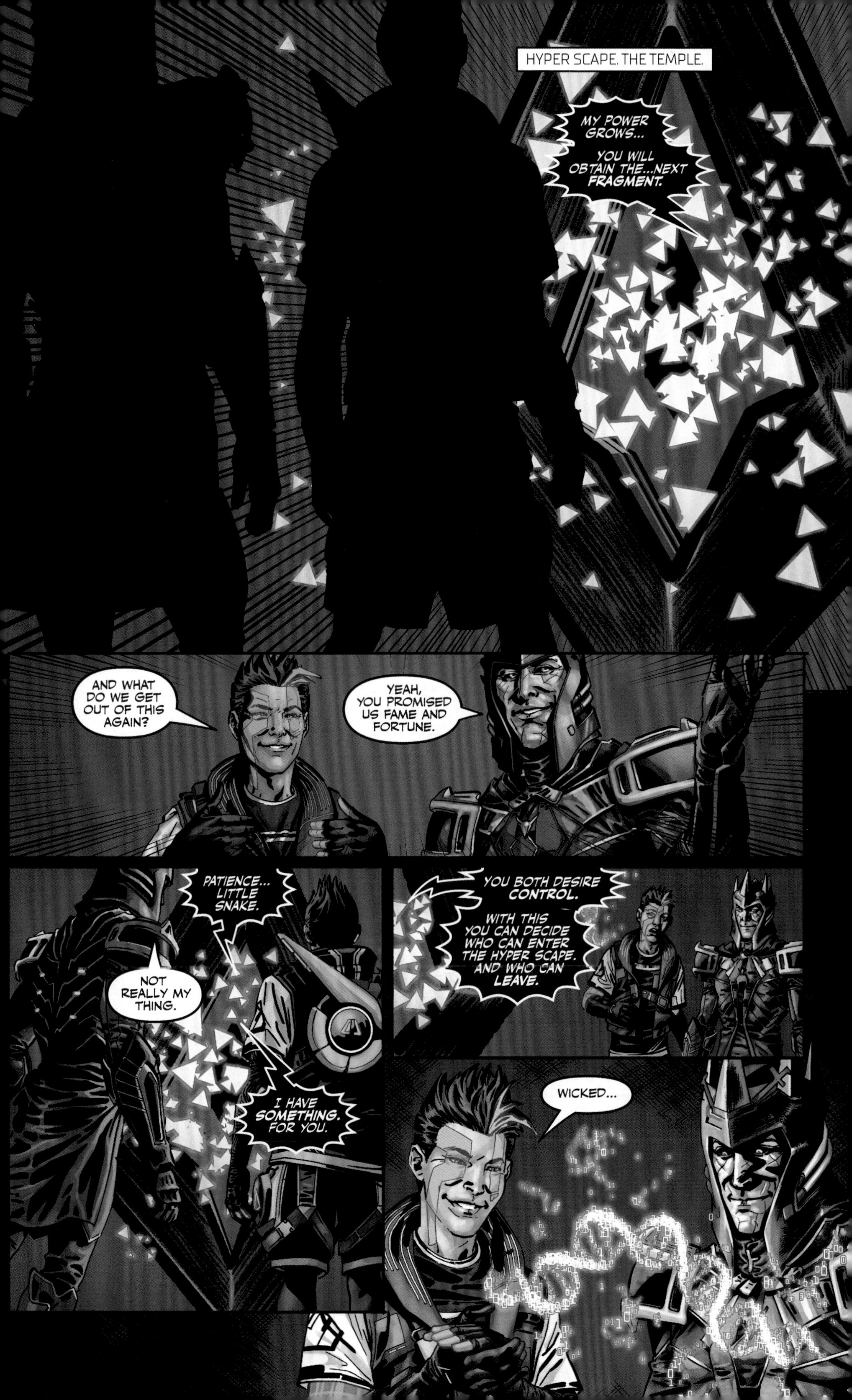
HYPER SCAPE. THE TEMPLE.
MY POWER GROWS... YOU WILL OBTAIN THE...NEXT FRAGMENT.
AND WHAT DO WE GET OUT OF THIS AGAIN?
YEAH, YOU PROMISED US FAME AND FORTUNE.
PATIENCE... LITTLE SNAKE.
NOT REALLY MY THING.
I HAVE SOMETHING. FOR YOU.
YOU BOTH DESIRE CONTROL.
WITH THIS YOU CAN DECIDE WHO CAN ENTER THE HYPER SCAPE. AND WHO CAN LEAVE.
WICKED...

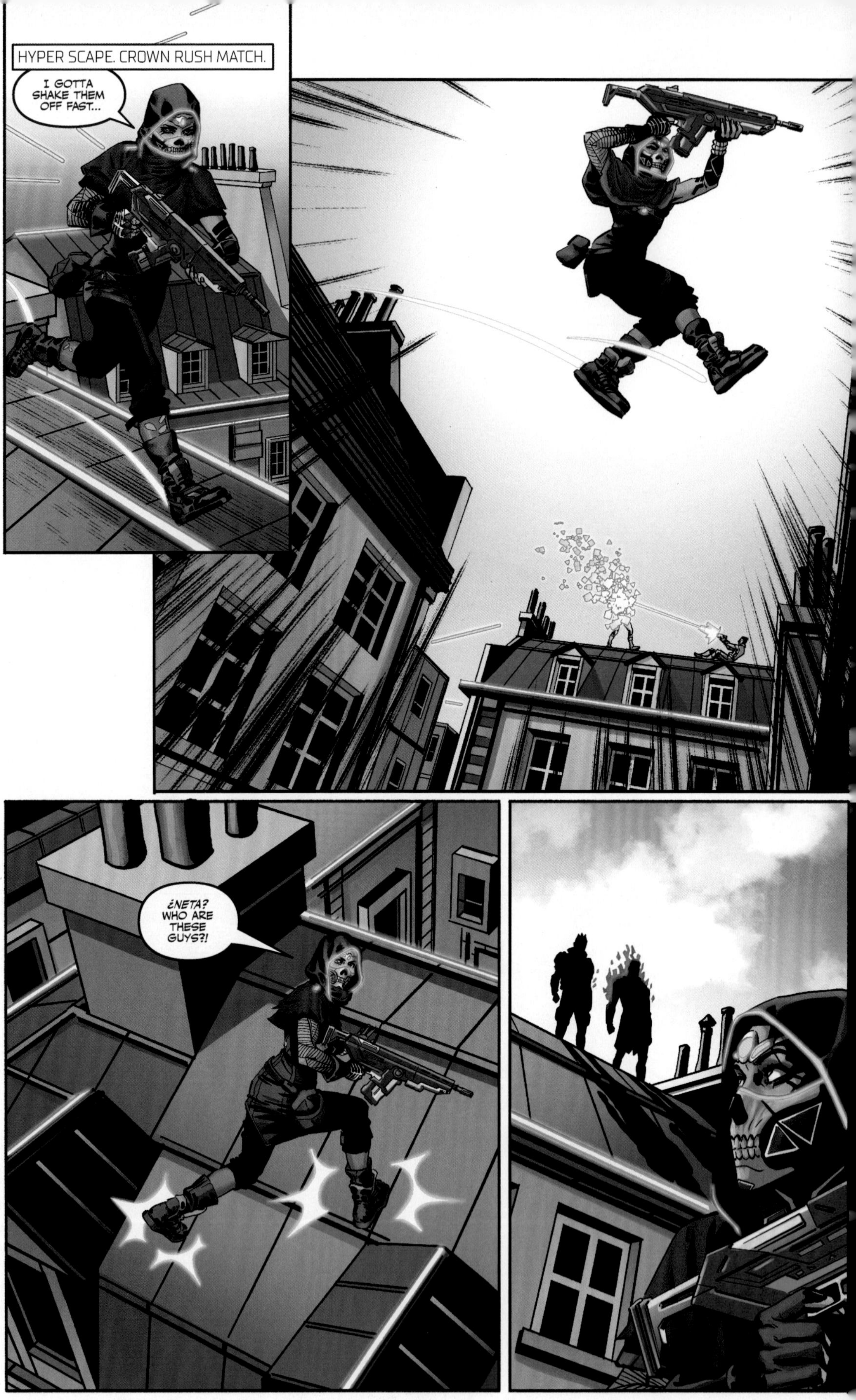
HYPER SCAPE. CROWN RUSH MATCH.
I GOTTA SHAKE THEM OFF FAST...
¿NETA? WHO ARE THESE GUYS?!

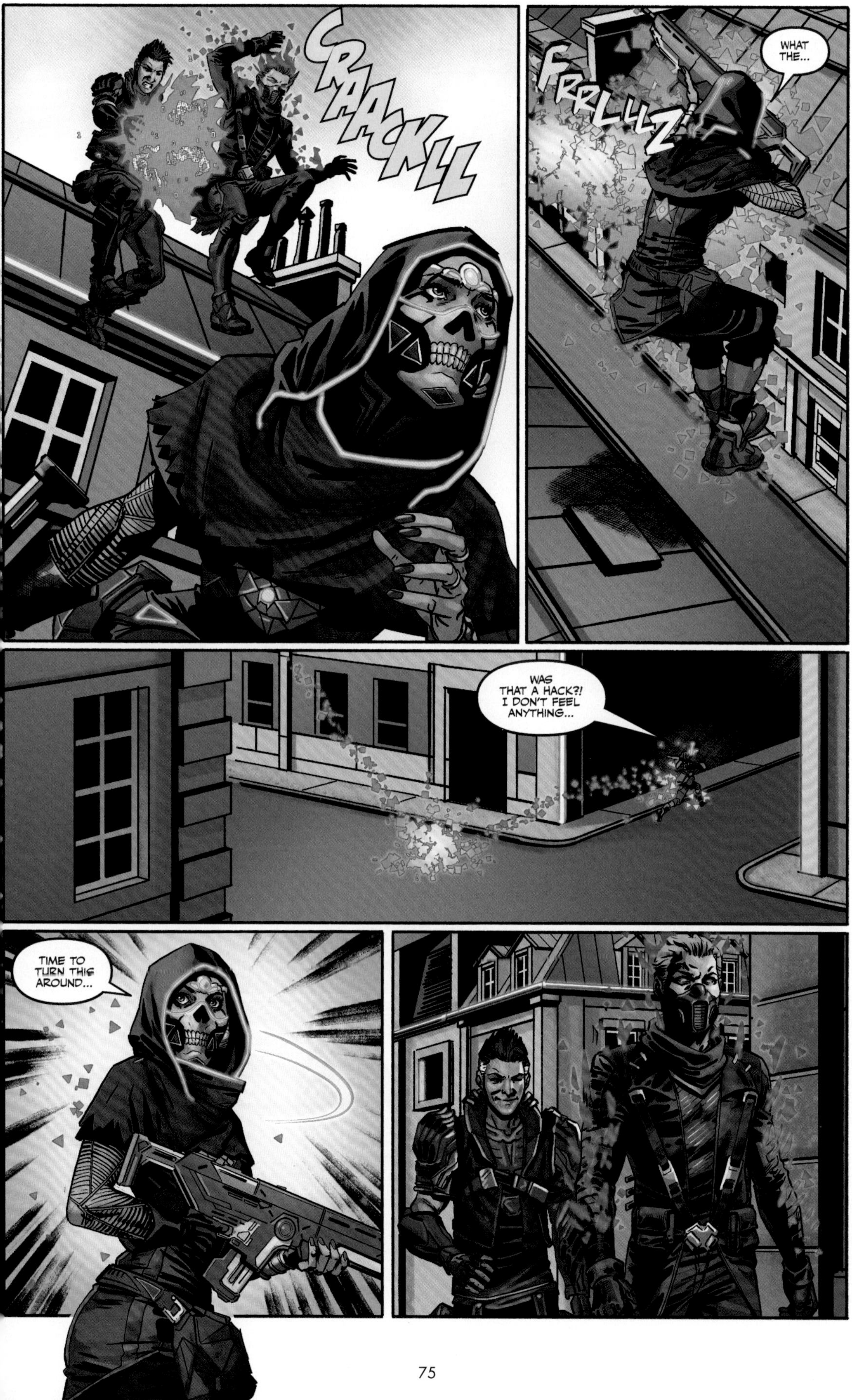
CRACKLL
FRRLLLZ
WHAT THE...
WAS THAT A HACK?! I DON'T FEEL ANYTHING...
TIME TO TURN THIS AROUND...

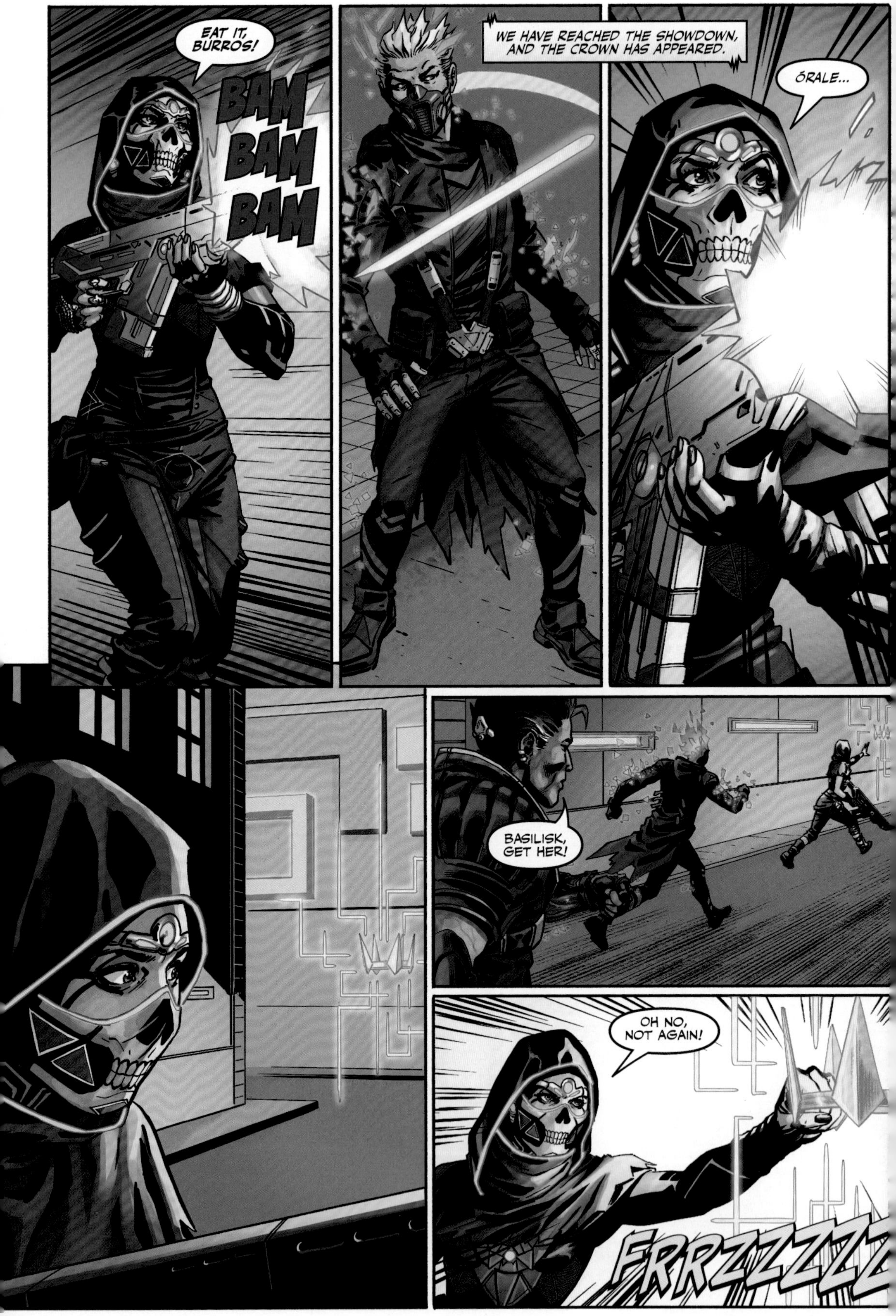
EAT IT, BURROS!
BAM BAM BAM
WE HAVE REACHED THE SHOWDOWN, AND THE CROWN HAS APPEARED.
ÓRALE...
BASILISK, GET HER!
OH NO, NOT AGAIN!
FRRZZZZZ

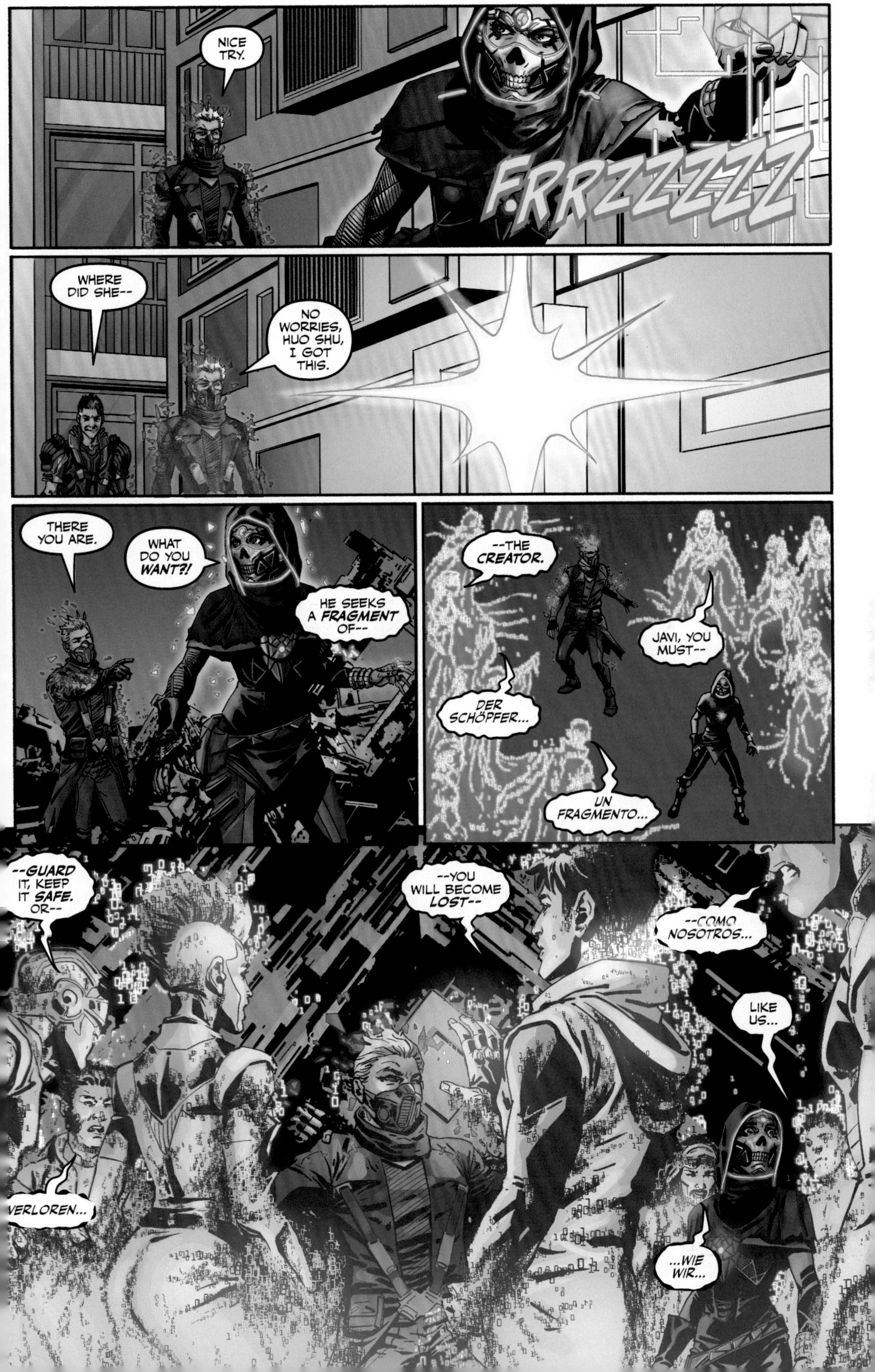
NICE TRY.
FRRZZZZZ
WHERE DID SHE--
NO WORRIES, HUO SHU, I GOT THIS.
THERE YOU ARE.
WHAT DO YOU WANT?!
HE SEEKS A FRAGMENT OF--
--THE CREATOR.
JAVI, YOU MUST--
DER SCHÖPFER...
UN FRAGMENTO...
--GUARD IT, KEEP IT SAFE. OR--
--YOU WILL BECOME LOST--
--COMO NOSOTROS...
LIKE US...
VERLOREN...
...WIE WIR...

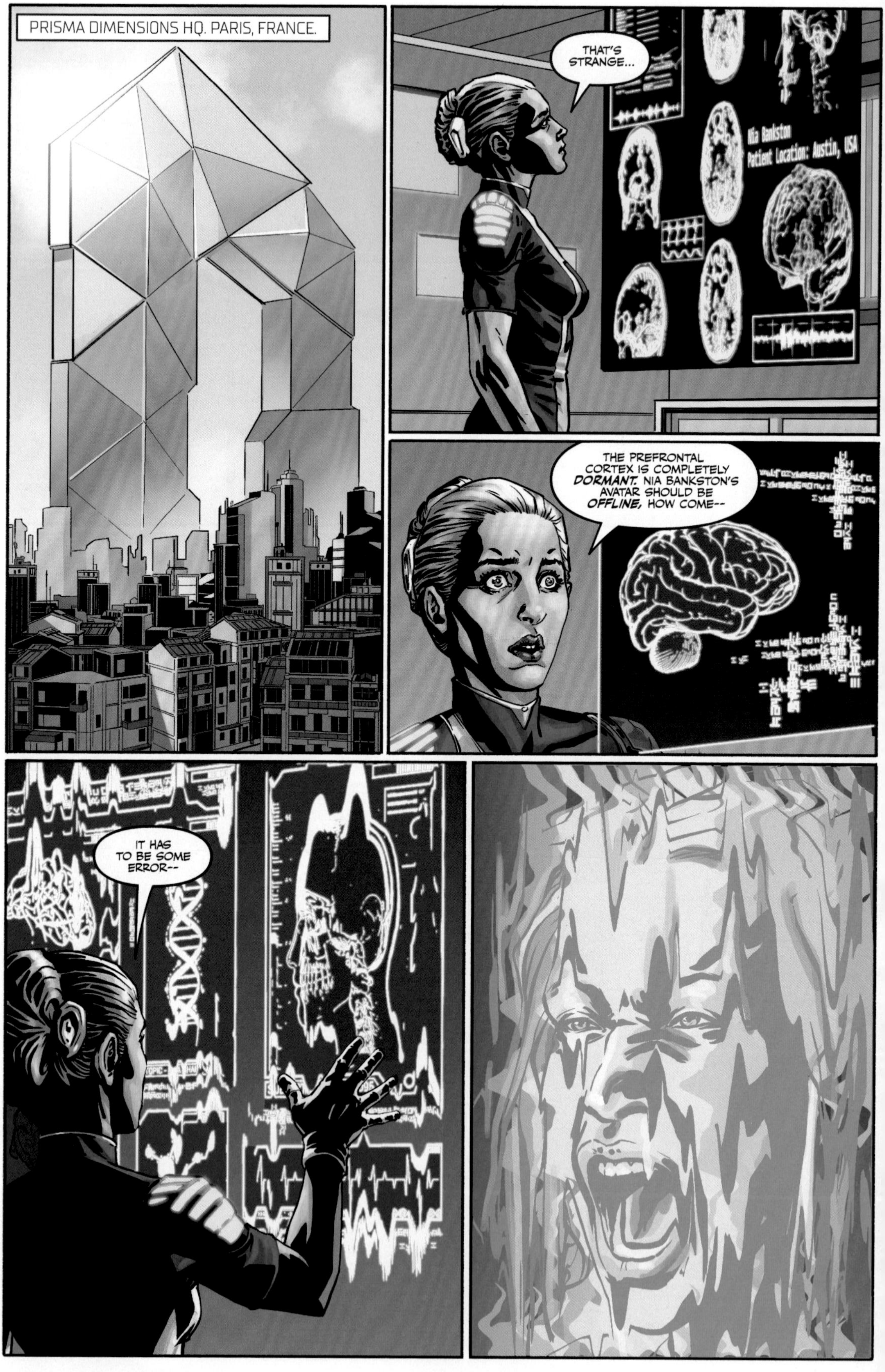
PRISMA DIMENSIONS HQ. PARIS, FRANCE.
THAT'S STRANGE...
Nia Bankston
Patient Location: Austin, USA
THE PREFRONTAL CORTEX IS COMPLETELY *DORMANT.* NIA BANKSTON'S AVATAR SHOULD BE *OFFLINE,* HOW COME--
IT HAS TO BE SOME ERROR--

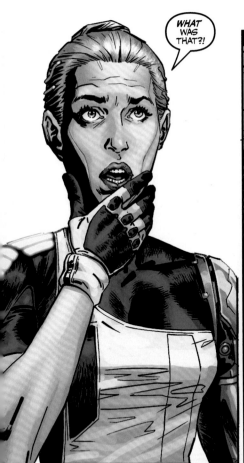

WHAT WAS THAT?!

I'VE NEVER SEEN ANYTHING LIKE THIS--

HOW CAN YOUR AVATAR STILL BE *ACTIVE?*

WHAT IS IT TRYING TO *TELL* ME?

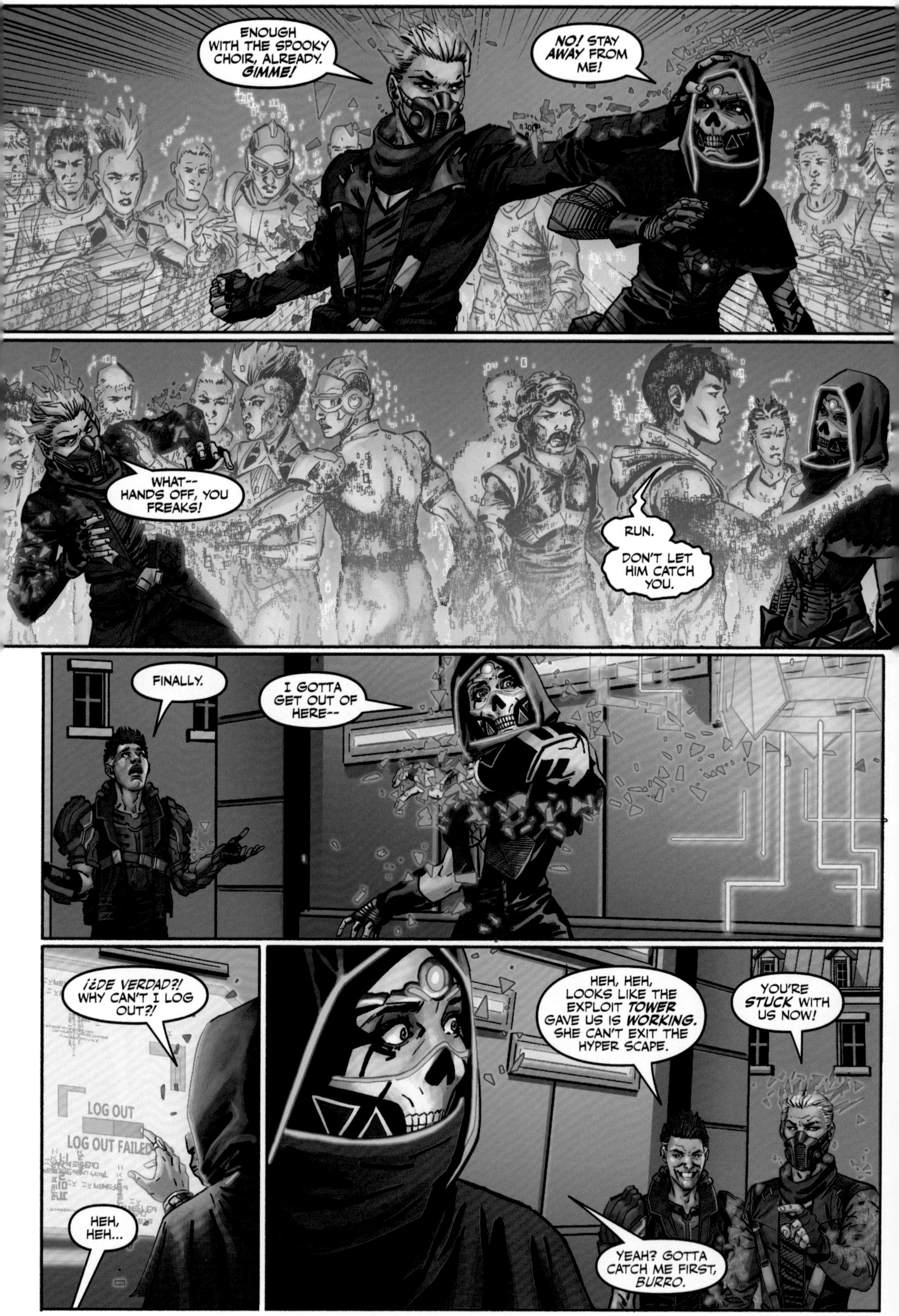
ENOUGH WITH THE SPOOKY CHOIR, ALREADY. GIMME!
NO! STAY AWAY FROM ME!
WHAT-- HANDS OFF, YOU FREAKS!
RUN.
DON'T LET HIM CATCH YOU.
FINALLY.
I GOTTA GET OUT OF HERE--
¡¿DE VERDAD?! WHY CAN'T I LOG OUT?!
LOG OUT
LOG OUT FAILED
HEH, HEH...
HEH, HEH, LOOKS LIKE THE EXPLOIT TOWER GAVE US IS WORKING. SHE CAN'T EXIT THE HYPER SCAPE.
YOU'RE STUCK WITH US NOW!
YEAH? GOTTA CATCH ME FIRST, BURRO.

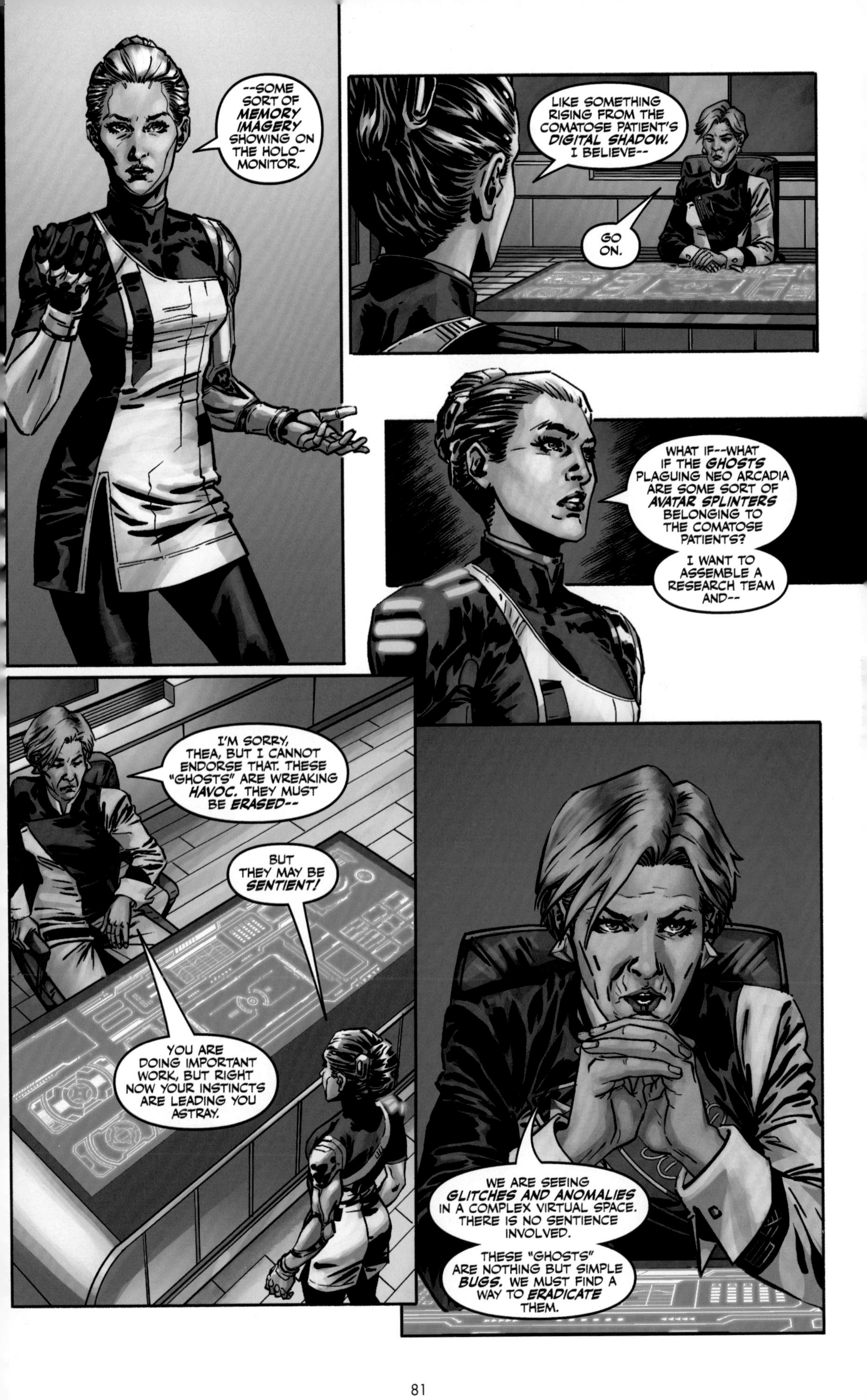
--SOME SORT OF MEMORY IMAGERY SHOWING ON THE HOLO-MONITOR.
LIKE SOMETHING RISING FROM THE COMATOSE PATIENT'S DIGITAL SHADOW. I BELIEVE--
GO ON.
WHAT IF--WHAT IF THE GHOSTS PLAGUING NEO ARCADIA ARE SOME SORT OF AVATAR SPLINTERS BELONGING TO THE COMATOSE PATIENTS?
I WANT TO ASSEMBLE A RESEARCH TEAM AND--
I'M SORRY, THEA, BUT I CANNOT ENDORSE THAT. THESE "GHOSTS" ARE WREAKING HAVOC. THEY MUST BE ERASED--
BUT THEY MAY BE SENTIENT!
YOU ARE DOING IMPORTANT WORK, BUT RIGHT NOW YOUR INSTINCTS ARE LEADING YOU ASTRAY.
WE ARE SEEING GLITCHES AND ANOMALIES IN A COMPLEX VIRTUAL SPACE. THERE IS NO SENTIENCE INVOLVED.
THESE "GHOSTS" ARE NOTHING BUT SIMPLE BUGS. WE MUST FIND A WAY TO ERADICATE THEM.

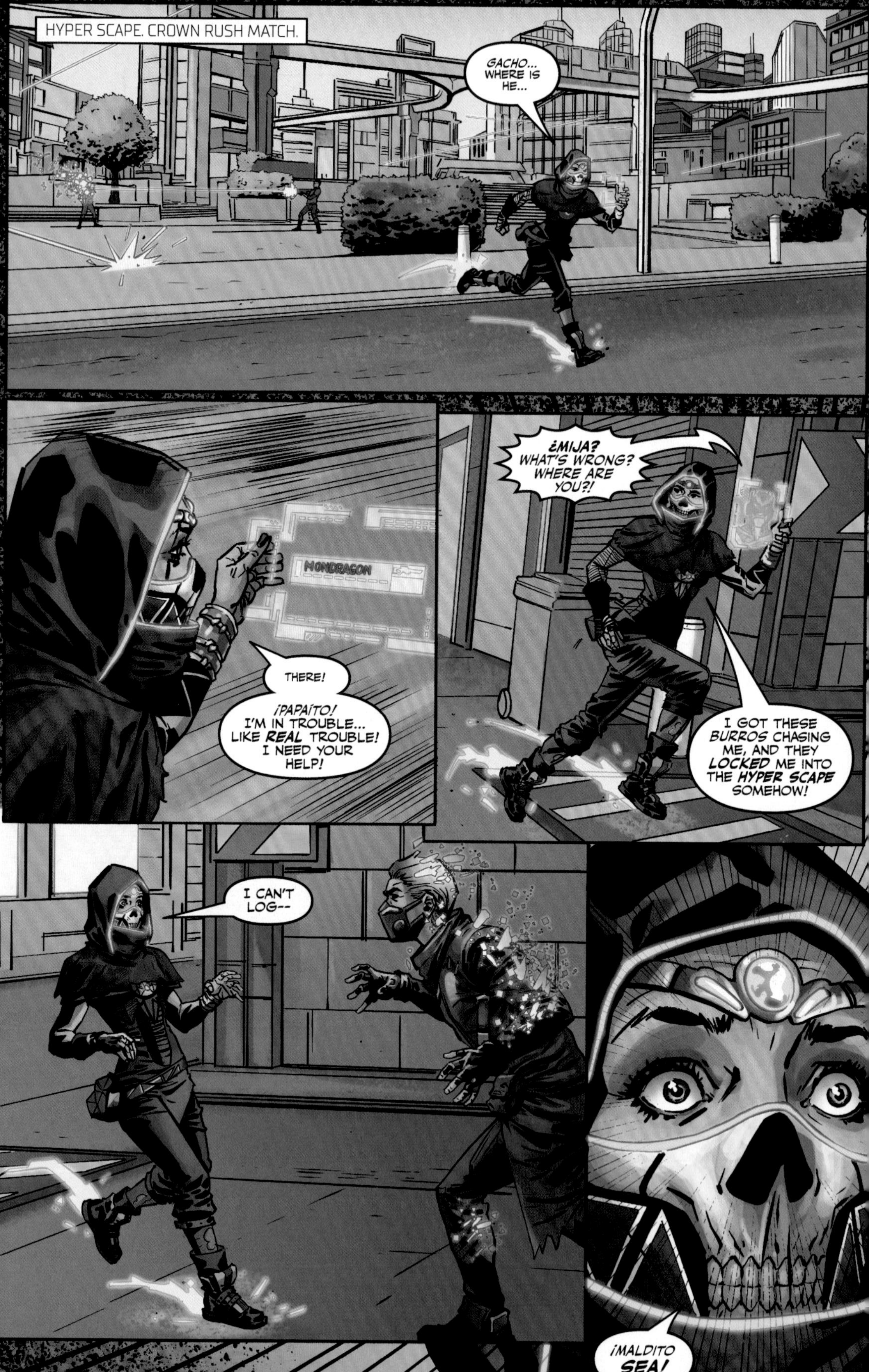
HYPER SCAPE. CROWN RUSH MATCH.
GACHO... WHERE IS HE...
THERE!
¡PAPAÍTO! I'M IN TROUBLE... LIKE REAL TROUBLE! I NEED YOUR HELP!
MONDRAGON
¿MIJA? WHAT'S WRONG? WHERE ARE YOU?!
I GOT THESE BURROS CHASING ME, AND THEY LOCKED ME INTO THE HYPER SCAPE SOMEHOW!
I CAN'T LOG--
¡MALDITO SEA!

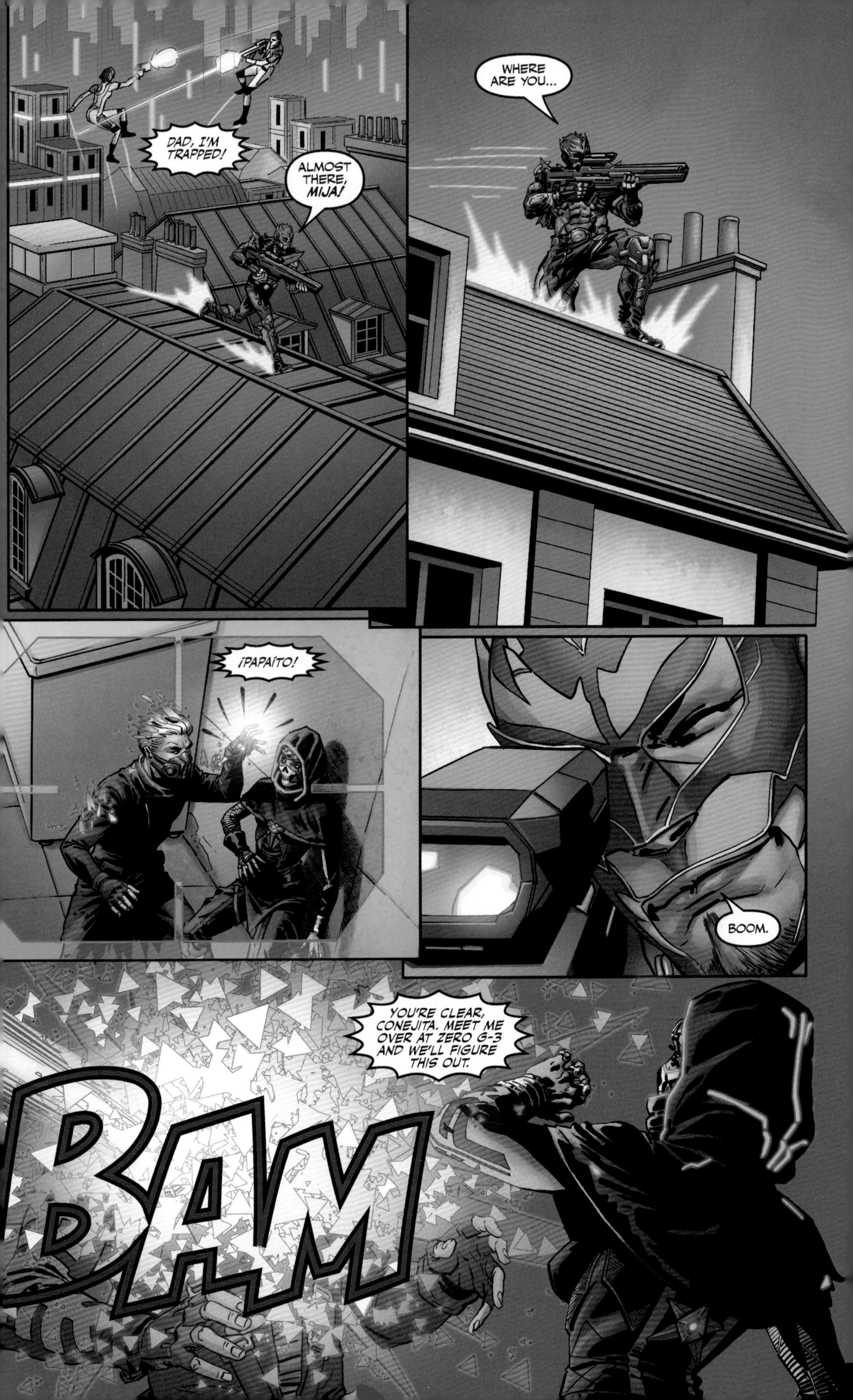
DAD, I'M TRAPPED!
ALMOST THERE, MIJA!
WHERE ARE YOU...
¡PAPAÍTO!
BOOM.
YOU'RE CLEAR, CONEJITA. MEET ME OVER AT ZERO G-3 AND WE'LL FIGURE THIS OUT.
BAM

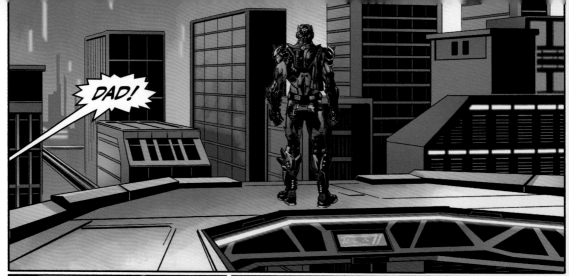

DAD!

I STILL CAN'T LOG OUT! THOSE *BURROS* *MESSED WITH* MY AVATAR SOMEHOW AND--

WE'LL PING PRISMA SECURITY, THEY'LL--

NO! I DON'T-- TRUST THEM...LET'S FIND *ACE*. HE'LL KNOW WHAT TO DO.

JAVI, THIS *VIRUS*, OR WHATEVER THE HELL IT IS, COULD ACTUALLY *KILL* YOU. WE HAVE TO--

WOOOOOOSH

ELIMINATED

THE MATCH IS OVER. LET'S MEET IN YOUR LOCKER!

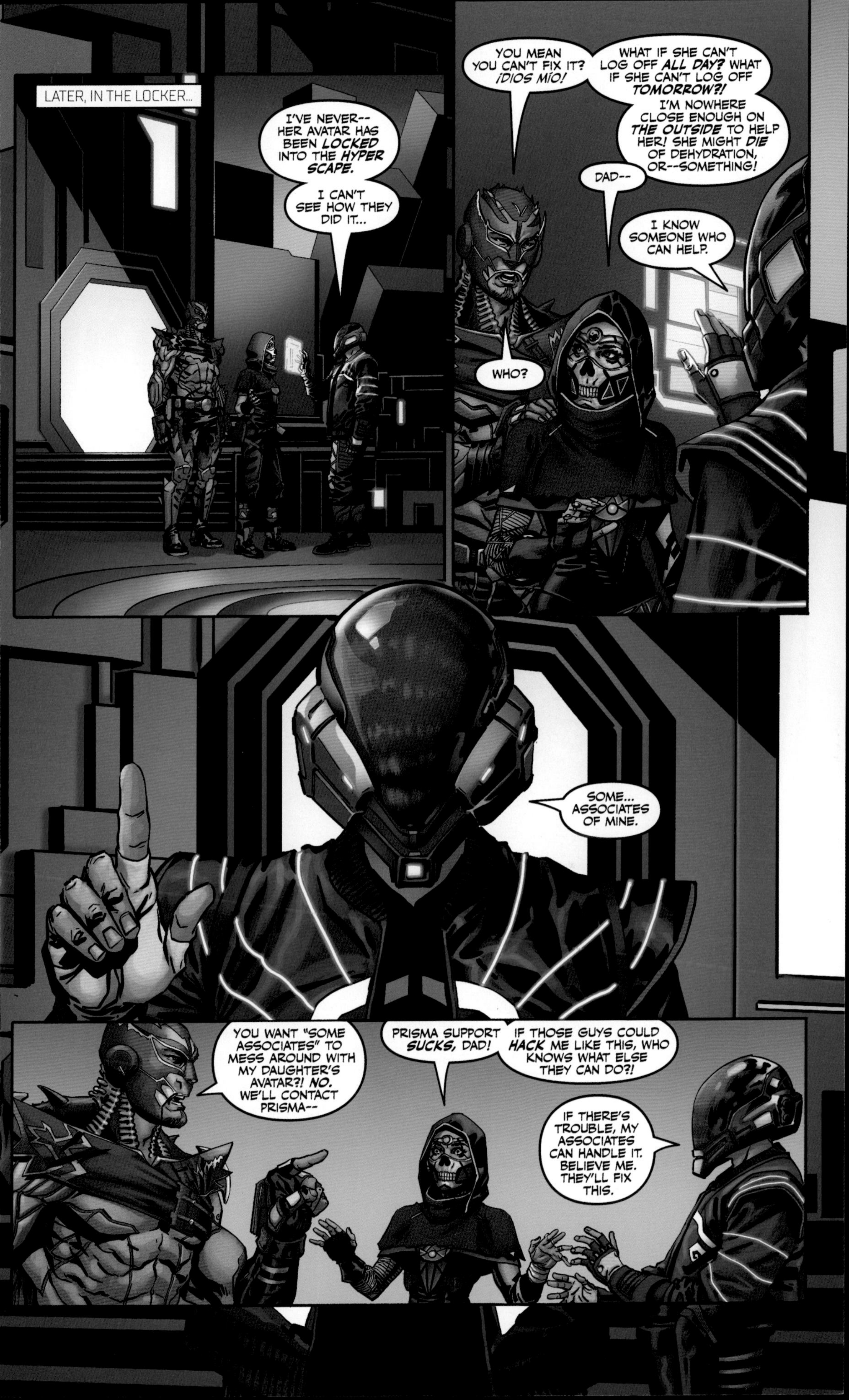
LATER, IN THE LOCKER...
I'VE NEVER-- HER AVATAR HAS BEEN LOCKED INTO THE HYPER SCAPE.
I CAN'T SEE HOW THEY DID IT...
YOU MEAN YOU CAN'T FIX IT? ¡DIOS MÍO!
WHAT IF SHE CAN'T LOG OFF ALL DAY? WHAT IF SHE CAN'T LOG OFF TOMORROW?!
I'M NOWHERE CLOSE ENOUGH ON THE OUTSIDE TO HELP HER! SHE MIGHT DIE OF DEHYDRATION, OR--SOMETHING!
DAD--
I KNOW SOMEONE WHO CAN HELP.
WHO?
SOME... ASSOCIATES OF MINE.
YOU WANT "SOME ASSOCIATES" TO MESS AROUND WITH MY DAUGHTER'S AVATAR?! NO. WE'LL CONTACT PRISMA--
PRISMA SUPPORT SUCKS, DAD!
IF THOSE GUYS COULD HACK ME LIKE THIS, WHO KNOWS WHAT ELSE THEY CAN DO?!
IF THERE'S TROUBLE, MY ASSOCIATES CAN HANDLE IT. BELIEVE ME. THEY'LL FIX THIS.

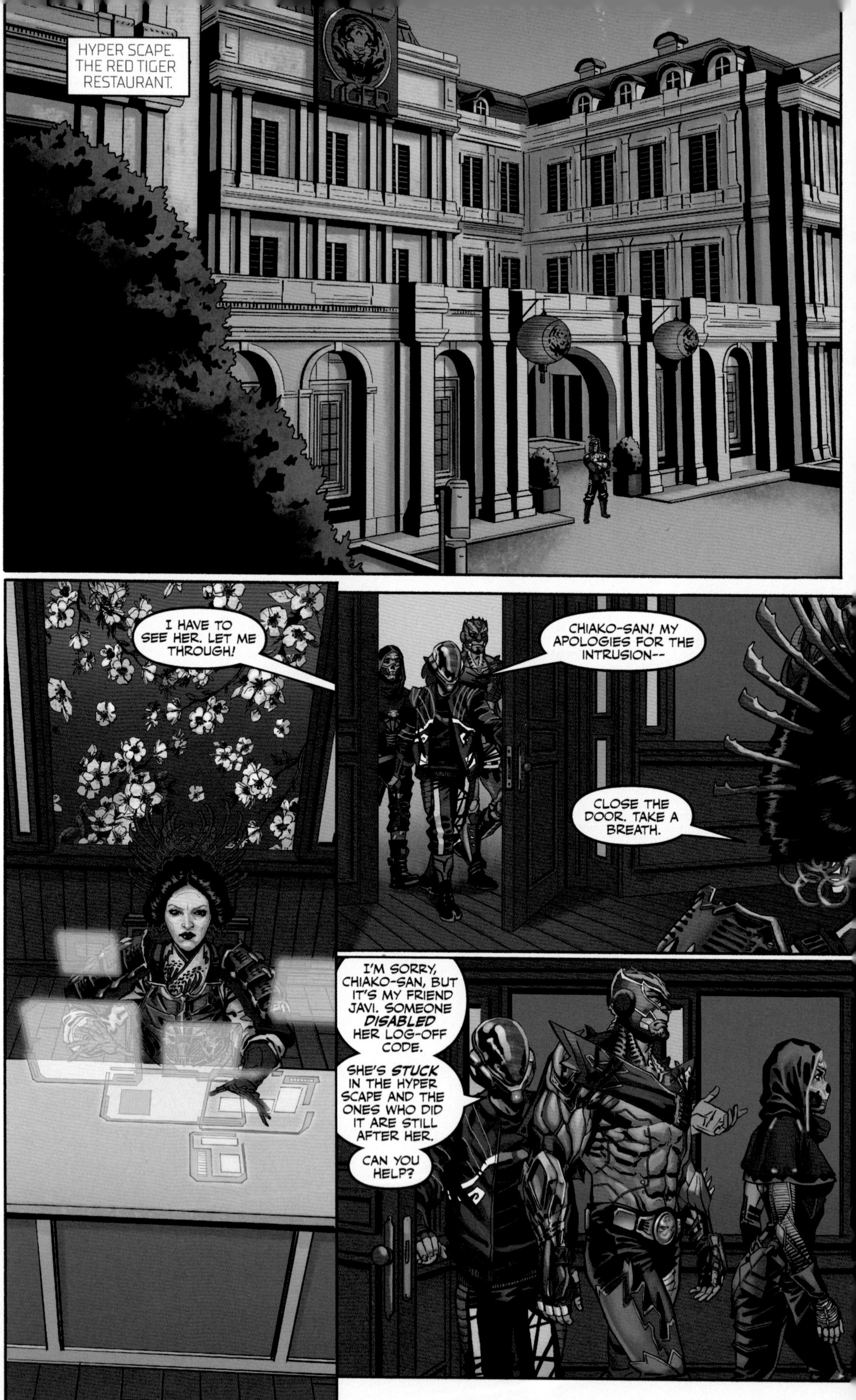
HYPER SCAPE. THE RED TIGER RESTAURANT.
TIGER
I HAVE TO SEE HER. LET ME THROUGH!
CHIAKO-SAN! MY APOLOGIES FOR THE INTRUSION--
CLOSE THE DOOR. TAKE A BREATH.
I'M SORRY, CHIAKO-SAN, BUT IT'S MY FRIEND JAVI. SOMEONE *DISABLED* HER LOG-OFF CODE.
SHE'S *STUCK* IN THE HYPER SCAPE AND THE ONES WHO DID IT ARE STILL AFTER HER.
CAN YOU HELP?

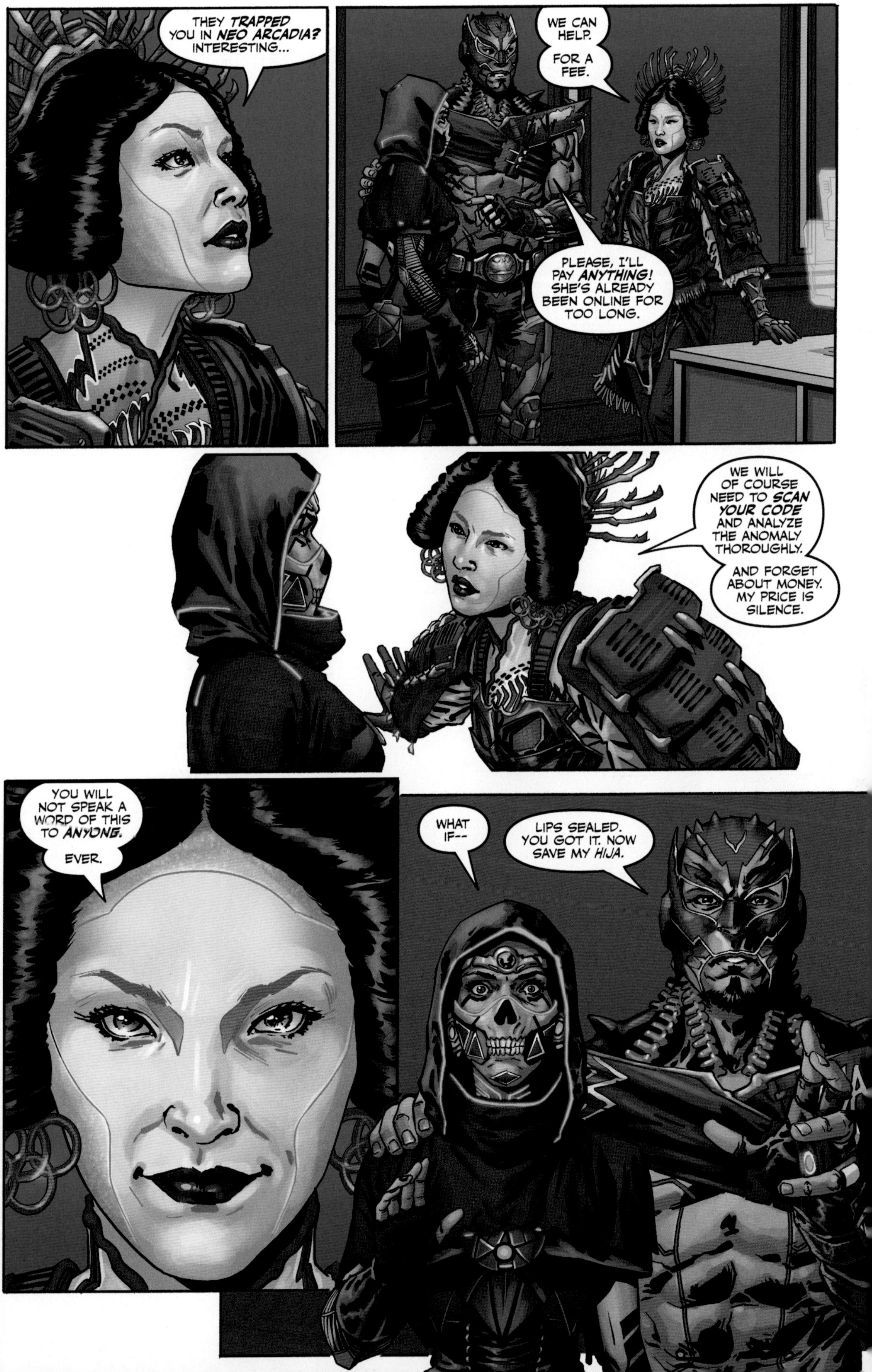
THEY TRAPPED YOU IN NEO ARCADIA? INTERESTING...
WE CAN HELP.
FOR A FEE.
PLEASE, I'LL PAY ANYTHING! SHE'S ALREADY BEEN ONLINE FOR TOO LONG.
WE WILL OF COURSE NEED TO SCAN YOUR CODE AND ANALYZE THE ANOMALY THOROUGHLY.
AND FORGET ABOUT MONEY. MY PRICE IS SILENCE.
YOU WILL NOT SPEAK A WORD OF THIS TO ANYONE.
EVER.
WHAT IF--
LIPS SEALED. YOU GOT IT. NOW SAVE MY HIJA.

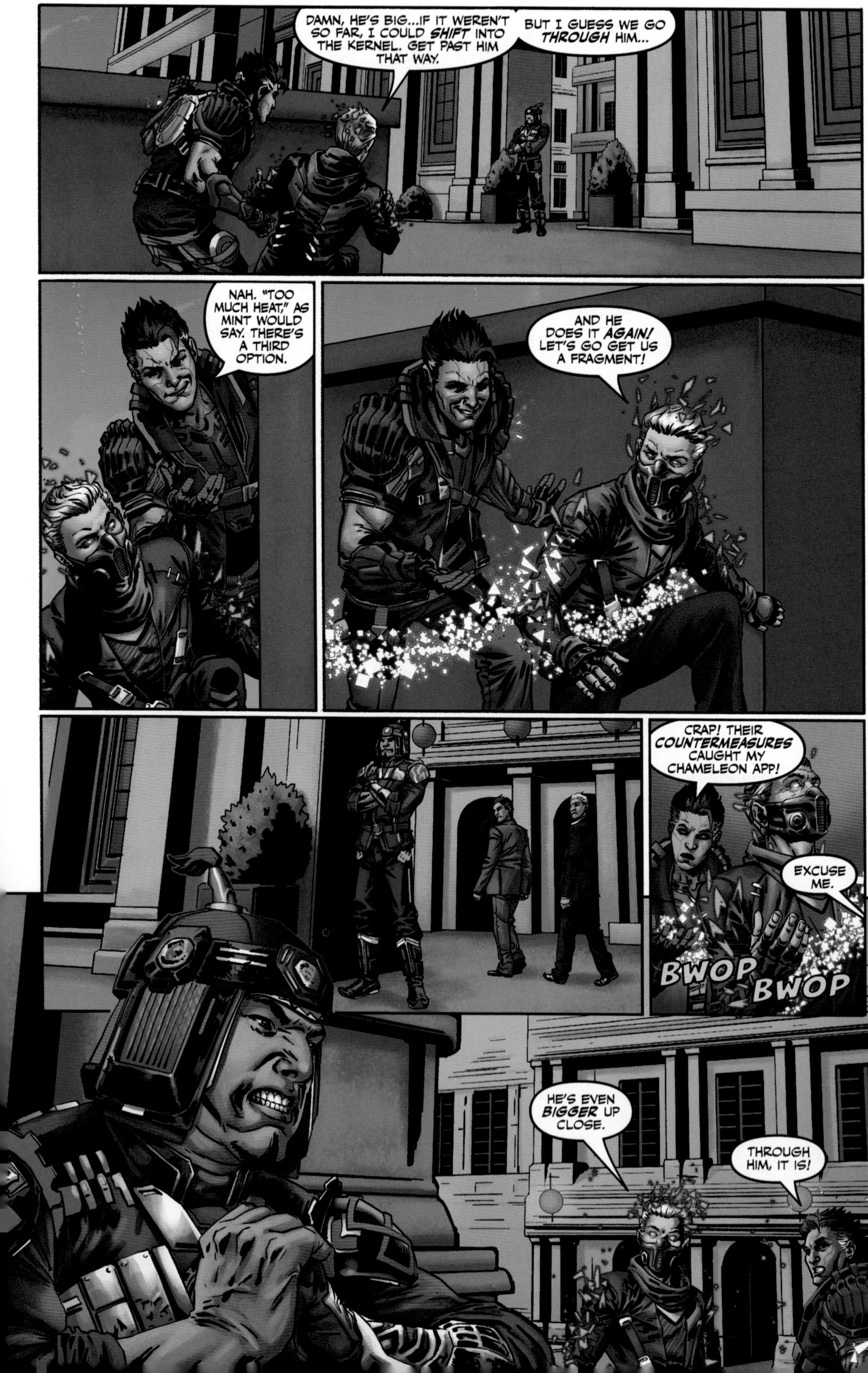
DAMN, HE'S BIG...IF IT WEREN'T SO FAR, I COULD SHIFT INTO THE KERNEL. GET PAST HIM THAT WAY.
BUT I GUESS WE GO THROUGH HIM...
NAH. "TOO MUCH HEAT," AS MINT WOULD SAY. THERE'S A THIRD OPTION.
AND HE DOES IT AGAIN! LET'S GO GET US A FRAGMENT!
CRAP! THEIR COUNTERMEASURES CAUGHT MY CHAMELEON APP!
EXCUSE ME.
BWOP
BWOP
HE'S EVEN BIGGER UP CLOSE.
THROUGH HIM, IT IS!

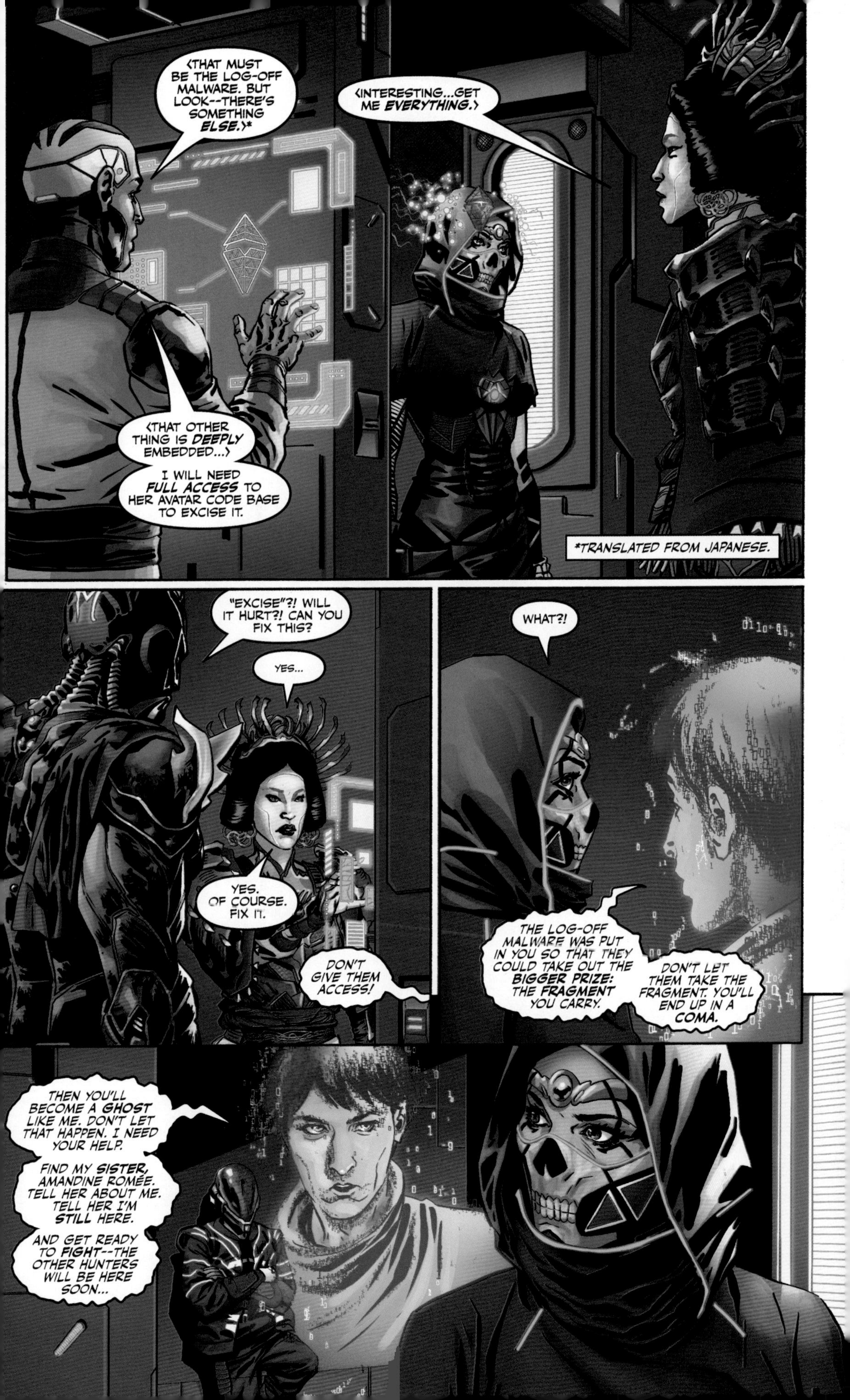
‹THAT MUST BE THE LOG-OFF MALWARE. BUT LOOK--THERE'S SOMETHING ELSE.›*
‹INTERESTING...GET ME EVERYTHING.›
‹THAT OTHER THING IS DEEPLY EMBEDDED...›
I WILL NEED FULL ACCESS TO HER AVATAR CODE BASE TO EXCISE IT.
*TRANSLATED FROM JAPANESE.
"EXCISE"?! WILL IT HURT?! CAN YOU FIX THIS?
YES...
YES. OF COURSE. FIX IT.
DON'T GIVE THEM ACCESS!
WHAT?!
THE LOG-OFF MALWARE WAS PUT IN YOU SO THAT THEY COULD TAKE OUT THE BIGGER PRIZE: THE FRAGMENT YOU CARRY.
DON'T LET THEM TAKE THE FRAGMENT. YOU'LL END UP IN A COMA.
THEN YOU'LL BECOME A GHOST LIKE ME. DON'T LET THAT HAPPEN. I NEED YOUR HELP.
FIND MY SISTER, AMANDINE ROMÉE. TELL HER ABOUT ME. TELL HER I'M STILL HERE.
AND GET READY TO FIGHT--THE OTHER HUNTERS WILL BE HERE SOON...

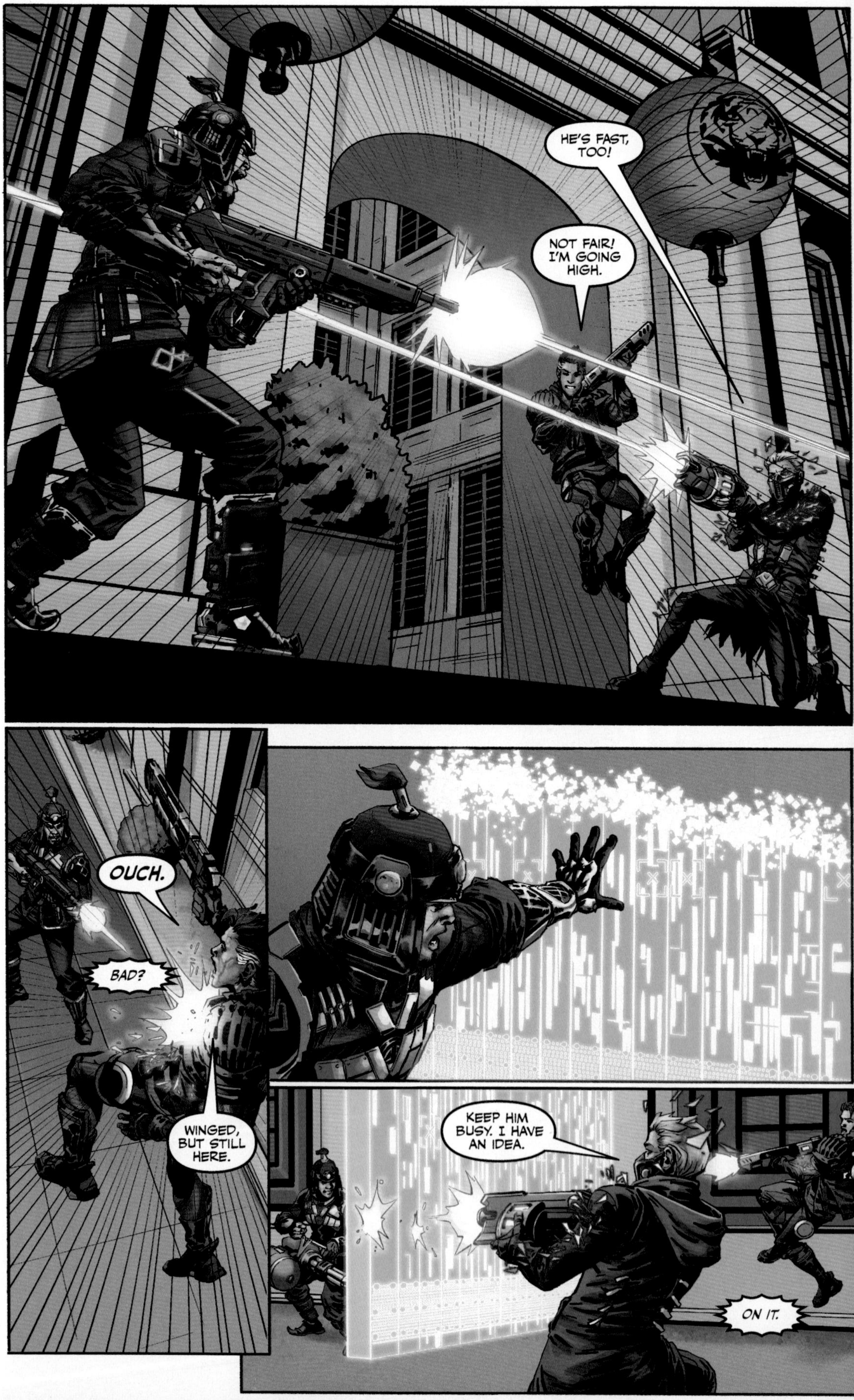
HE'S FAST, TOO!
NOT FAIR! I'M GOING HIGH.
OUCH.
BAD?
WINGED, BUT STILL HERE.
KEEP HIM BUSY. I HAVE AN IDEA.
ON IT.

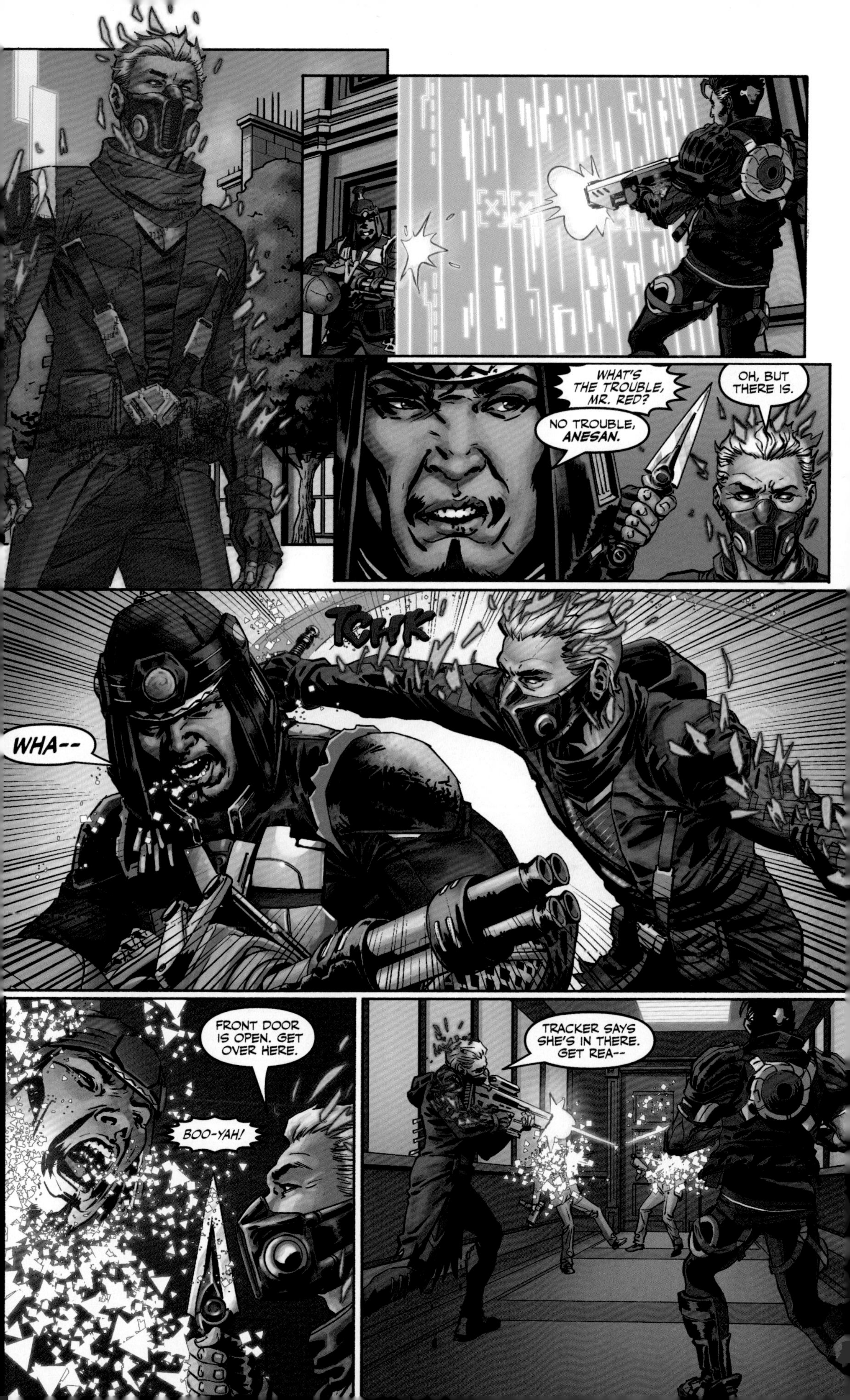
WHAT'S THE TROUBLE, MR. RED?
NO TROUBLE, ANESAN.
OH, BUT THERE IS.
TCHK
WHA--
FRONT DOOR IS OPEN. GET OVER HERE.
BOO-YAH!
TRACKER SAYS SHE'S IN THERE. GET REA--

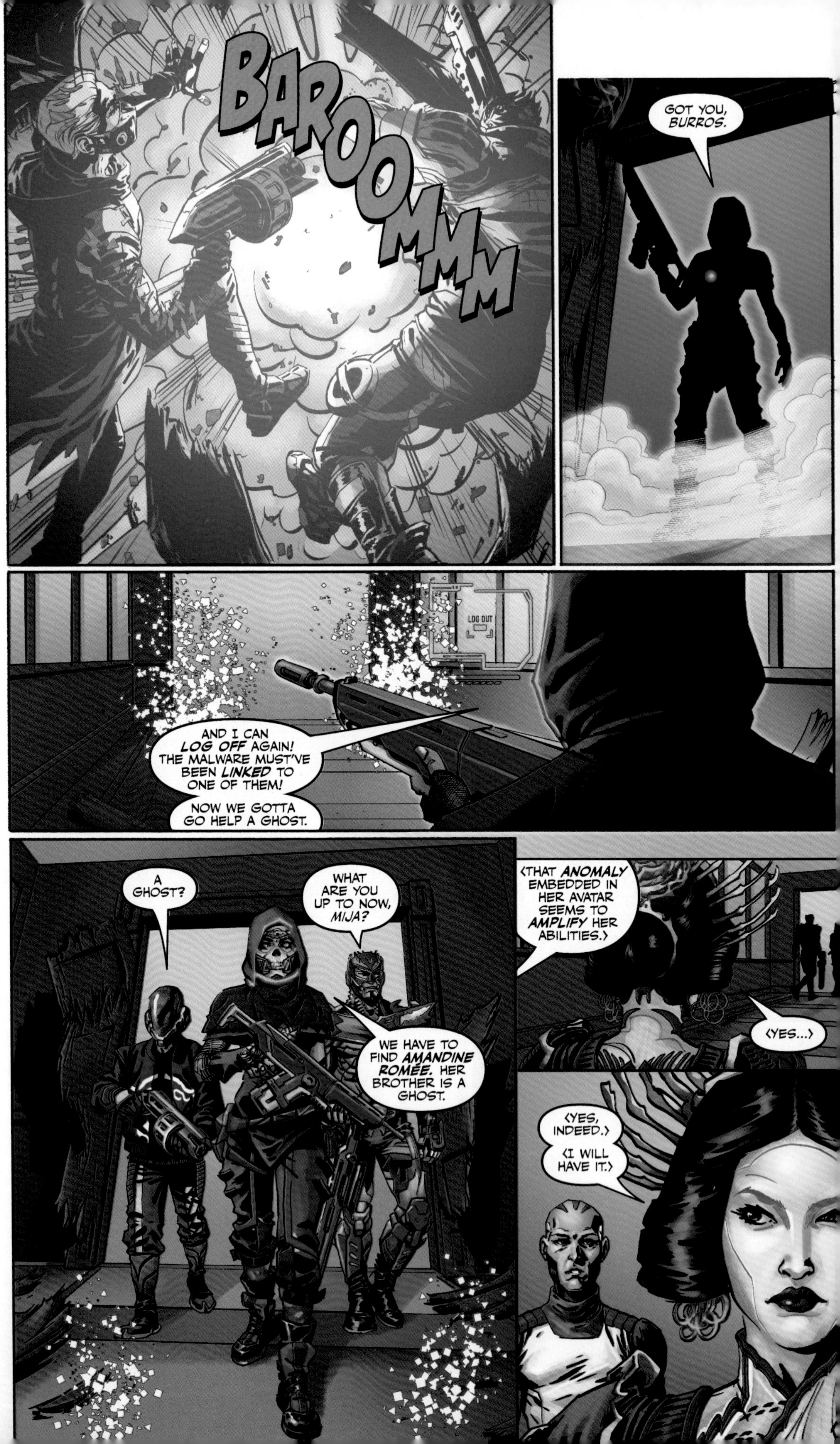
BAROOOMMMM
GOT YOU, BURROS.
LOG OUT
AND I CAN LOG OFF AGAIN! THE MALWARE MUST'VE BEEN LINKED TO ONE OF THEM!
NOW WE GOTTA GO HELP A GHOST.
A GHOST?
WHAT ARE YOU UP TO NOW, MIJA?
WE HAVE TO FIND AMANDINE ROMÉE. HER BROTHER IS A GHOST.
<THAT ANOMALY EMBEDDED IN HER AVATAR SEEMS TO AMPLIFY HER ABILITIES.>
<YES...>
<YES, INDEED.>
<I WILL HAVE IT.>

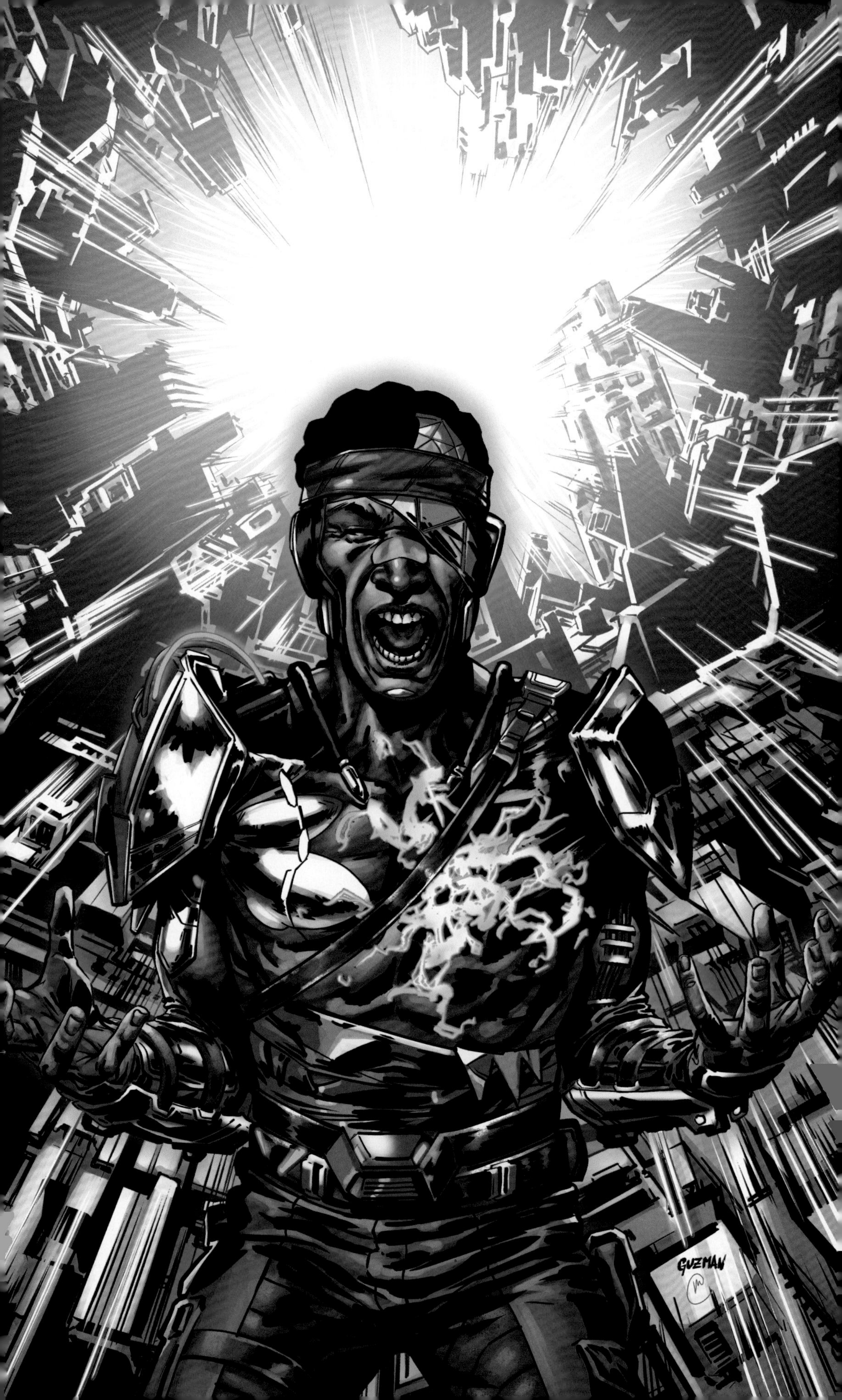
GUZMAN

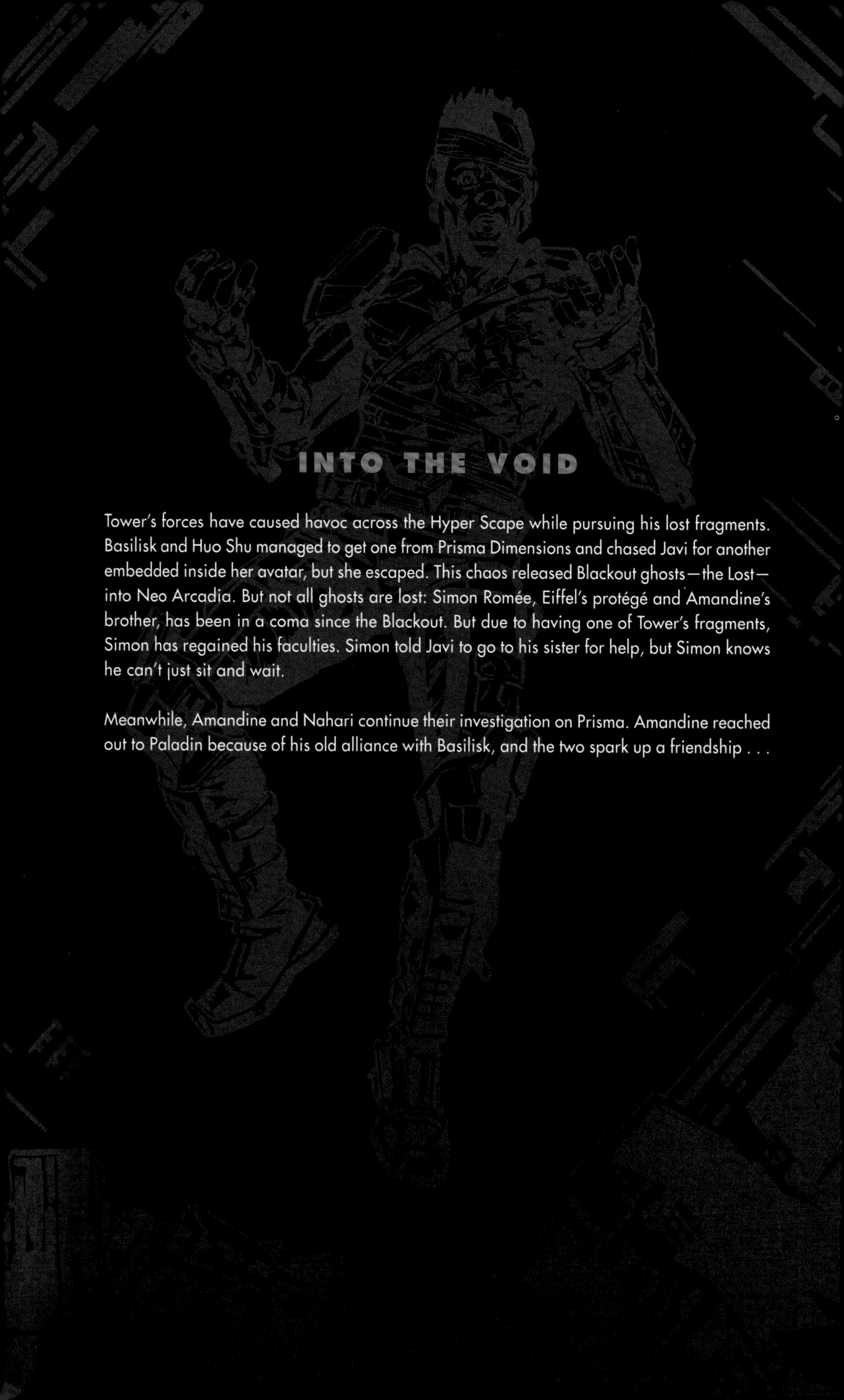

INTO THE VOID

Tower's forces have caused havoc across the Hyper Scape while pursuing his lost fragments. Basilisk and Huo Shu managed to get one from Prisma Dimensions and chased Javi for another embedded inside her avatar, but she escaped. This chaos released Blackout ghosts—the Lost—into Neo Arcadia. But not all ghosts are lost: Simon Romée, Eiffel's protégé and Amandine's brother, has been in a coma since the Blackout. But due to having one of Tower's fragments, Simon has regained his faculties. Simon told Javi to go to his sister for help, but Simon knows he can't just sit and wait.

Meanwhile, Amandine and Nahari continue their investigation on Prisma. Amandine reached out to Paladin because of his old alliance with Basilisk, and the two spark up a friendship . . .

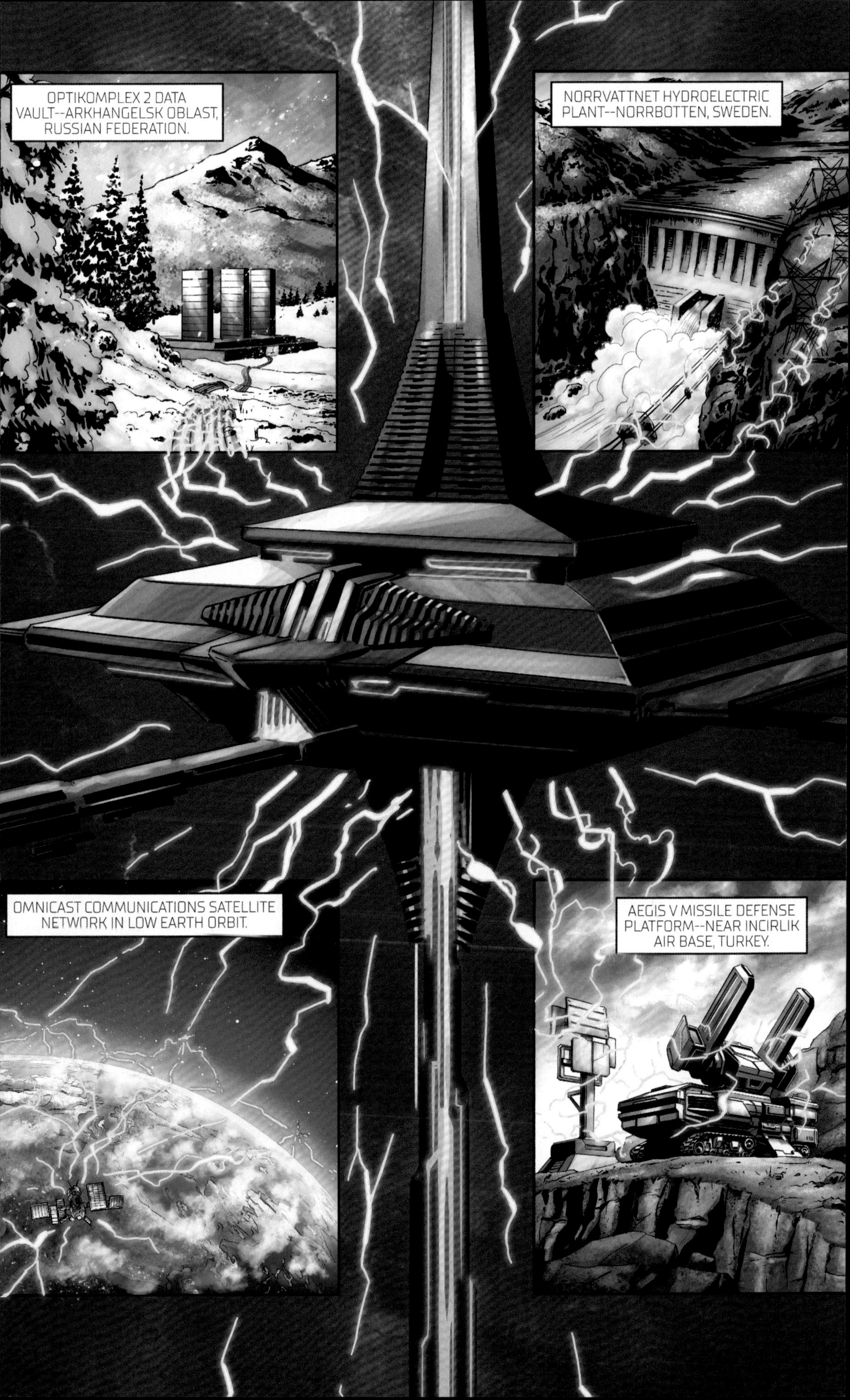
OPTIKOMPLEX 2 DATA VAULT--ARKHANGELSK OBLAST, RUSSIAN FEDERATION.
NORRVATTNET HYDROELECTRIC PLANT--NORRBOTTEN, SWEDEN.
OMNICAST COMMUNICATIONS SATELLITE NETWORK IN LOW EARTH ORBIT.
AEGIS V MISSILE DEFENSE PLATFORM--NEAR INCIRLIK AIR BASE, TURKEY.

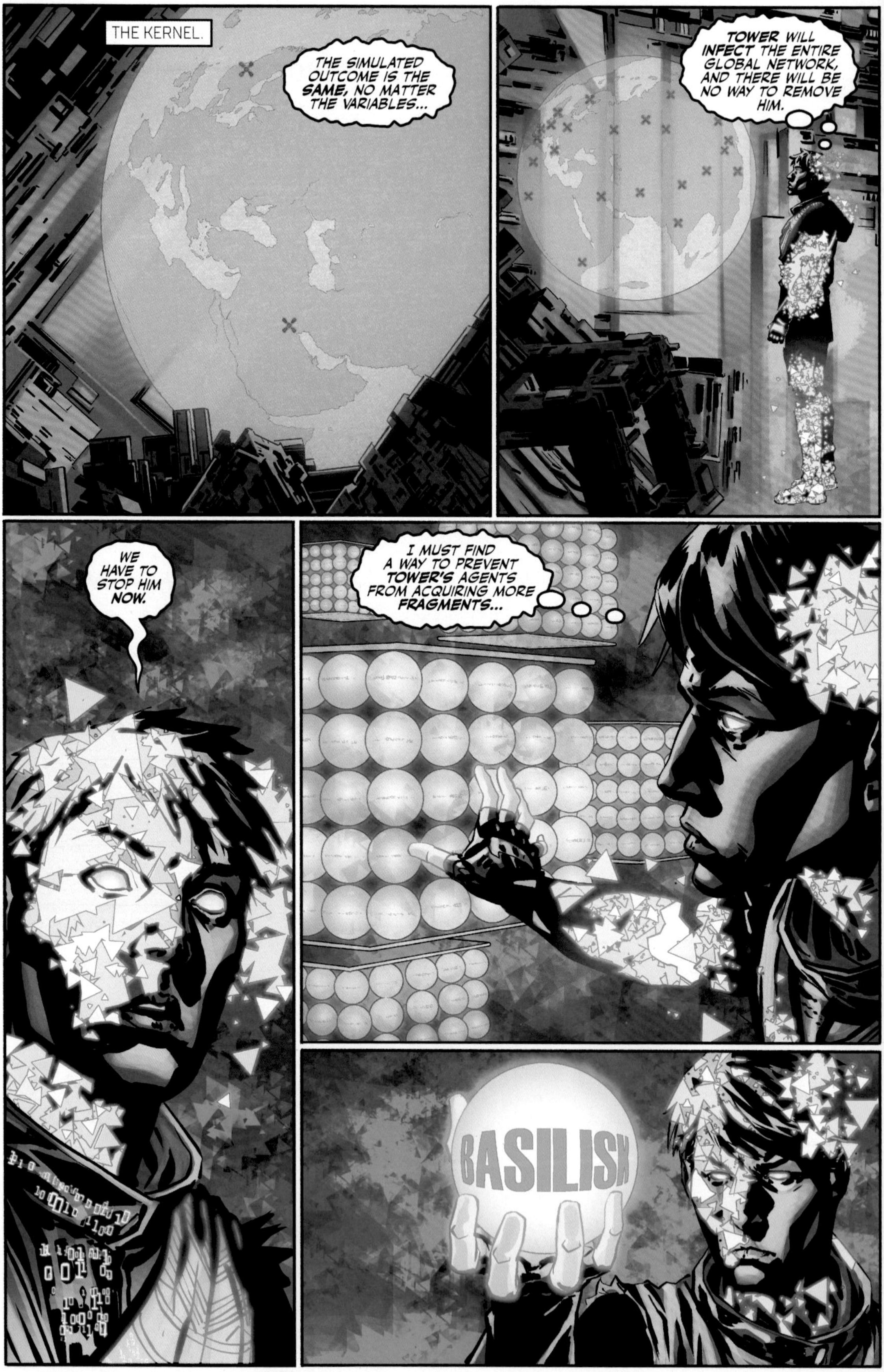
THE KERNEL.
THE SIMULATED OUTCOME IS THE SAME, NO MATTER THE VARIABLES...
TOWER WILL INFECT THE ENTIRE GLOBAL NETWORK, AND THERE WILL BE NO WAY TO REMOVE HIM.
WE HAVE TO STOP HIM NOW.
I MUST FIND A WAY TO PREVENT TOWER'S AGENTS FROM ACQUIRING MORE FRAGMENTS...
BASILISK

HYPER SCAPE ID: Basilisk

NAME: Giang Tran

AGE: 20

MAJOR CONTACTS

MINOR CONTACTS

FAMILY: Katherine [Mother] Daniel [Father]

INCOME SEGMENT: Low 45th percentile

RESIDENCE: Austin, Rep. of Texas

LET'S SEE WHO YOUR FRIENDS ARE...

AND IDENTIFY ANY ANOMALIES...

PALADIN, HUH?

MAJOR CONTACTS

Paladin Rook

Berry Huo Shu

MINOR CONTACTS

WHAT IS SO SPECIAL ABOUT YOU...

MAJOR CONTACTS

Rook Paladin

Berry Huo Shu

Hours Played Together
Season 1: 203.5
Season 2: 7.2
Season 3: 0

NAME: Giang Tran

HYPER SCAPE ID: Basilisk

AGE: 20

HYPER SCAPE ID: Paladin

NAME: Julian Jayden Bankston

AGE: 20

FAMILY: Katherine [Mother] Daniel [Father]

INCOME SEGMENT: Low 45th percentile

FAMILY: Nia [Mother] Gabriella [Sister]

RESIDENCE: Austin, Rep. of Texas

INCOME SEGMENT: Very Low percen

HMM...THE TWO OF YOU USED TO BE CLOSE...

BUT YOU HAVEN'T PLAYED TOGETHER SINCE BASILISK BECAME *TOWER'S ERRAND BOY.* INTERESTING...

RESIDENCE: Austin, Rep. of Texas

AGE: 20

HYPER SCAPE ID: Paladin

AGE: 20

I NEED SOMETHING TO WORK WITH...

THERE...

INCOME SEGMENT: w 45th percentile

FAMILY: Nia [Mother] Gabriella [Sister]

RESIDENCE: Austin, Rep.

INCOME SEGMEN Very Low percent

GABRIELLA BANKSTON, EDUCATION SUBSCRIPTION FEE, **OVERDUE**

JE TE TIENS!

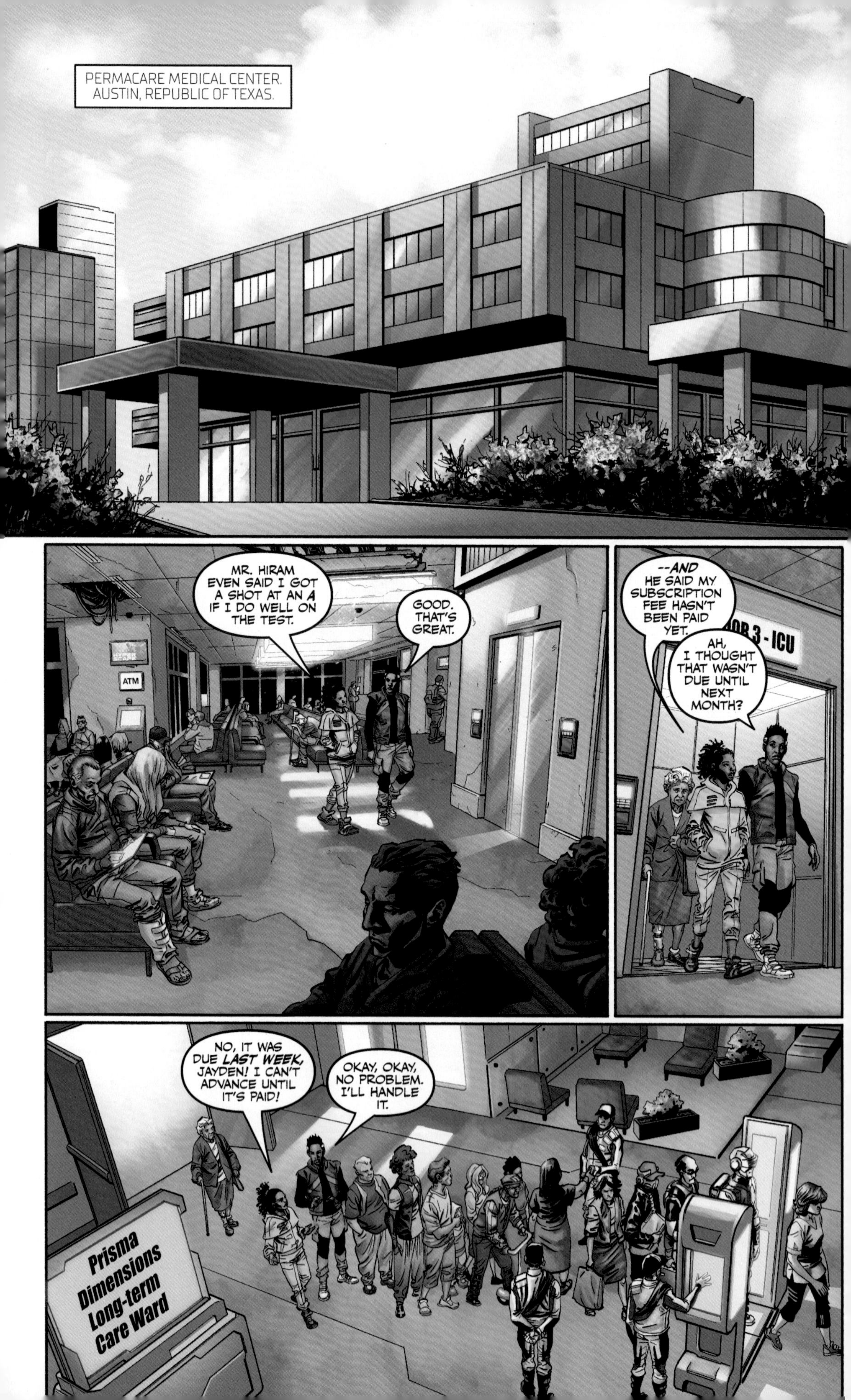
PERMACARE MEDICAL CENTER.
AUSTIN, REPUBLIC OF TEXAS.
ATM
MR. HIRAM EVEN SAID I GOT A SHOT AT AN *A* IF I DO WELL ON THE TEST.
GOOD. THAT'S GREAT.
--*AND* HE SAID MY SUBSCRIPTION FEE HASN'T BEEN PAID YET.
OR 3 - ICU
AH, I THOUGHT THAT WASN'T DUE UNTIL NEXT MONTH?
NO, IT WAS DUE *LAST WEEK,* JAYDEN! I CAN'T ADVANCE UNTIL IT'S PAID!
OKAY, OKAY, NO PROBLEM. I'LL HANDLE IT.
Prisma Dimensions Long-term Care Ward

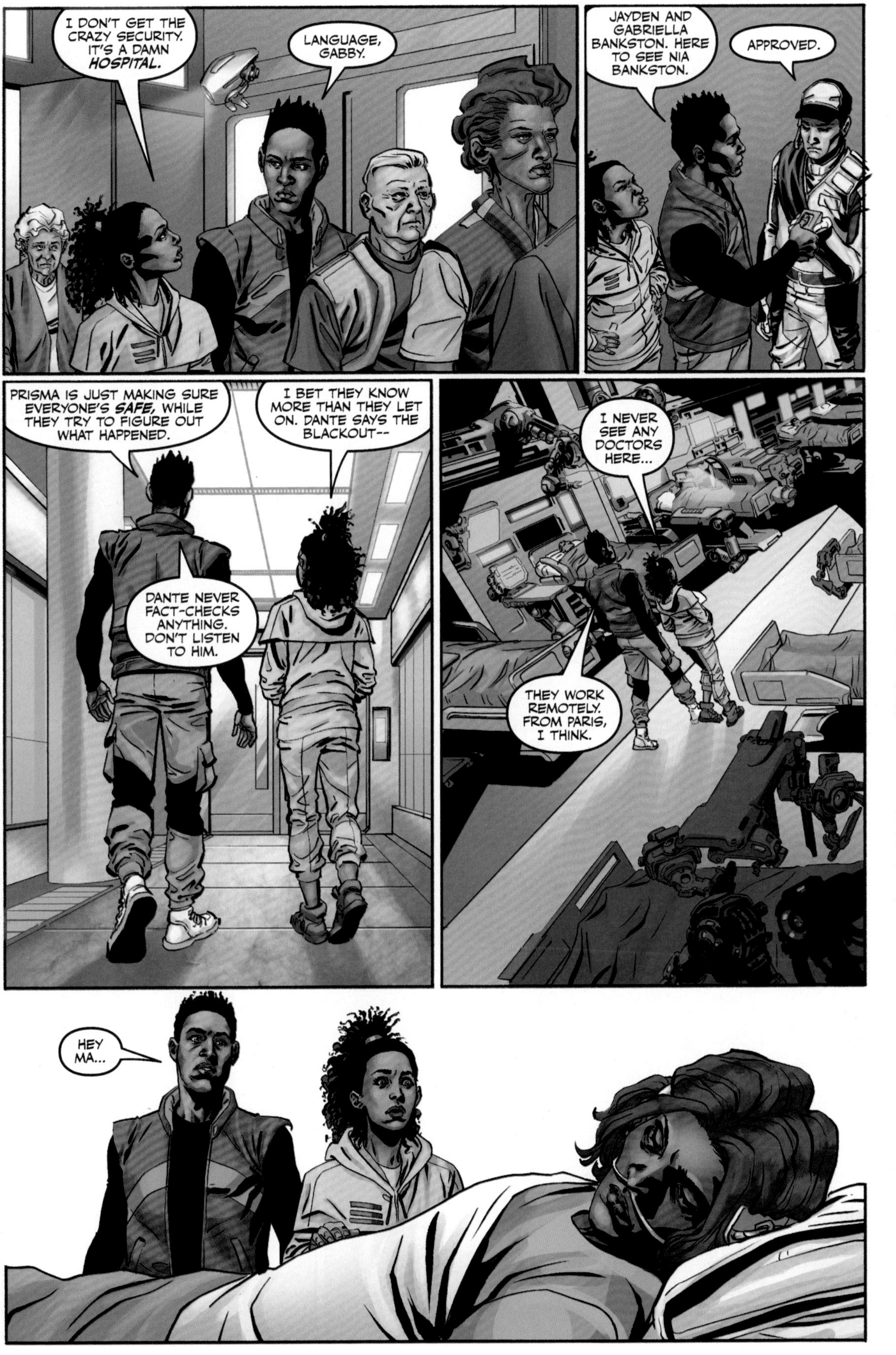
I DON'T GET THE CRAZY SECURITY. IT'S A DAMN *HOSPITAL.*
LANGUAGE, GABBY.
JAYDEN AND GABRIELLA BANKSTON. HERE TO SEE NIA BANKSTON.
APPROVED.
PRISMA IS JUST MAKING SURE EVERYONE'S *SAFE,* WHILE THEY TRY TO FIGURE OUT WHAT HAPPENED.
I BET THEY KNOW MORE THAN THEY LET ON. DANTE SAYS THE BLACKOUT--
DANTE NEVER FACT-CHECKS ANYTHING. DON'T LISTEN TO HIM.
I NEVER SEE ANY DOCTORS HERE...
THEY WORK REMOTELY. FROM PARIS, I THINK.
HEY MA...

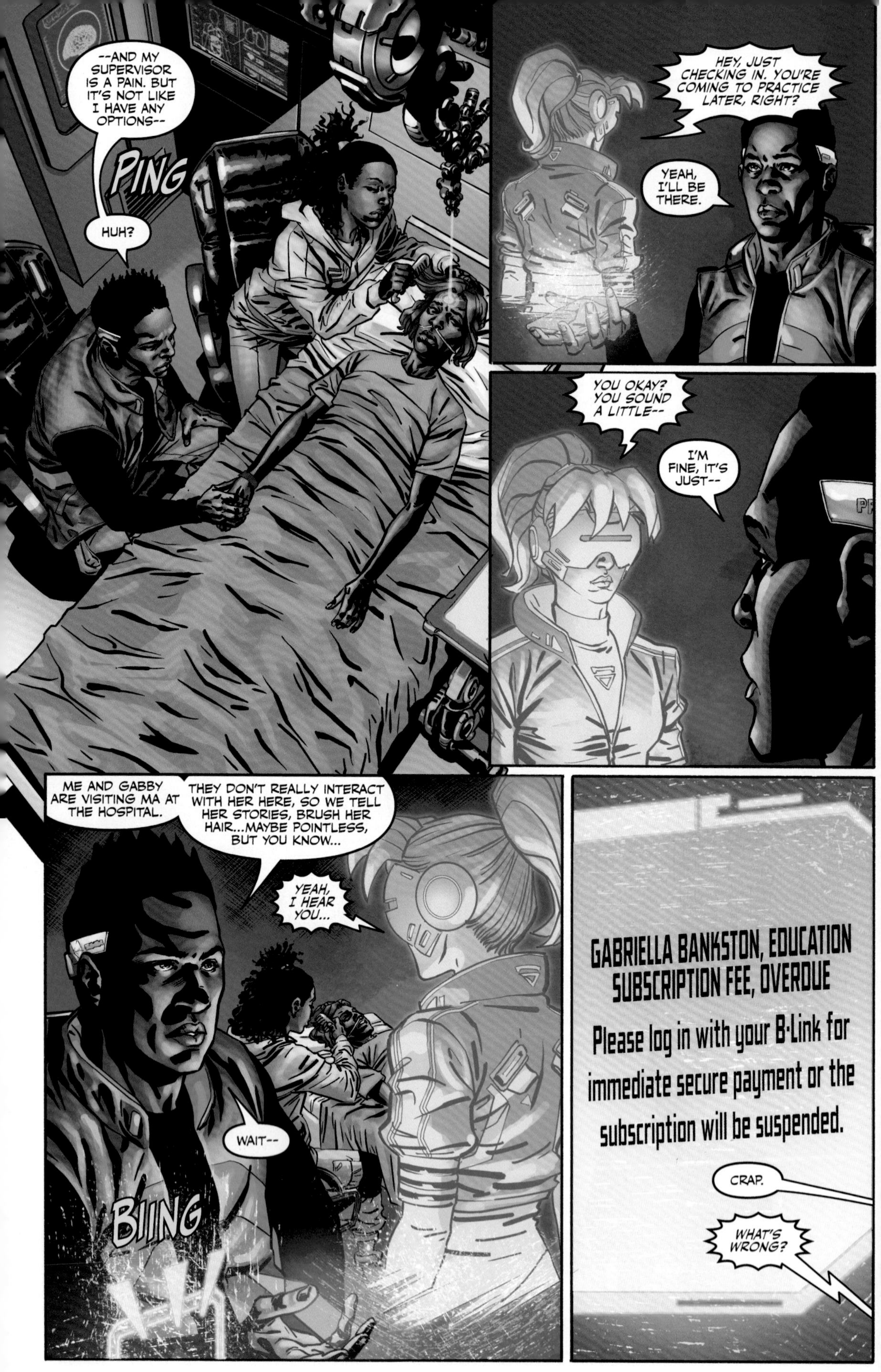
--AND MY SUPERVISOR IS A PAIN. BUT IT'S NOT LIKE I HAVE ANY OPTIONS--
PING
HUH?
HEY, JUST CHECKING IN. YOU'RE COMING TO PRACTICE LATER, RIGHT?
YEAH, I'LL BE THERE.
YOU OKAY? YOU SOUND A LITTLE--
I'M FINE, IT'S JUST--
ME AND GABBY ARE VISITING MA AT THE HOSPITAL.
THEY DON'T REALLY INTERACT WITH HER HERE, SO WE TELL HER STORIES, BRUSH HER HAIR...MAYBE POINTLESS, BUT YOU KNOW...
YEAH, I HEAR YOU...
WAIT--
BIING
GABRIELLA BANKSTON, EDUCATION SUBSCRIPTION FEE, OVERDUE
Please log in with your B-Link for immediate secure payment or the subscription will be suspended.
CRAP.
WHAT'S WRONG?

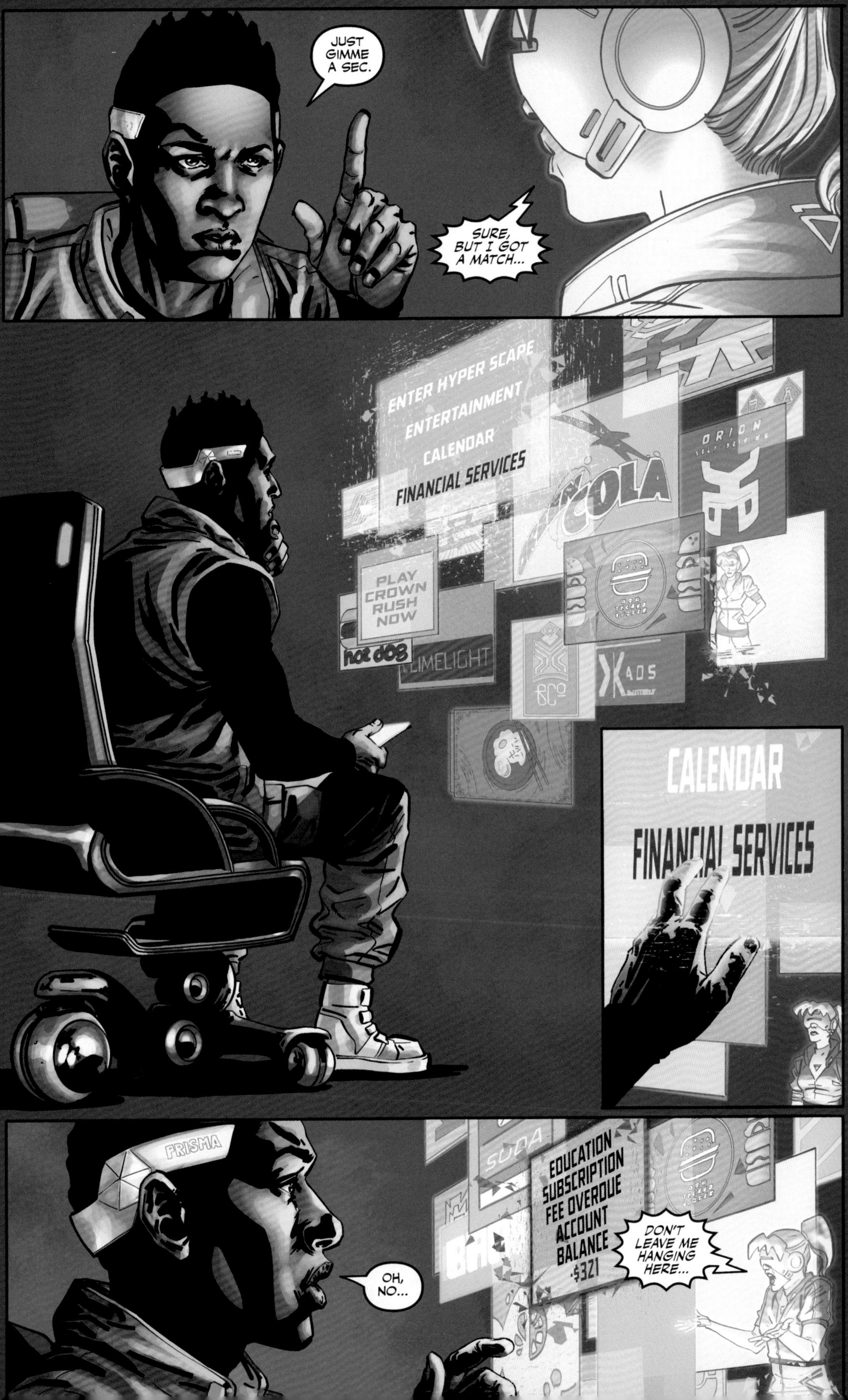
JUST GIMME A SEC.
SURE, BUT I GOT A MATCH...
ENTER HYPER SCAPE
ENTERTAINMENT
CALENDAR
FINANCIAL SERVICES
COLA
ORION
PLAY CROWN RUSH NOW
hot dog
LIMELIGHT
KADS
CALENDAR
FINANCIAL SERVICES
PRISMA
SODA
EDUCATION SUBSCRIPTION FEE OVERDUE ACCOUNT BALANCE -$321
OH, NO...
DON'T LEAVE ME HANGING HERE...

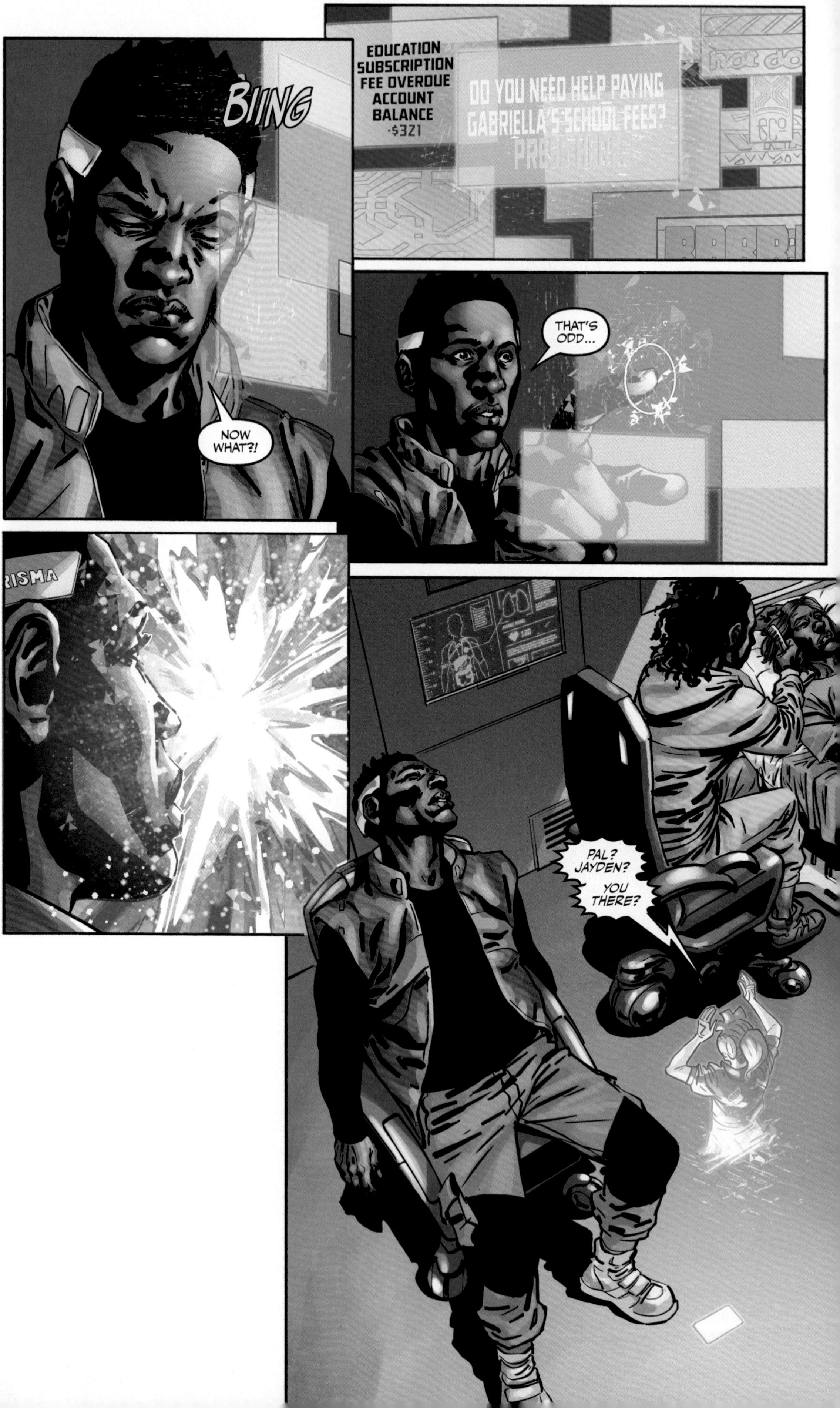
BIING
EDUCATION SUBSCRIPTION FEE OVERDUE ACCOUNT BALANCE -$321
DO YOU NEED HELP PAYING GABRIELLA'S SCHOOL FEES?
NOW WHAT?!
THAT'S ODD...
RISMA
PAL? JAYDEN?
YOU THERE?

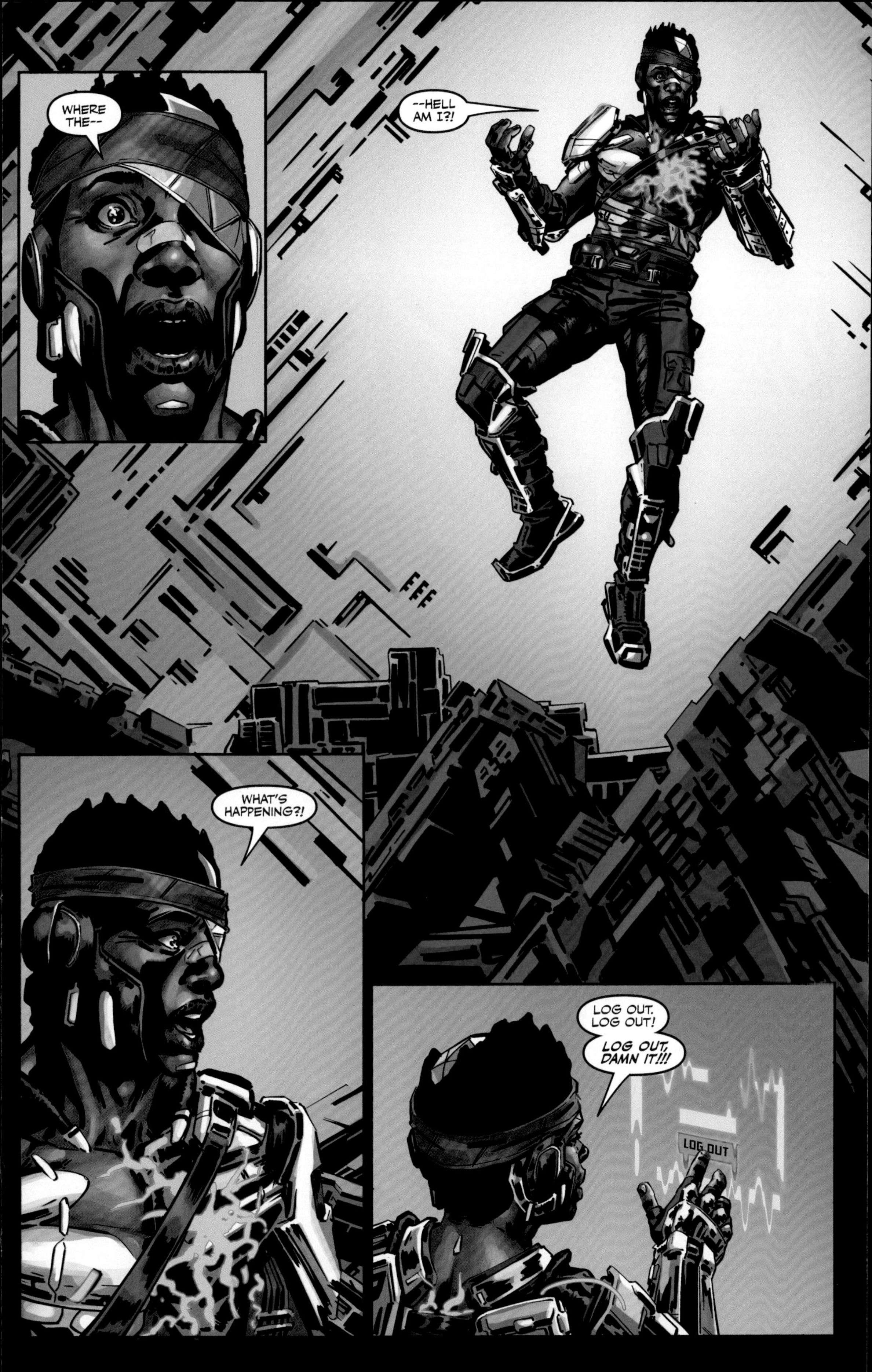
WHERE THE--
--HELL AM I?!
WHAT'S HAPPENING?!
LOG OUT. LOG OUT!
LOG OUT, DAMN IT!!!
LOG OUT

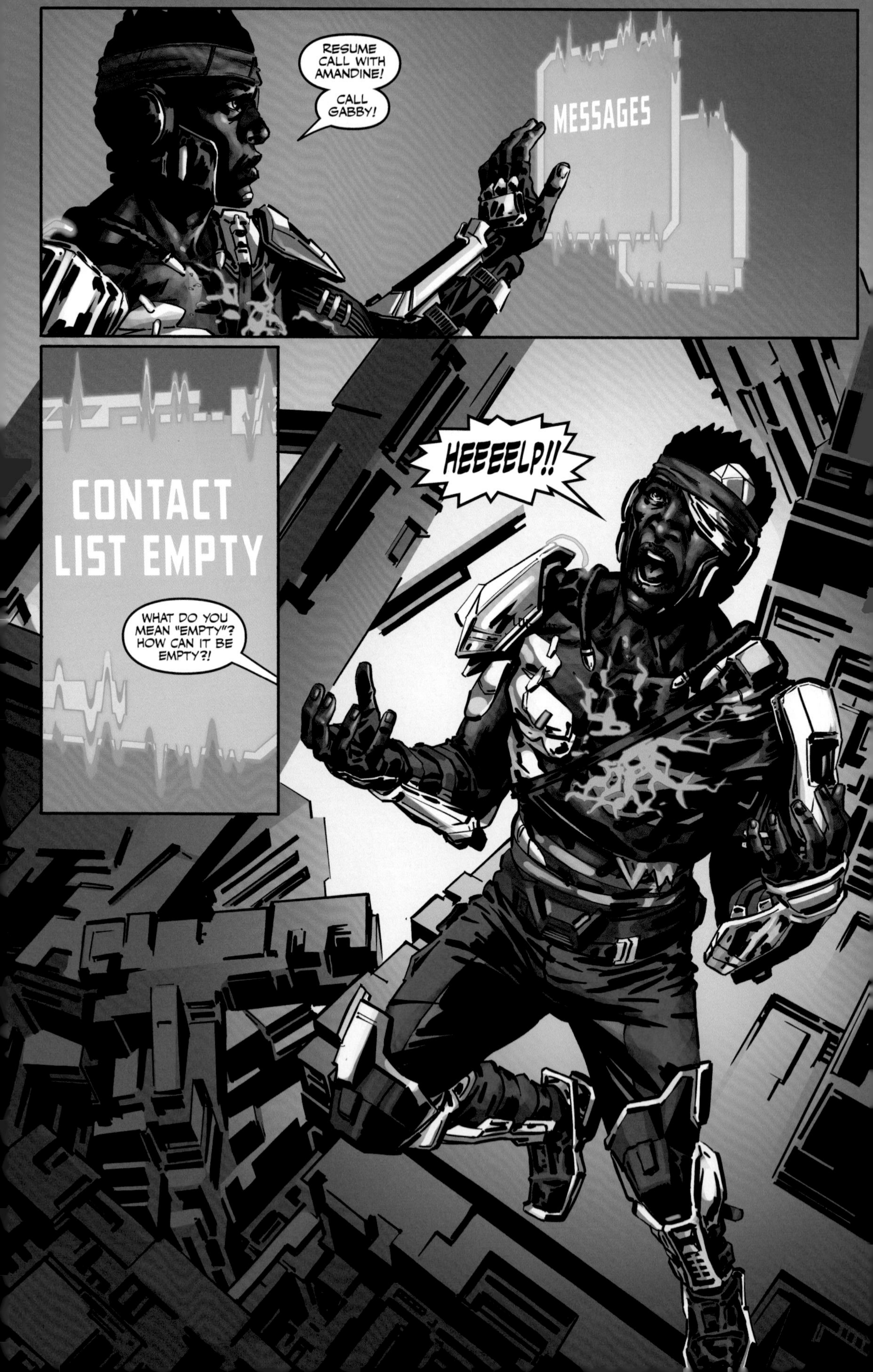
RESUME CALL WITH AMANDINE!
CALL GABBY!
MESSAGES
CONTACT LIST EMPTY
HEEEEELP!!
WHAT DO YOU MEAN "EMPTY"? HOW CAN IT BE EMPTY?!

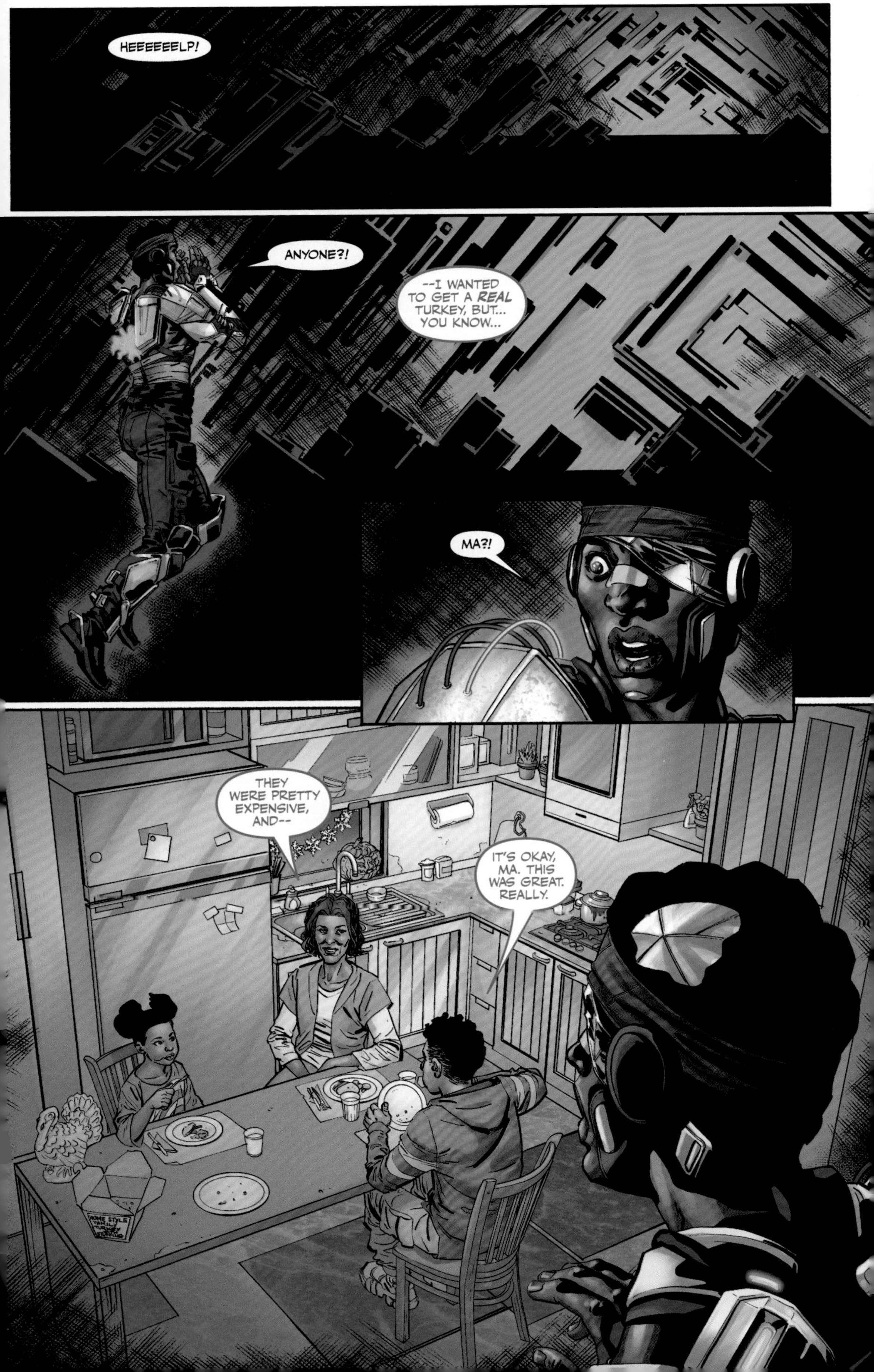
HEEEEEEELP!
ANYONE?!
--I WANTED TO GET A *REAL* TURKEY, BUT... YOU KNOW...
MA?!
THEY WERE PRETTY EXPENSIVE, AND--
IT'S OKAY, MA. THIS WAS GREAT. REALLY.

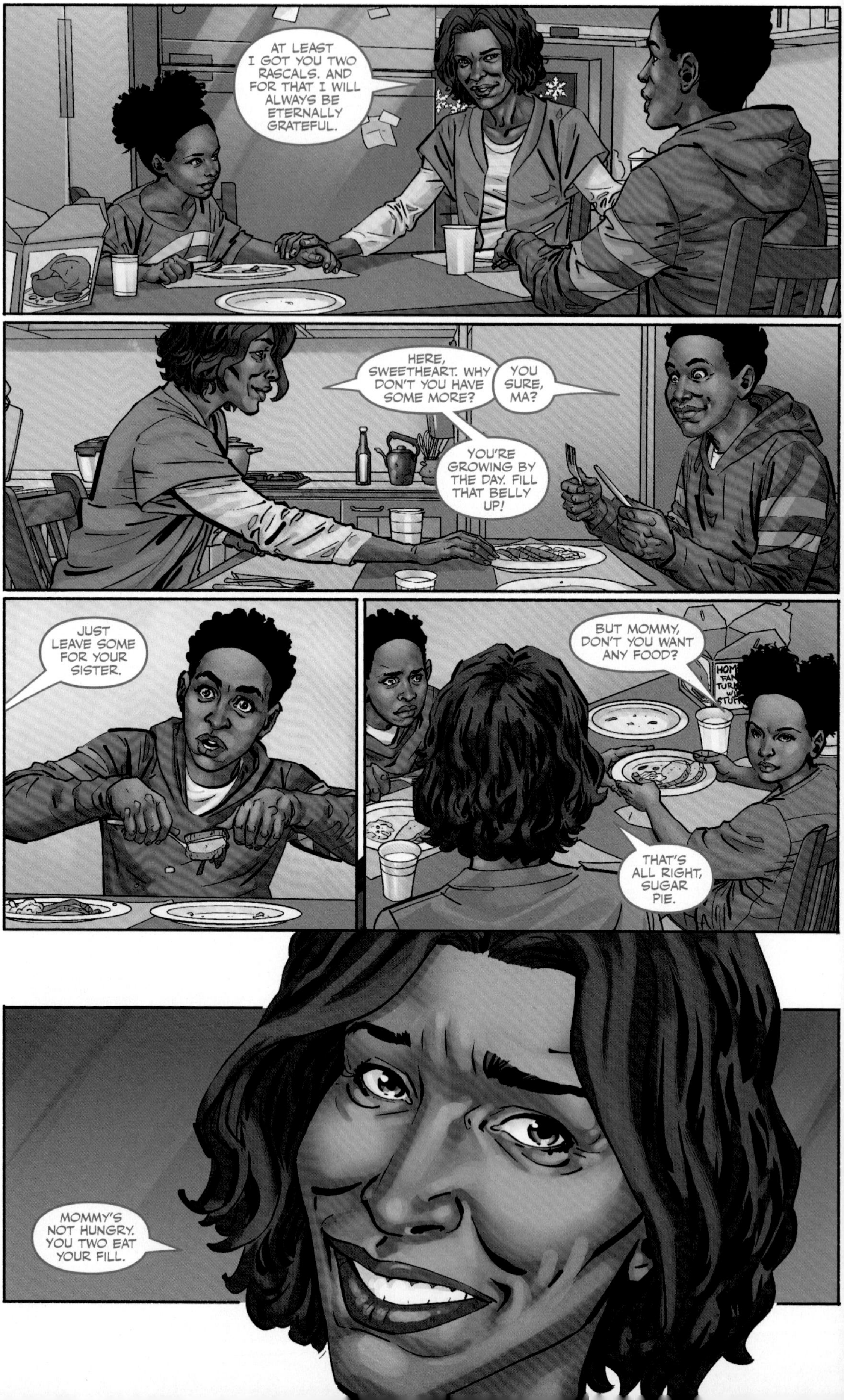
AT LEAST I GOT YOU TWO RASCALS. AND FOR THAT I WILL ALWAYS BE ETERNALLY GRATEFUL.
HERE, SWEETHEART. WHY DON'T YOU HAVE SOME MORE?
YOU'RE GROWING BY THE DAY. FILL THAT BELLY UP!
YOU SURE, MA?
JUST LEAVE SOME FOR YOUR SISTER.
BUT MOMMY, DON'T YOU WANT ANY FOOD?
THAT'S ALL RIGHT, SUGAR PIE.
MOMMY'S NOT HUNGRY. YOU TWO EAT YOUR FILL.

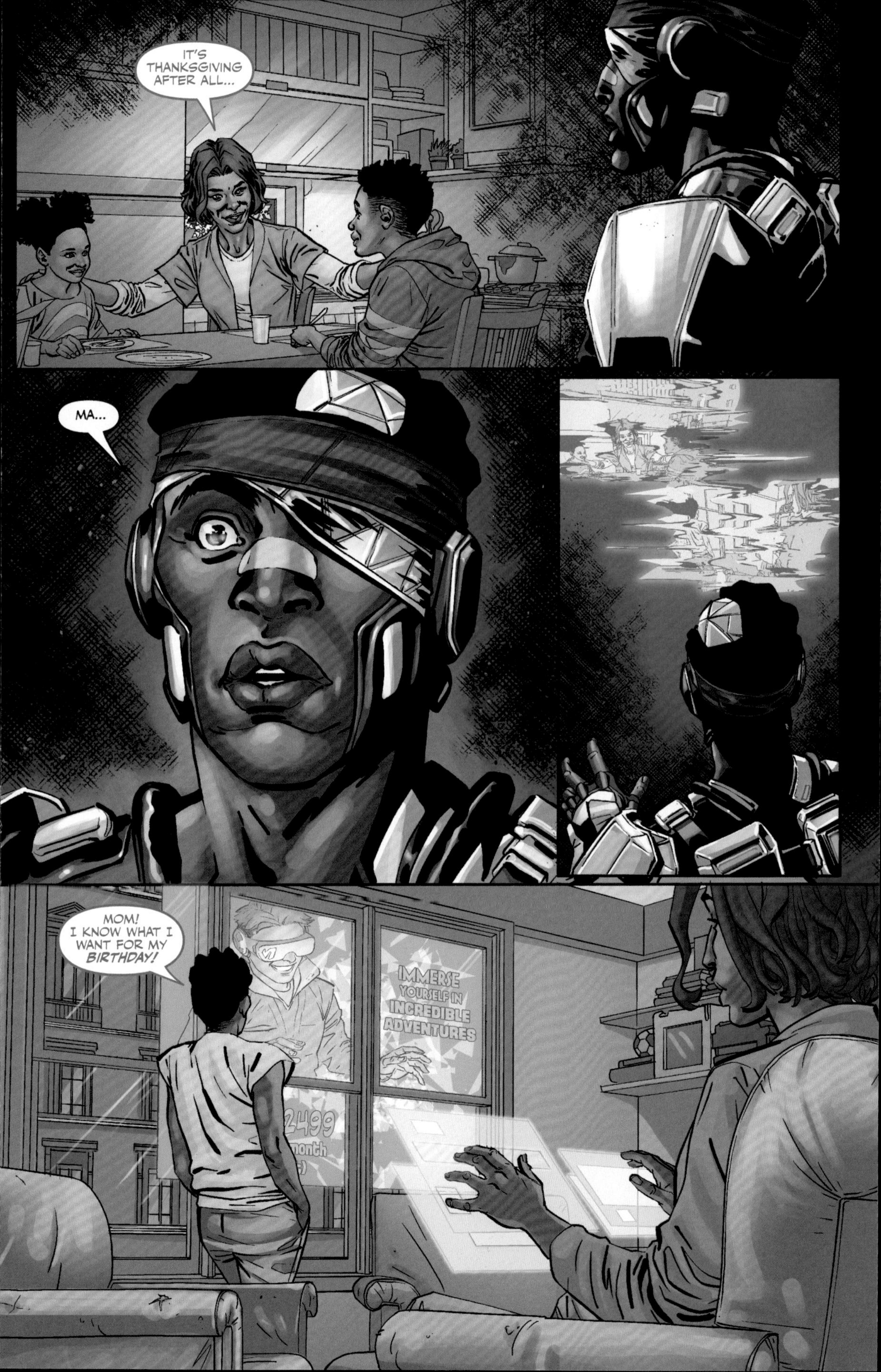
IT'S THANKSGIVING AFTER ALL...
MA...
MOM! I KNOW WHAT I WANT FOR MY *BIRTHDAY!*
IMMERSE YOURSELF IN INCREDIBLE ADVENTURES

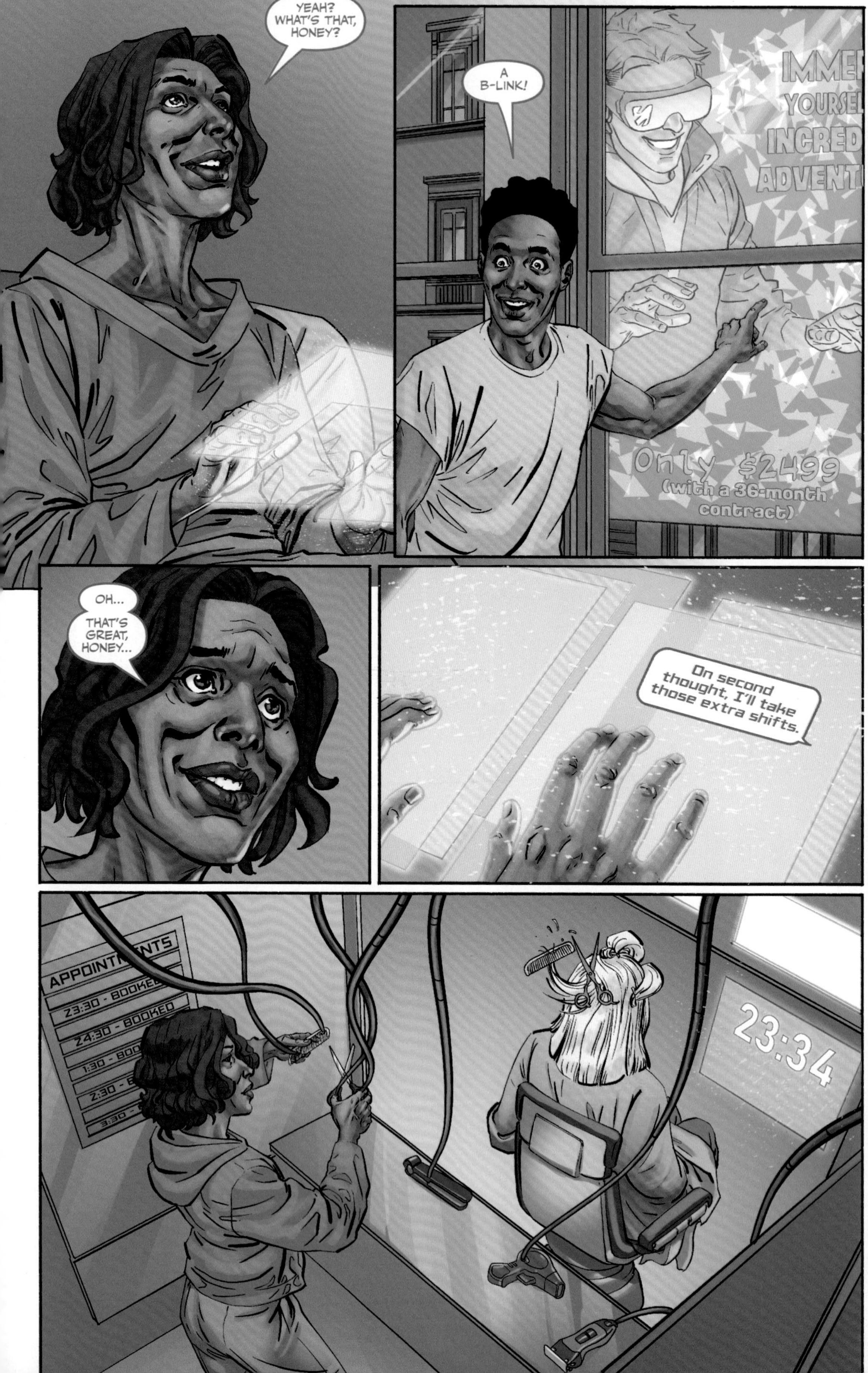
YEAH? WHAT'S THAT, HONEY?
A B-LINK!
Only $2499
(with a 36-month contract)
OH... THAT'S GREAT, HONEY...
On second thought, I'll take those extra shifts.
23:30 - BOOKED
24:30 - BOOKED
23:34

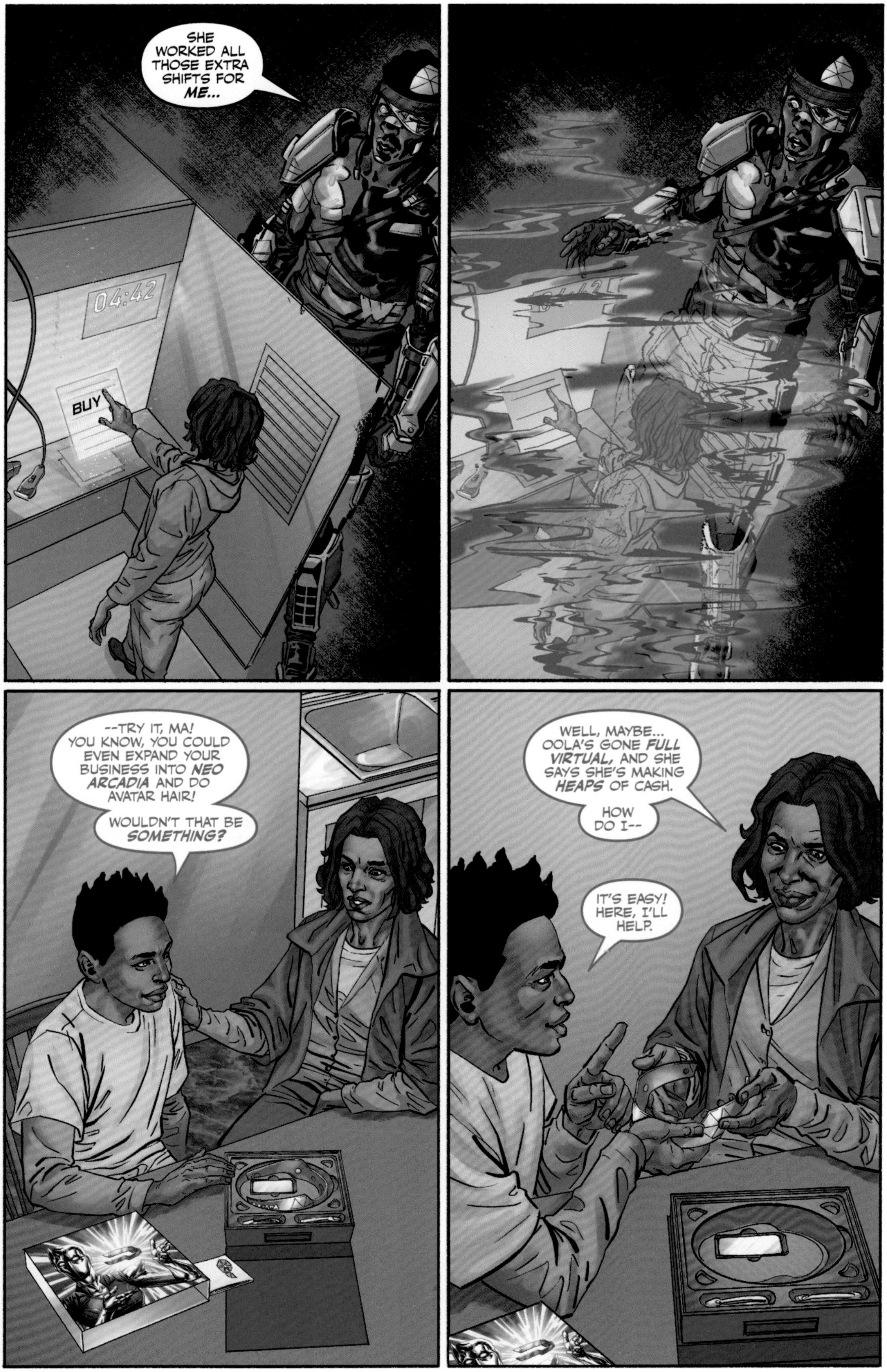
SHE WORKED ALL THOSE EXTRA SHIFTS FOR ME...
04:42
BUY
--TRY IT, MA! YOU KNOW, YOU COULD EVEN EXPAND YOUR BUSINESS INTO NEO ARCADIA AND DO AVATAR HAIR!
WOULDN'T THAT BE SOMETHING?
WELL, MAYBE... OOLA'S GONE FULL VIRTUAL, AND SHE SAYS SHE'S MAKING HEAPS OF CASH.
HOW DO I--
IT'S EASY! HERE, I'LL HELP.

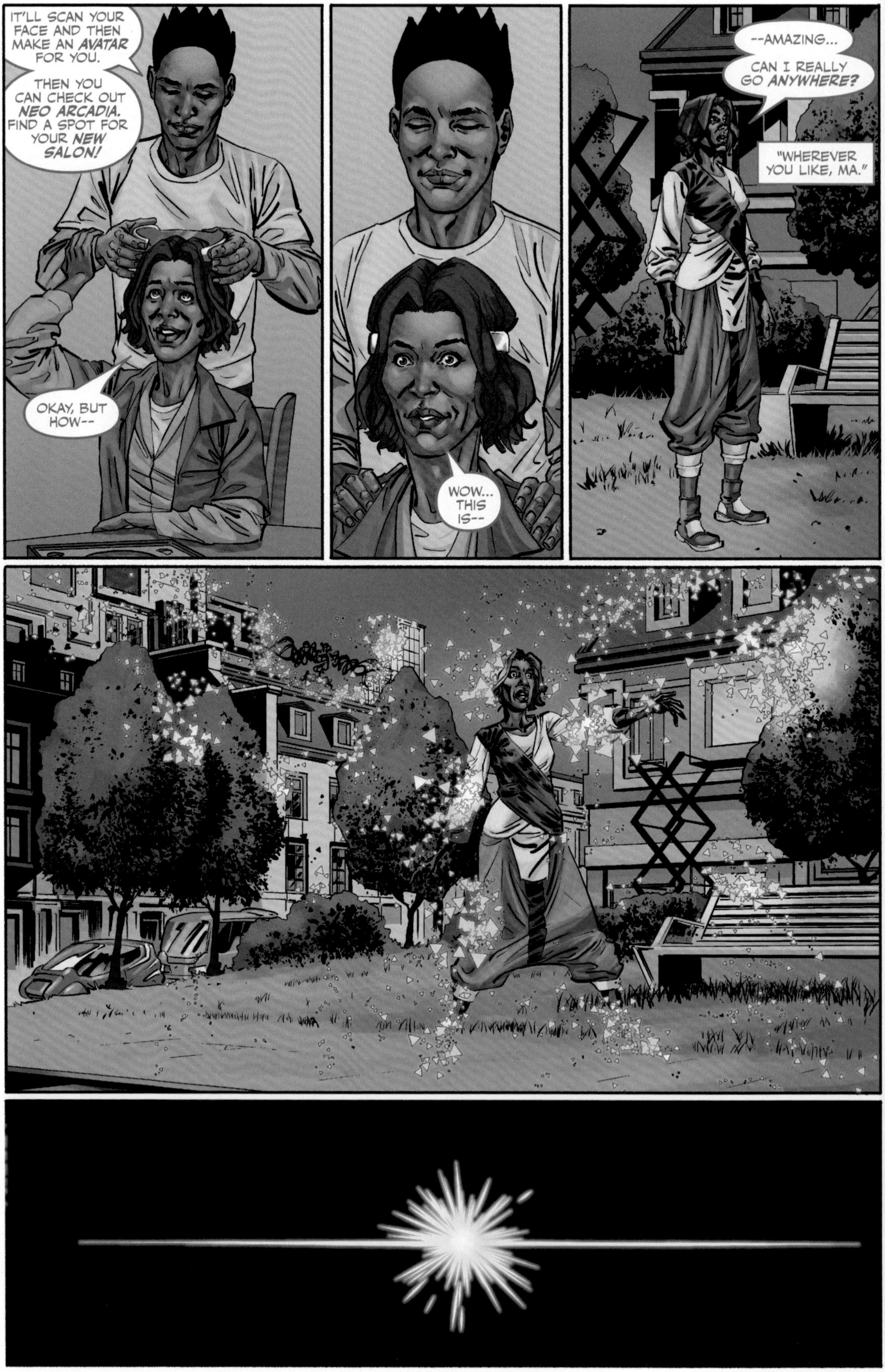
IT'LL SCAN YOUR FACE AND THEN MAKE AN AVATAR FOR YOU.
THEN YOU CAN CHECK OUT NEO ARCADIA. FIND A SPOT FOR YOUR NEW SALON!
OKAY, BUT HOW--
WOW... THIS IS--
--AMAZING...
CAN I REALLY GO ANYWHERE?
"WHEREVER YOU LIKE, MA."

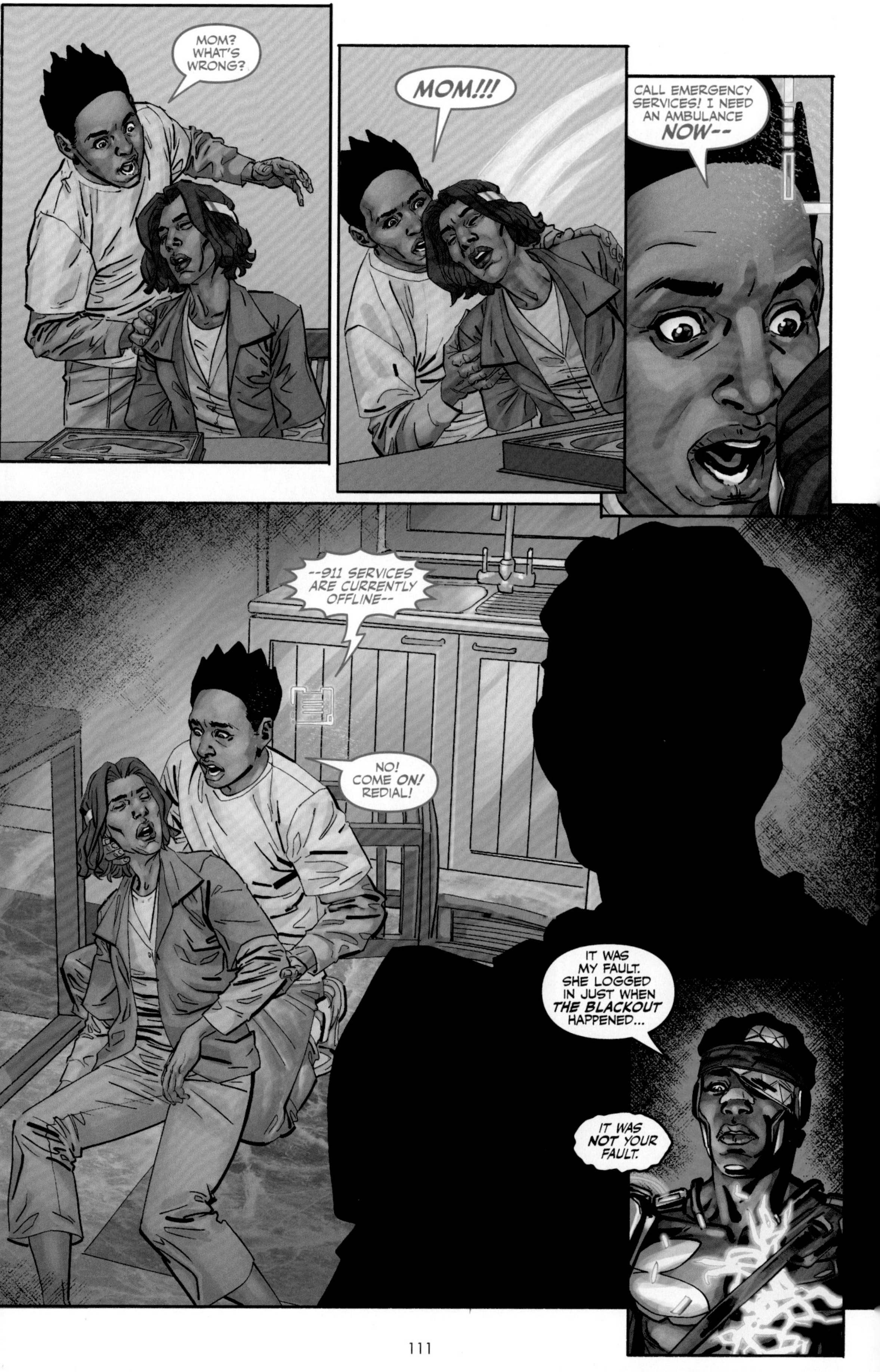
MOM? WHAT'S WRONG?
MOM!!!
CALL EMERGENCY SERVICES! I NEED AN AMBULANCE NOW--
--911 SERVICES ARE CURRENTLY OFFLINE--
NO! COME ON! REDIAL!
IT WAS MY FAULT. SHE LOGGED IN JUST WHEN THE BLACKOUT HAPPENED...
IT WAS NOT YOUR FAULT.

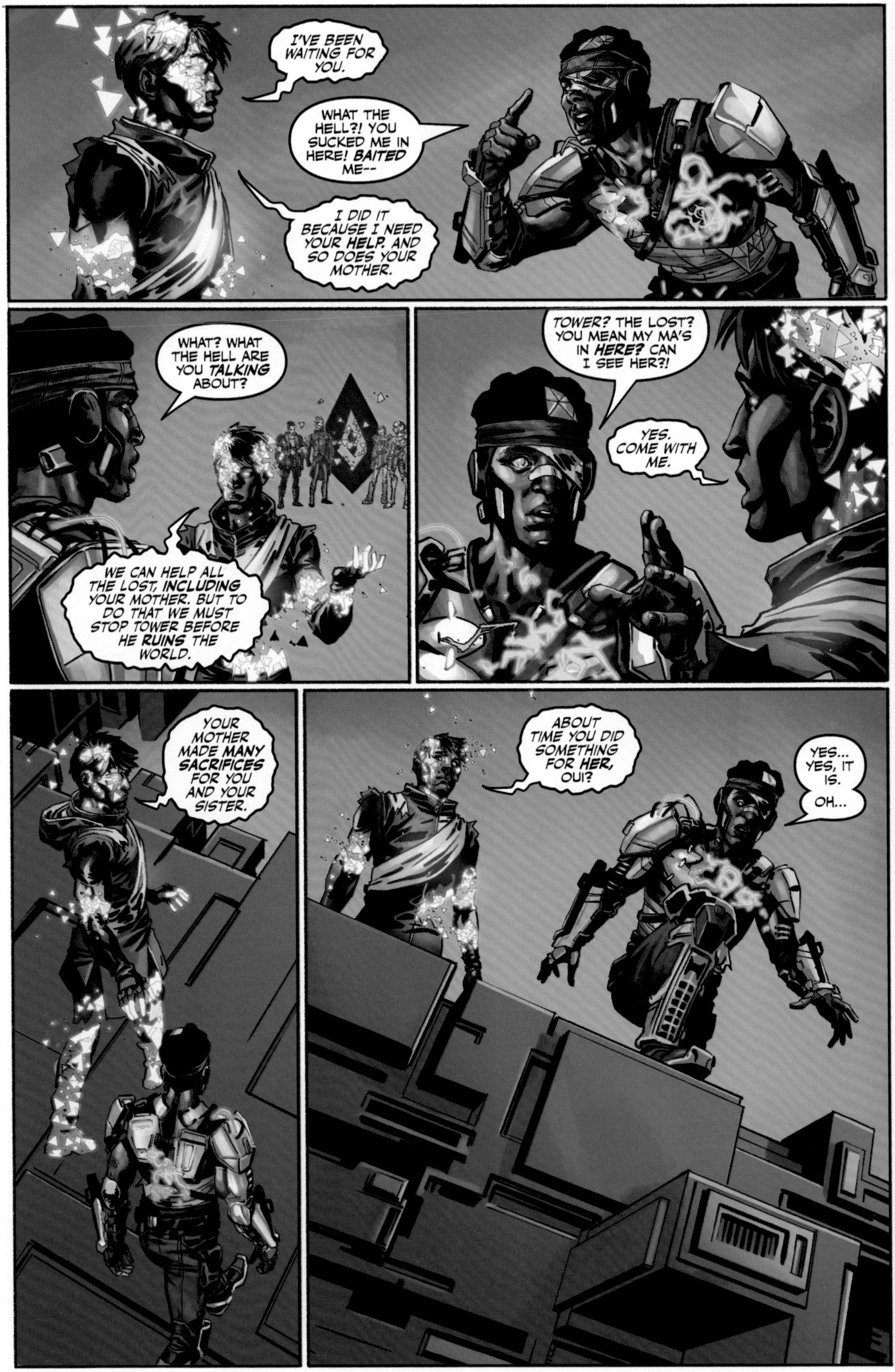
I'VE BEEN WAITING FOR YOU.
WHAT THE HELL?! YOU SUCKED ME IN HERE! BAITED ME--
I DID IT BECAUSE I NEED YOUR HELP. AND SO DOES YOUR MOTHER.
WHAT? WHAT THE HELL ARE YOU TALKING ABOUT?
WE CAN HELP ALL THE LOST, INCLUDING YOUR MOTHER. BUT TO DO THAT WE MUST STOP TOWER BEFORE HE RUINS THE WORLD.
TOWER? THE LOST? YOU MEAN MY MA'S IN HERE? CAN I SEE HER?!
YES. COME WITH ME.
YOUR MOTHER MADE MANY SACRIFICES FOR YOU AND YOUR SISTER.
ABOUT TIME YOU DID SOMETHING FOR HER, OUI?
YES... YES, IT IS.
OH...

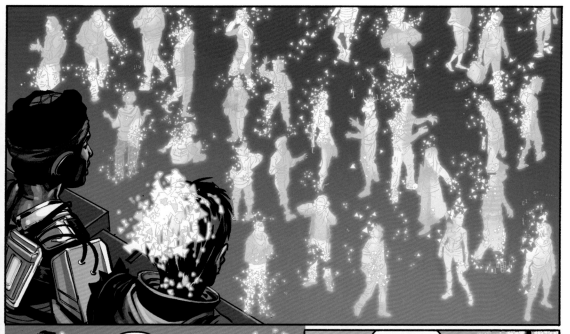

MA?

THERE YOU ARE, JAYDEN. I WAS WORRIED YOU'D BE *LATE* AGAIN.

MA...GOD, I'M SO SORRY... PLEASE...

DINNER'S ALMOST READY. CAN YOU PLEASE FETCH YOUR SISTER?

WHAT? BUT--

BUT IT'S *ME*, MA. I'M *HERE*.

GABBY'S BEEN WATCHING HOLOS ALL DAY. IT'S TIME FOR A BREAK.

CAN'T YOU HEAR ME?

WHY CAN'T SHE HEAR ME?!

SHE'S LOST IN MEMORIES OF HER OWN. BUT YOU CAN HELP HER.

YOU MUST PREVENT *BASILISK* FROM TAKING MORE *FRAGMENTS* TO TOWER.

THEN WE STAND A CHANCE. THEN WE CAN SAVE THEM.

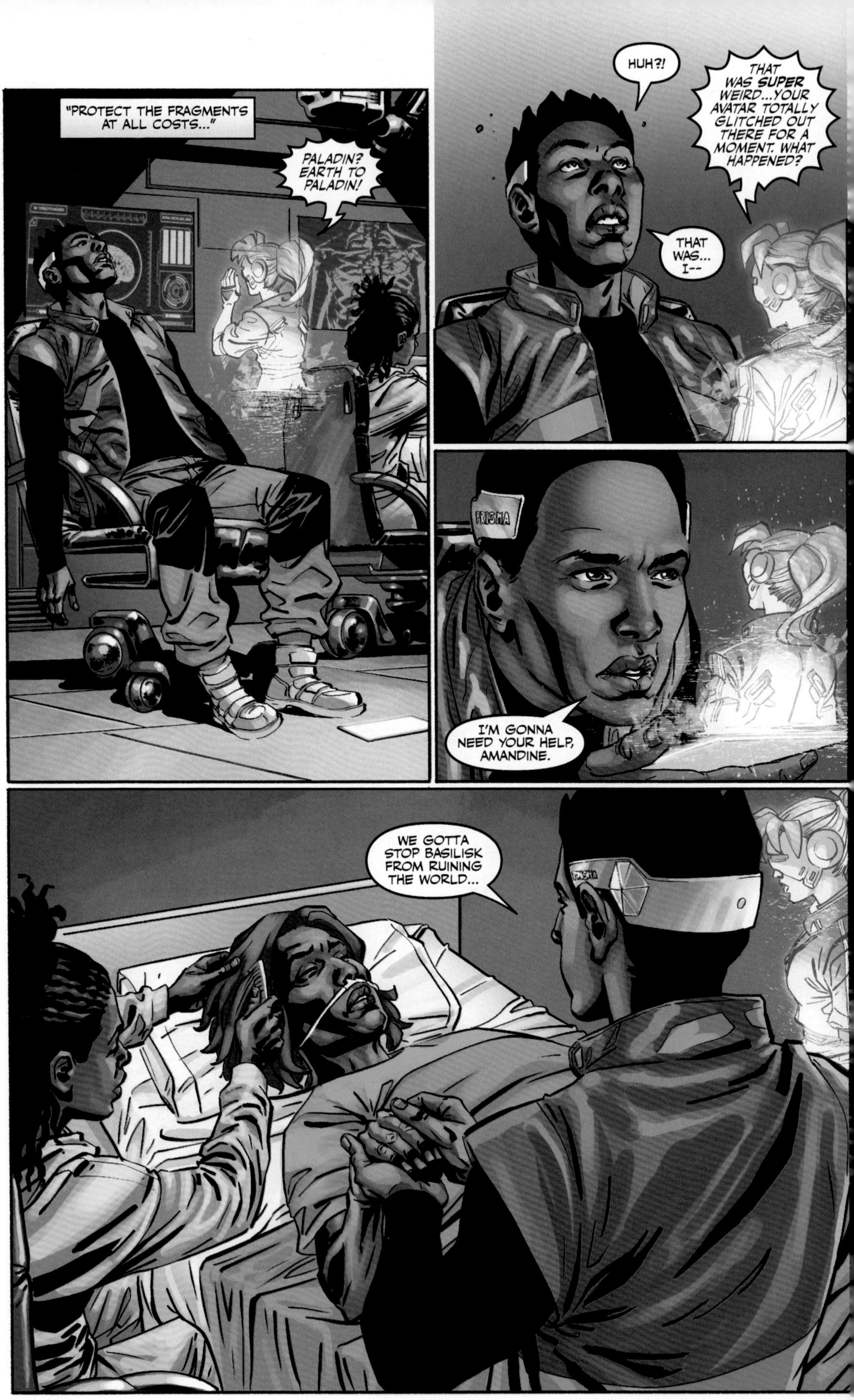
"PROTECT THE FRAGMENTS AT ALL COSTS..."
PALADIN? EARTH TO PALADIN!
HUH?!
THAT WAS SUPER WEIRD...YOUR AVATAR TOTALLY GLITCHED OUT THERE FOR A MOMENT. WHAT HAPPENED?
THAT WAS... I--
PRISMA
I'M GONNA NEED YOUR HELP, AMANDINE.
WE GOTTA STOP BASILISK FROM RUINING THE WORLD...

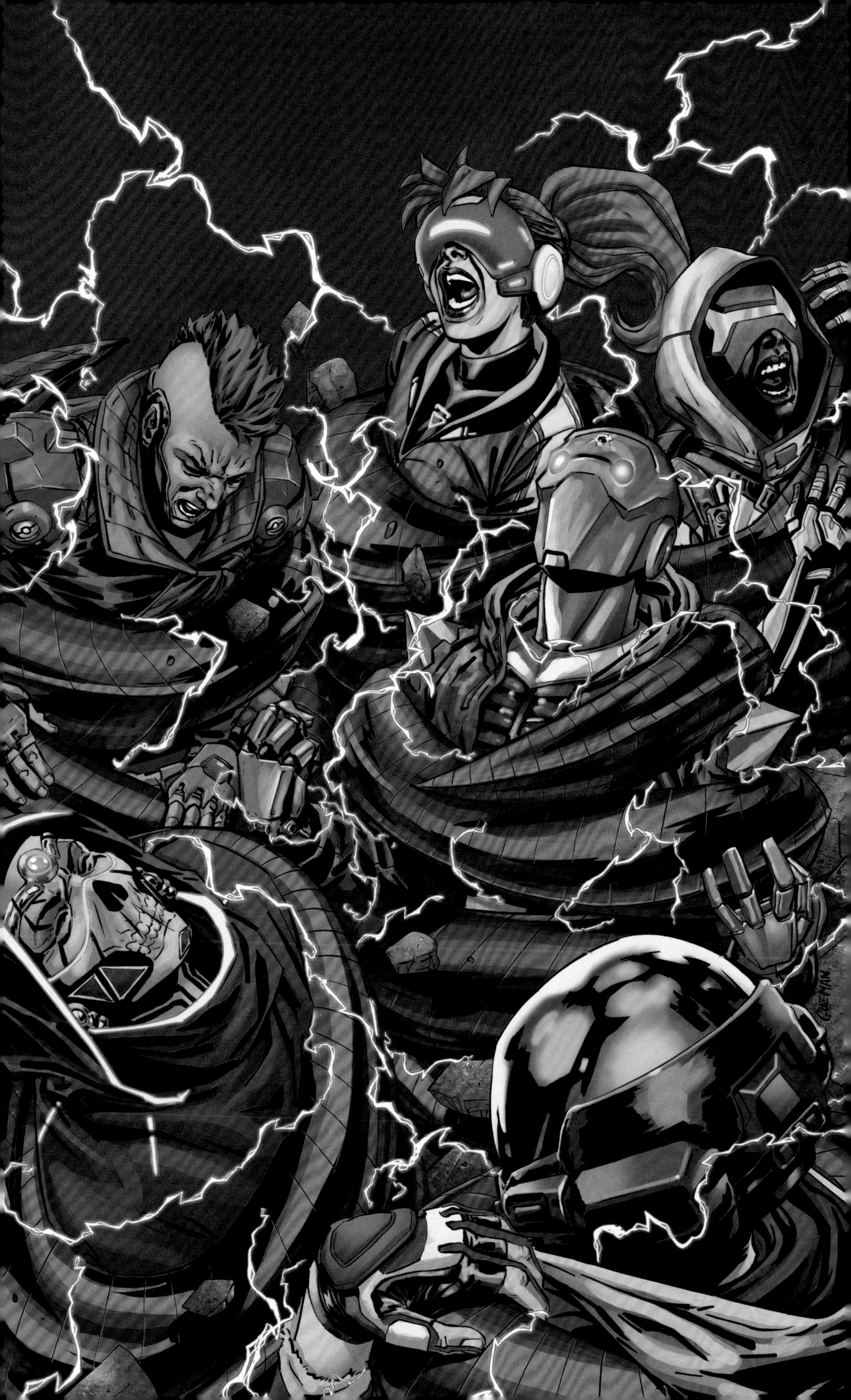
GUZMAN

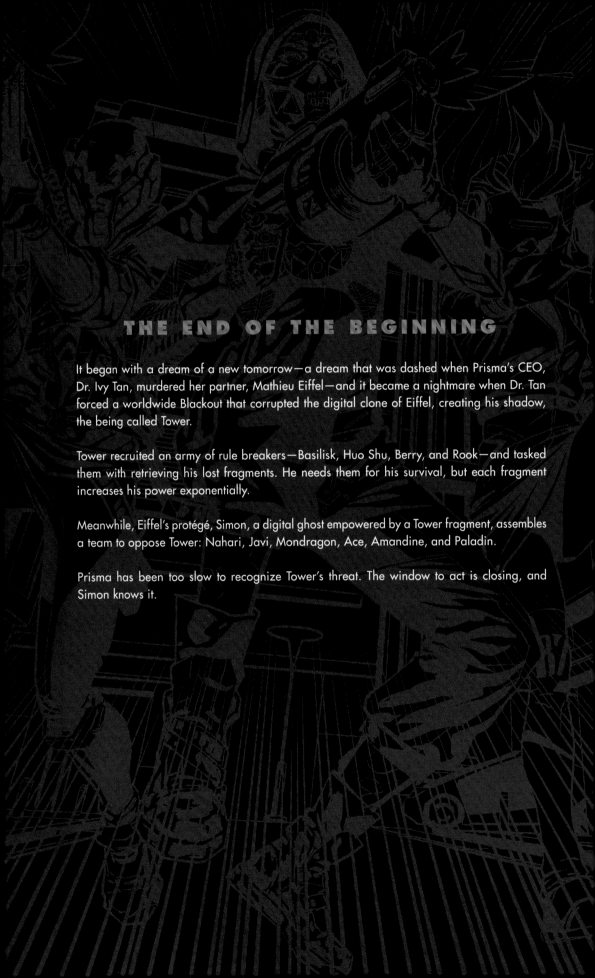

THE END OF THE BEGINNING

It began with a dream of a new tomorrow—a dream that was dashed when Prisma's CEO, Dr. Ivy Tan, murdered her partner, Mathieu Eiffel—and it became a nightmare when Dr. Tan forced a worldwide Blackout that corrupted the digital clone of Eiffel, creating his shadow, the being called Tower.

Tower recruited an army of rule breakers—Basilisk, Huo Shu, Berry, and Rook—and tasked them with retrieving his lost fragments. He needs them for his survival, but each fragment increases his power exponentially.

Meanwhile, Eiffel's protégé, Simon, a digital ghost empowered by a Tower fragment, assembles a team to oppose Tower: Nahari, Javi, Mondragon, Ace, Amandine, and Paladin.

Prisma has been too slow to recognize Tower's threat. The window to act is closing, and Simon knows it.

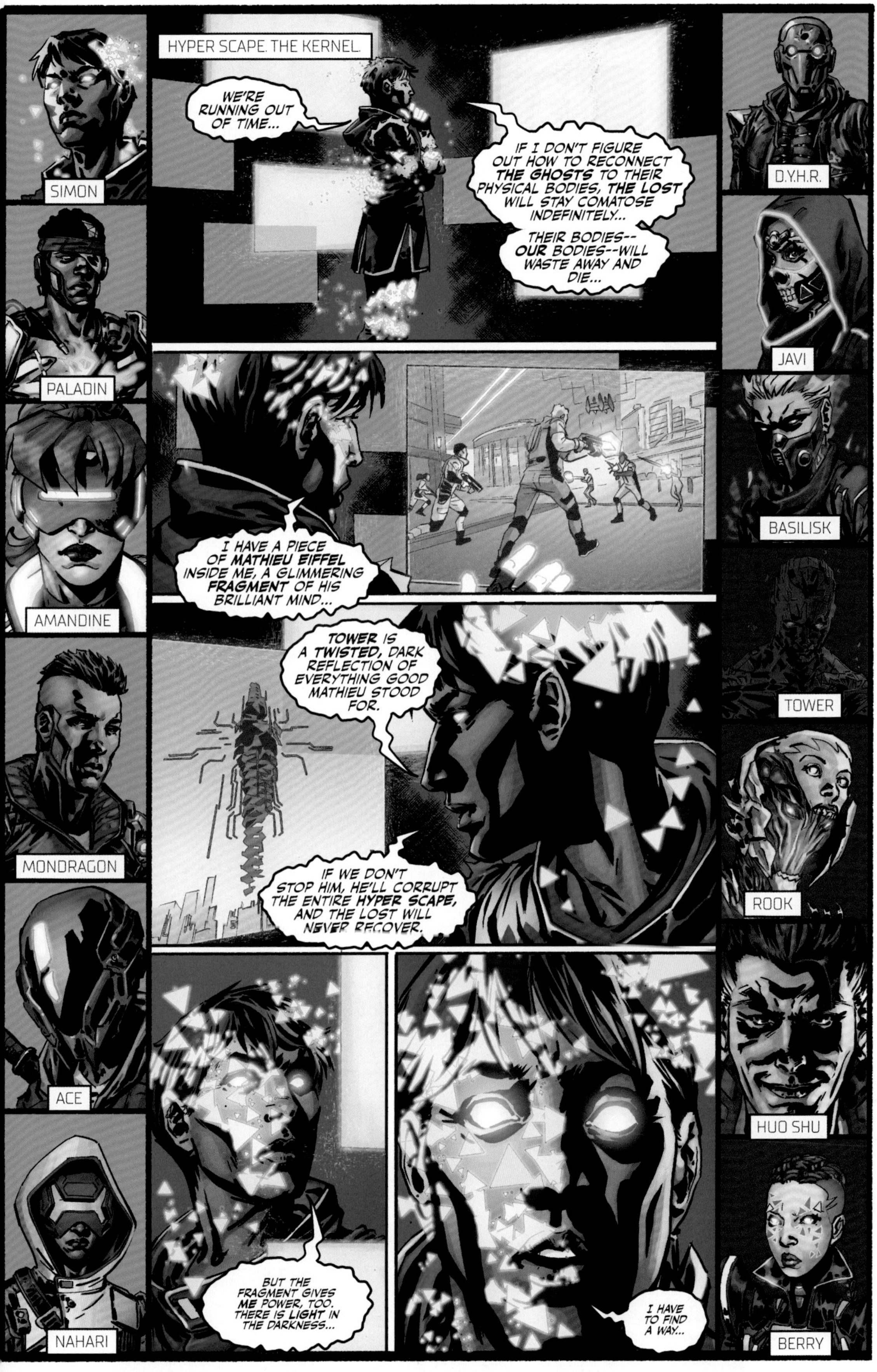

HYPER SCAPE. THE KERNEL.
WE'RE RUNNING OUT OF TIME...
IF I DON'T FIGURE OUT HOW TO RECONNECT THE GHOSTS TO THEIR PHYSICAL BODIES, THE LOST WILL STAY COMATOSE INDEFINITELY...
THEIR BODIES-- OUR BODIES--WILL WASTE AWAY AND DIE...
I HAVE A PIECE OF MATHIEU EIFFEL INSIDE ME, A GLIMMERING FRAGMENT OF HIS BRILLIANT MIND...
TOWER IS A TWISTED, DARK REFLECTION OF EVERYTHING GOOD MATHIEU STOOD FOR.
IF WE DON'T STOP HIM, HE'LL CORRUPT THE ENTIRE HYPER SCAPE, AND THE LOST WILL NEVER RECOVER.
BUT THE FRAGMENT GIVES ME POWER, TOO. THERE IS LIGHT IN THE DARKNESS...
I HAVE TO FIND A WAY...
SIMON
PALADIN
AMANDINE
MONDRAGON
ACE
NAHARI
D.Y.H.R.
JAVI
BASILISK
TOWER
ROOK
HUO SHU
BERRY

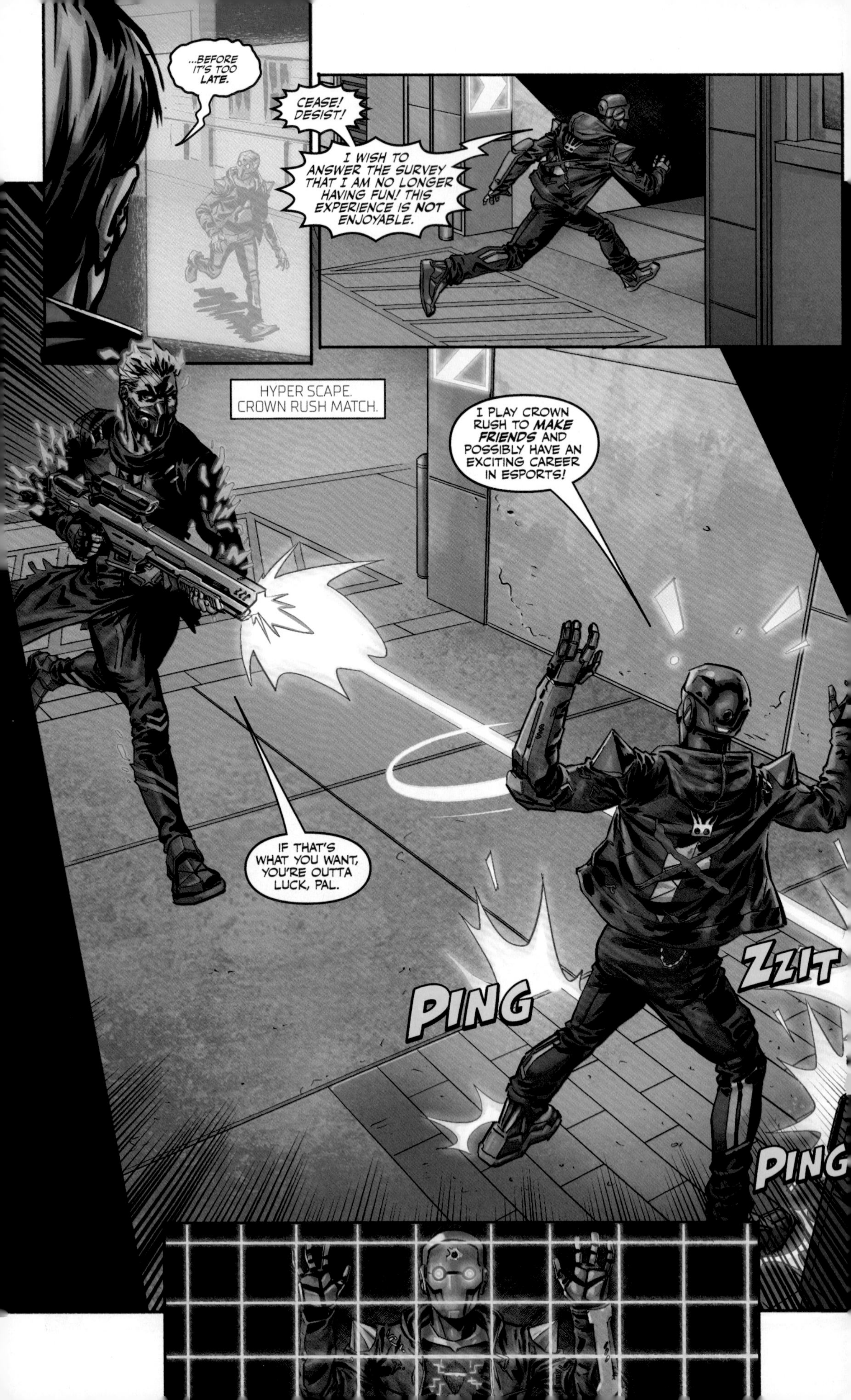
...BEFORE IT'S TOO LATE.
CEASE! DESIST!
I WISH TO ANSWER THE SURVEY THAT I AM NO LONGER HAVING FUN! THIS EXPERIENCE IS NOT ENJOYABLE.
HYPER SCAPE. CROWN RUSH MATCH.
I PLAY CROWN RUSH TO MAKE FRIENDS AND POSSIBLY HAVE AN EXCITING CAREER IN ESPORTS!
IF THAT'S WHAT YOU WANT, YOU'RE OUTTA LUCK, PAL.
PING
ZZIT
PING

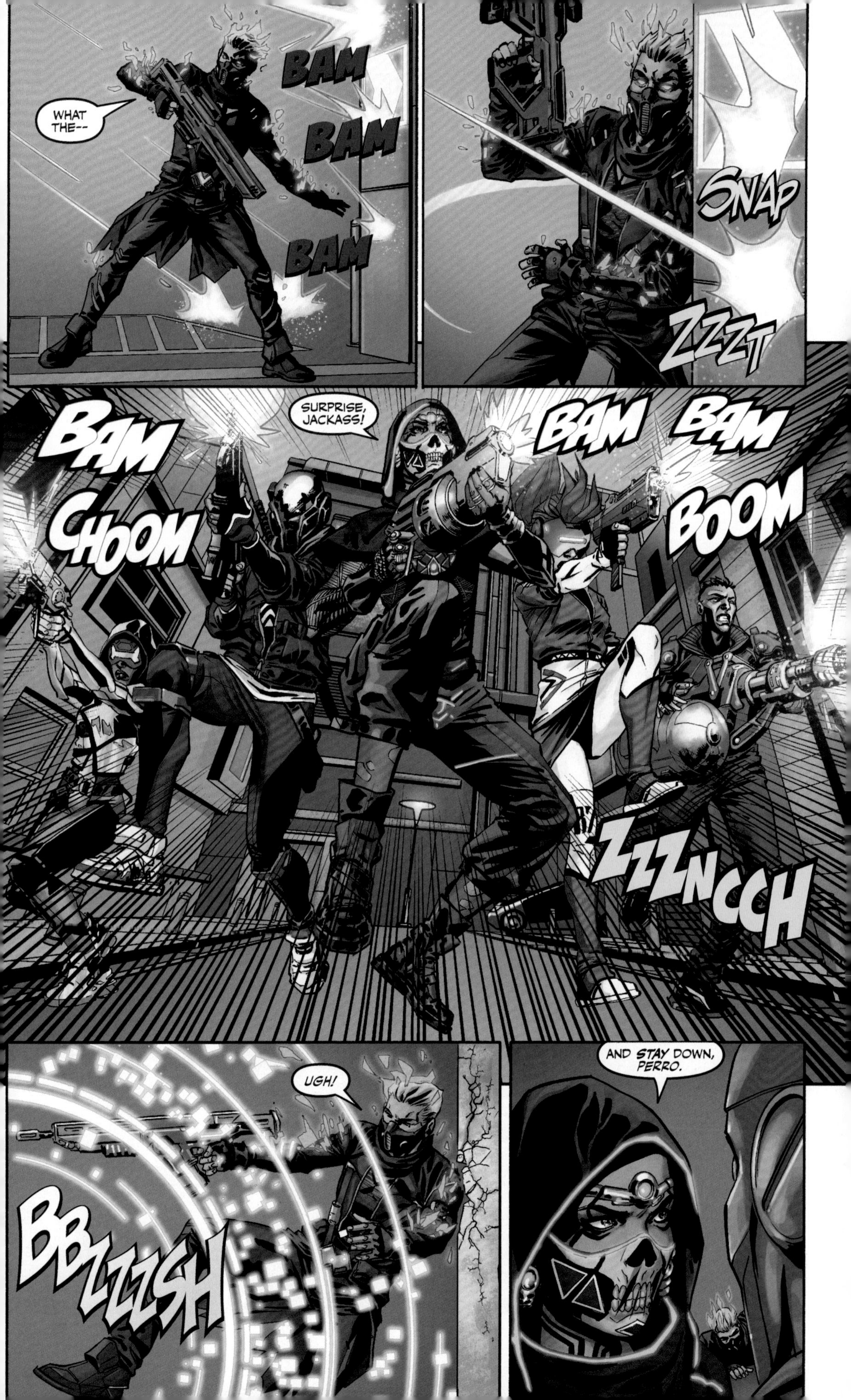
WHAT THE--
BAM
BAM
BAM
SNAP
ZZZT
BAM
CHOOM
SURPRISE, JACKASS!
BAM BAM
BOOM
ZZZNCCH
UGH!
BBZZZSH
AND STAY DOWN, PERRO.

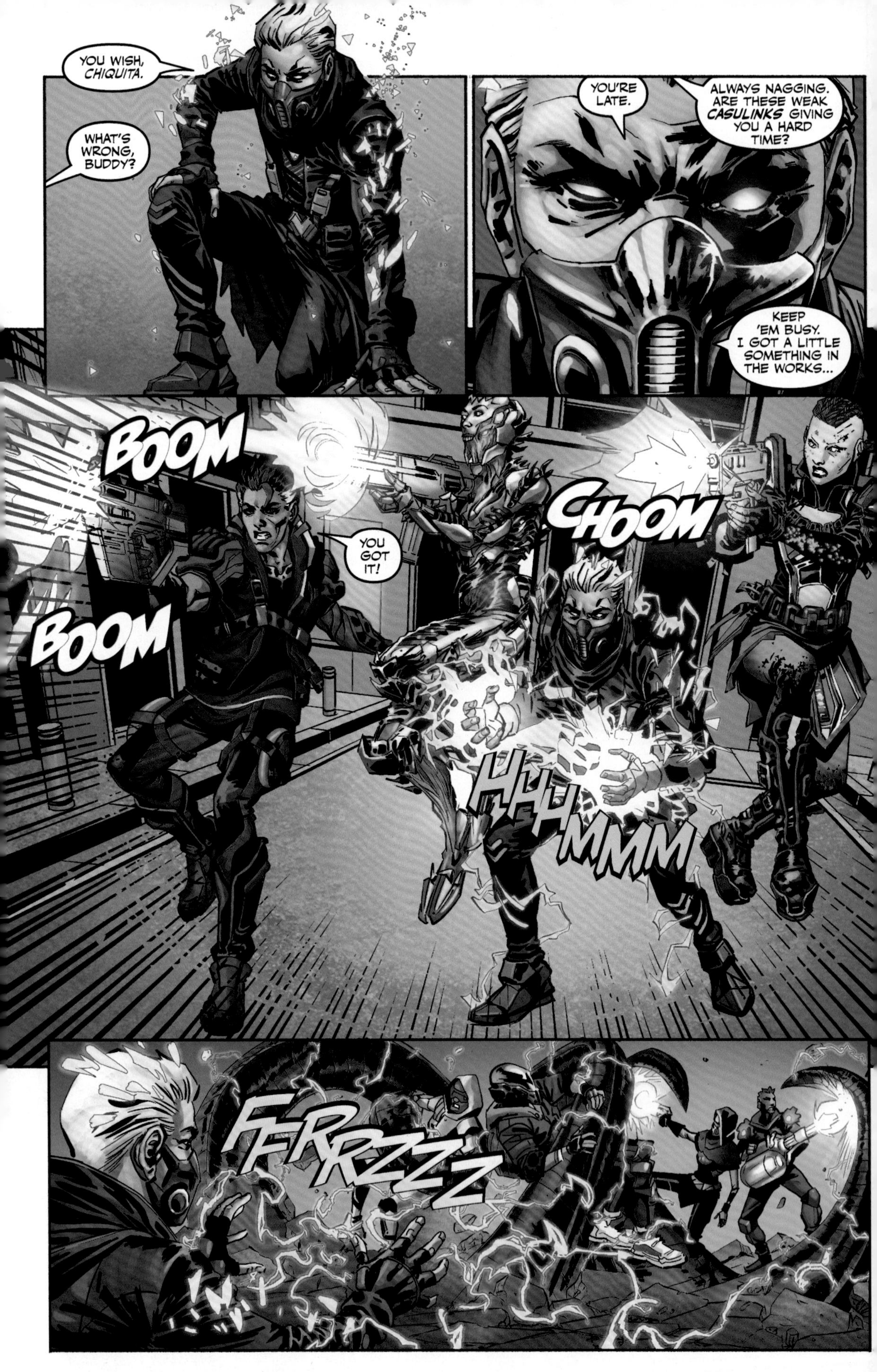
YOU WISH, CHIQUITA.
WHAT'S WRONG, BUDDY?
YOU'RE LATE.
ALWAYS NAGGING. ARE THESE WEAK CASULINKS GIVING YOU A HARD TIME?
KEEP 'EM BUSY. I GOT A LITTLE SOMETHING IN THE WORKS...
BOOM
BOOM
YOU GOT IT!
CHOOM
HHUMMMM
FFRZZZZ

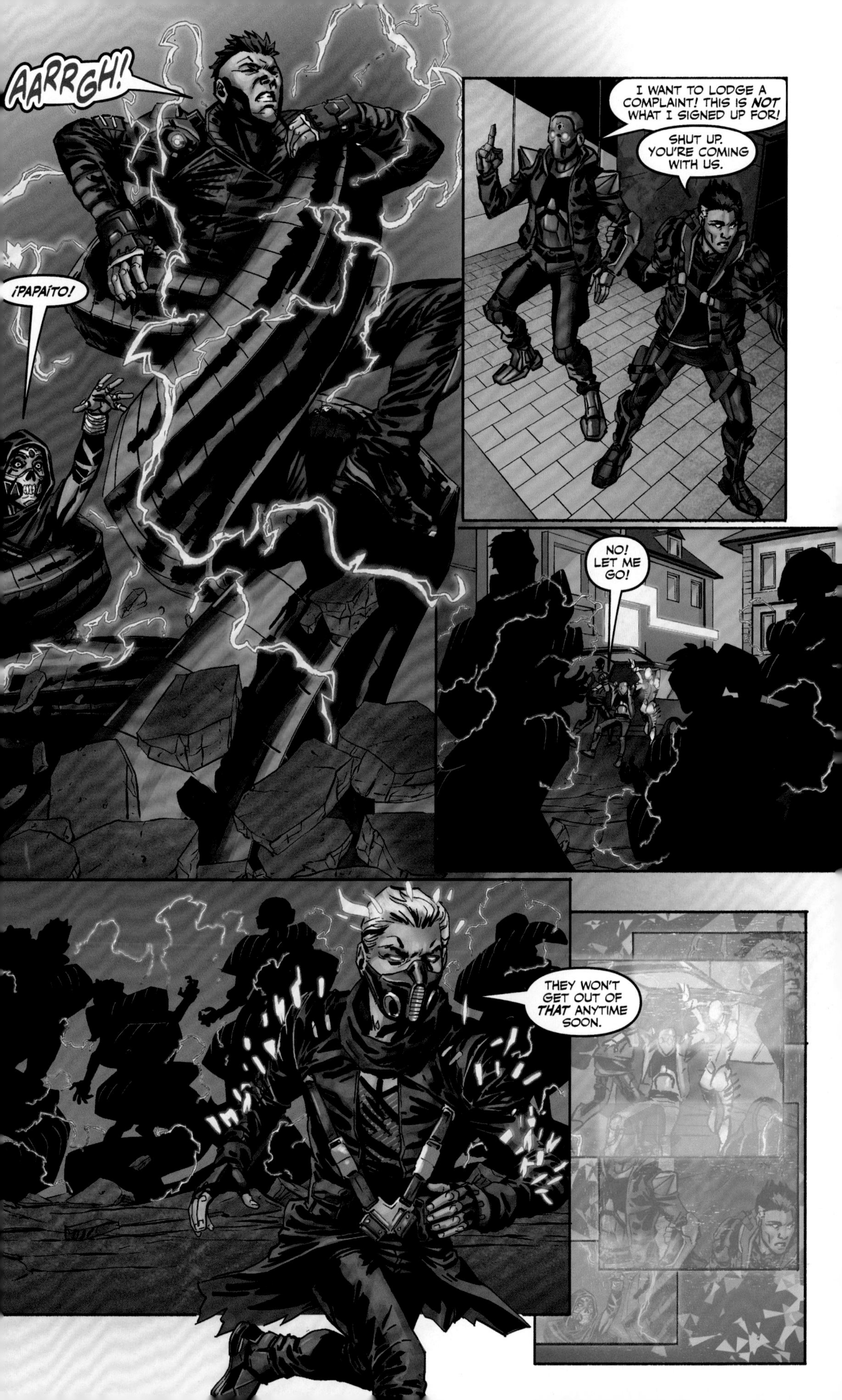
AARRGH!
¡PAPAÍTO!
I WANT TO LODGE A COMPLAINT! THIS IS *NOT* WHAT I SIGNED UP FOR!
SHUT UP. YOU'RE COMING WITH US.
NO! LET ME GO!
THEY WON'T GET OUT OF *THAT* ANYTIME SOON.

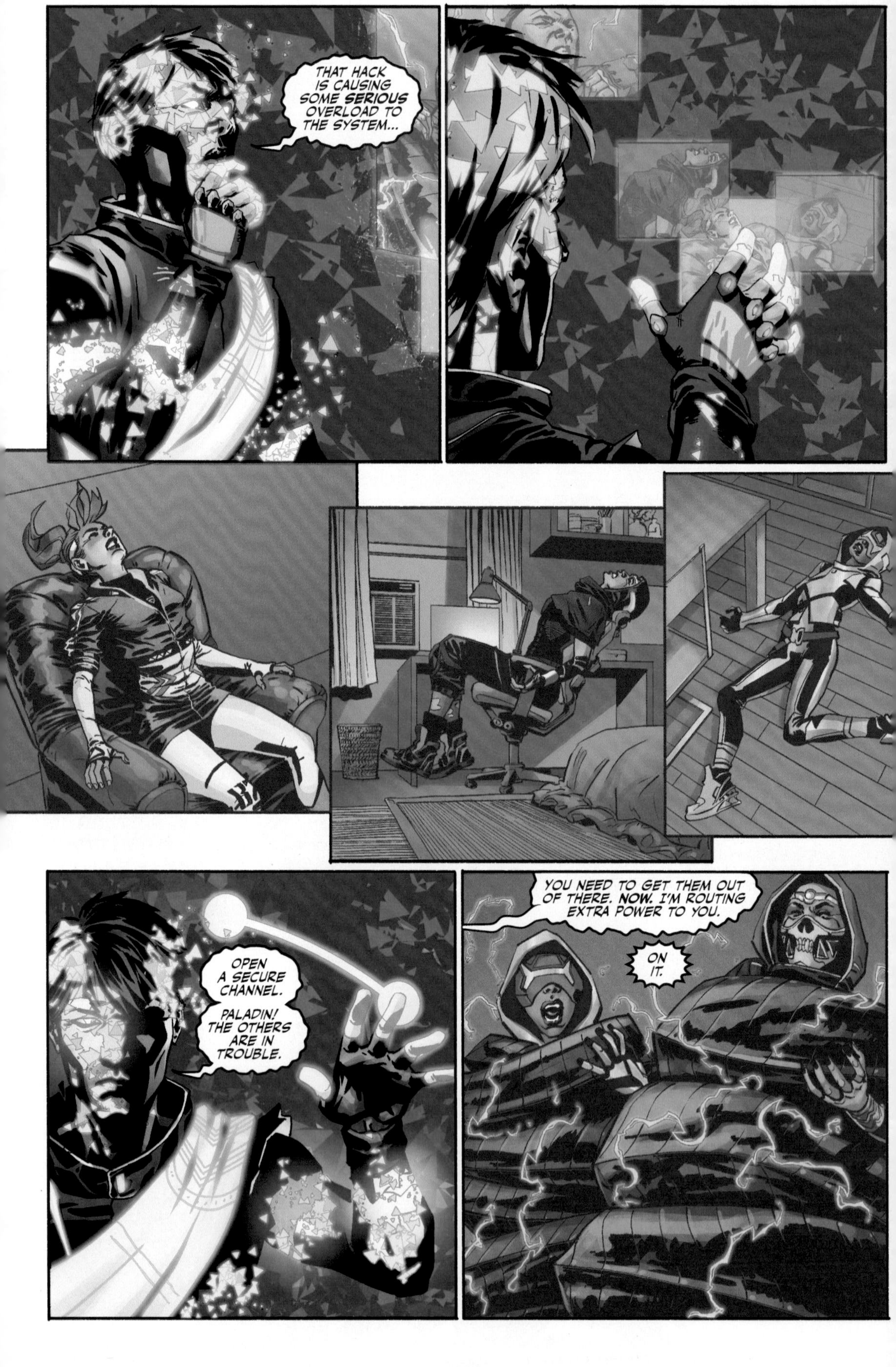
THAT HACK IS CAUSING SOME SERIOUS OVERLOAD TO THE SYSTEM...
OPEN A SECURE CHANNEL.
PALADIN! THE OTHERS ARE IN TROUBLE.
YOU NEED TO GET THEM OUT OF THERE. NOW. I'M ROUTING EXTRA POWER TO YOU.
ON IT.

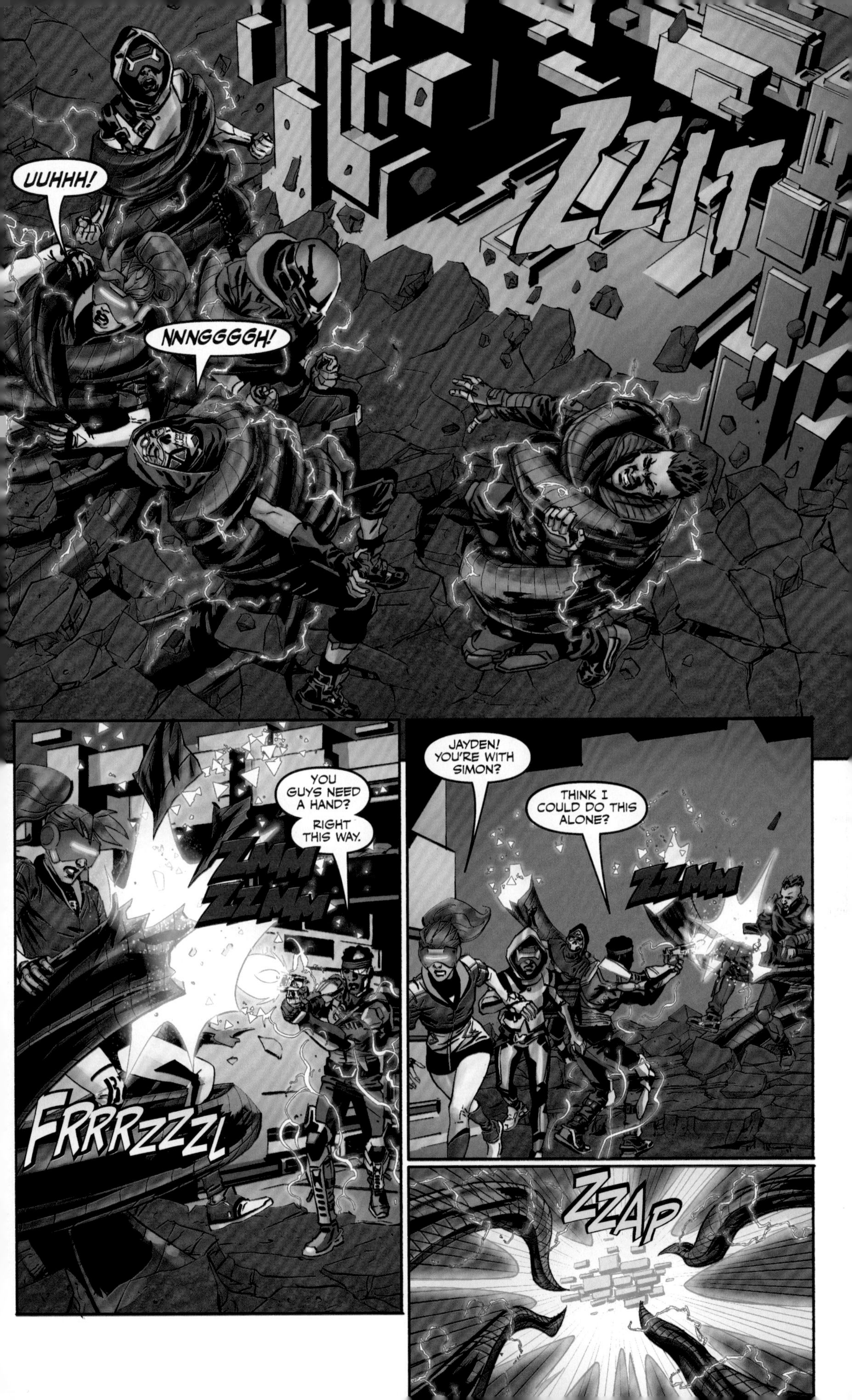
UUHHH!
ZZIT
NNNGGGGH!
YOU GUYS NEED A HAND?
RIGHT THIS WAY.
ZMM
ZZMM
FRRRZZZL
JAYDEN! YOU'RE WITH SIMON?
THINK I COULD DO THIS ALONE?
ZZMM
ZZAP

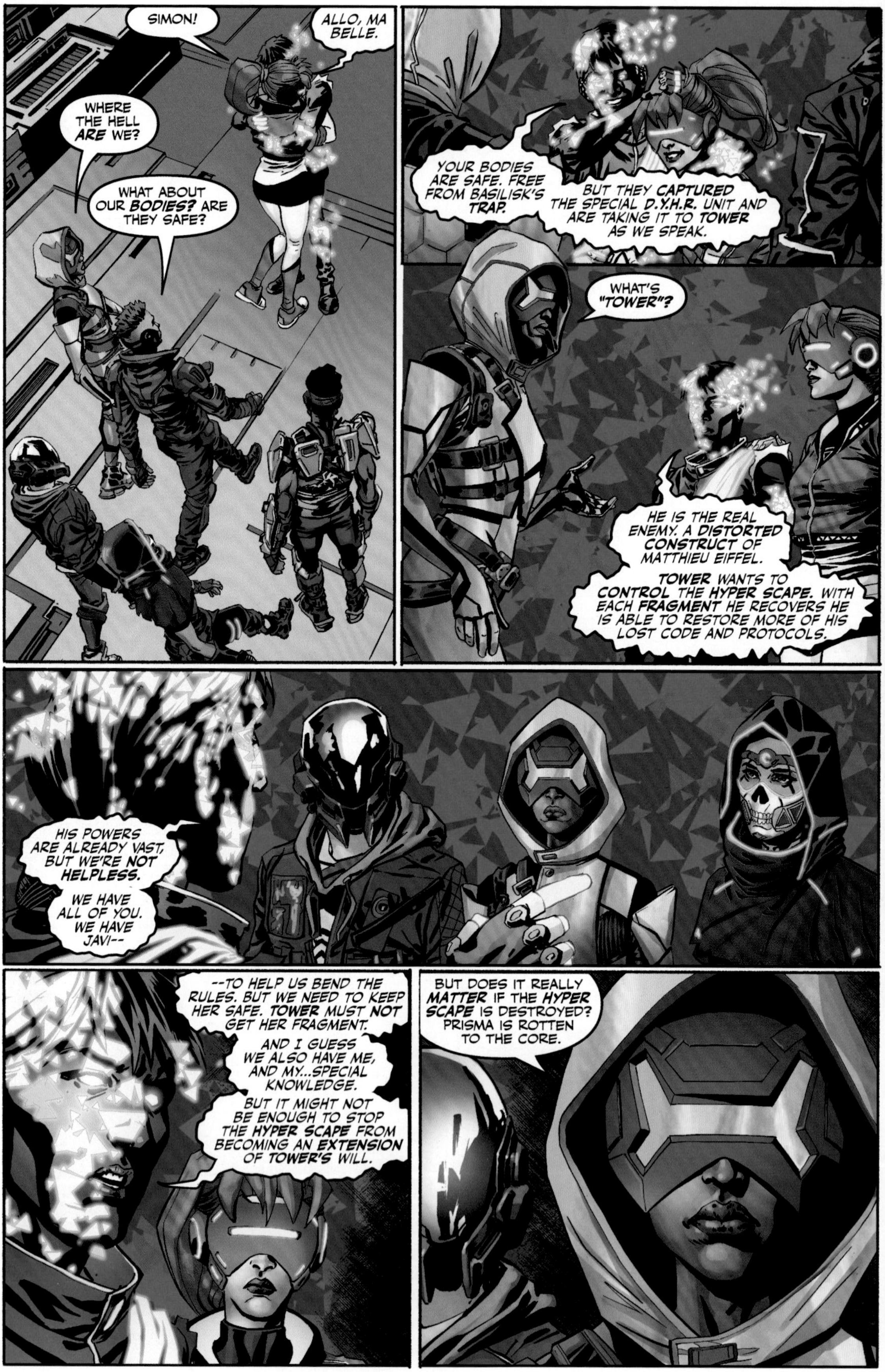
SIMON!
ALLO, MA BELLE.
WHERE THE HELL ARE WE?
WHAT ABOUT OUR BODIES? ARE THEY SAFE?
YOUR BODIES ARE SAFE. FREE FROM BASILISK'S TRAP.
BUT THEY CAPTURED THE SPECIAL D.Y.H.R. UNIT AND ARE TAKING IT TO TOWER AS WE SPEAK.
WHAT'S "TOWER"?
HE IS THE REAL ENEMY. A DISTORTED CONSTRUCT OF MATTHIEU EIFFEL.
TOWER WANTS TO CONTROL THE HYPER SCAPE. WITH EACH FRAGMENT HE RECOVERS HE IS ABLE TO RESTORE MORE OF HIS LOST CODE AND PROTOCOLS.
HIS POWERS ARE ALREADY VAST, BUT WE'RE NOT HELPLESS.
WE HAVE ALL OF YOU. WE HAVE JAVI--
--TO HELP US BEND THE RULES. BUT WE NEED TO KEEP HER SAFE. TOWER MUST NOT GET HER FRAGMENT.
AND I GUESS WE ALSO HAVE ME, AND MY...SPECIAL KNOWLEDGE.
BUT IT MIGHT NOT BE ENOUGH TO STOP THE HYPER SCAPE FROM BECOMING AN EXTENSION OF TOWER'S WILL.
BUT DOES IT REALLY MATTER IF THE HYPER SCAPE IS DESTROYED? PRISMA IS ROTTEN TO THE CORE.

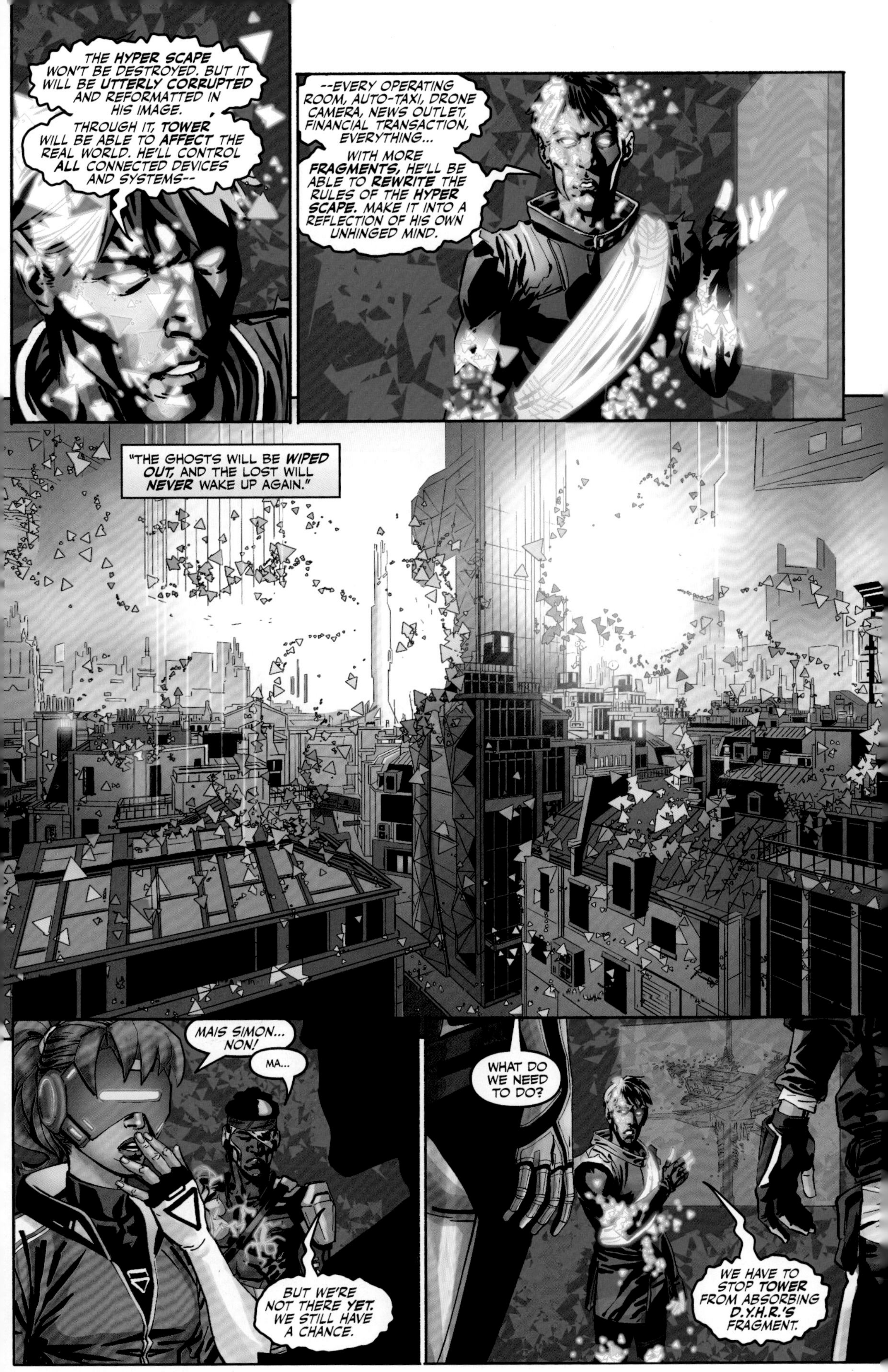
THE HYPER SCAPE WON'T BE DESTROYED. BUT IT WILL BE UTTERLY CORRUPTED AND REFORMATTED IN HIS IMAGE.
THROUGH IT, TOWER WILL BE ABLE TO AFFECT THE REAL WORLD. HE'LL CONTROL ALL CONNECTED DEVICES AND SYSTEMS--
--EVERY OPERATING ROOM, AUTO-TAXI, DRONE CAMERA, NEWS OUTLET, FINANCIAL TRANSACTION, EVERYTHING...
WITH MORE FRAGMENTS, HE'LL BE ABLE TO REWRITE THE RULES OF THE HYPER SCAPE. MAKE IT INTO A REFLECTION OF HIS OWN UNHINGED MIND.
"THE GHOSTS WILL BE WIPED OUT, AND THE LOST WILL NEVER WAKE UP AGAIN."
MAIS SIMON... NON!
MA...
BUT WE'RE NOT THERE YET. WE STILL HAVE A CHANCE.
WHAT DO WE NEED TO DO?
WE HAVE TO STOP TOWER FROM ABSORBING D.Y.H.R.'S FRAGMENT.

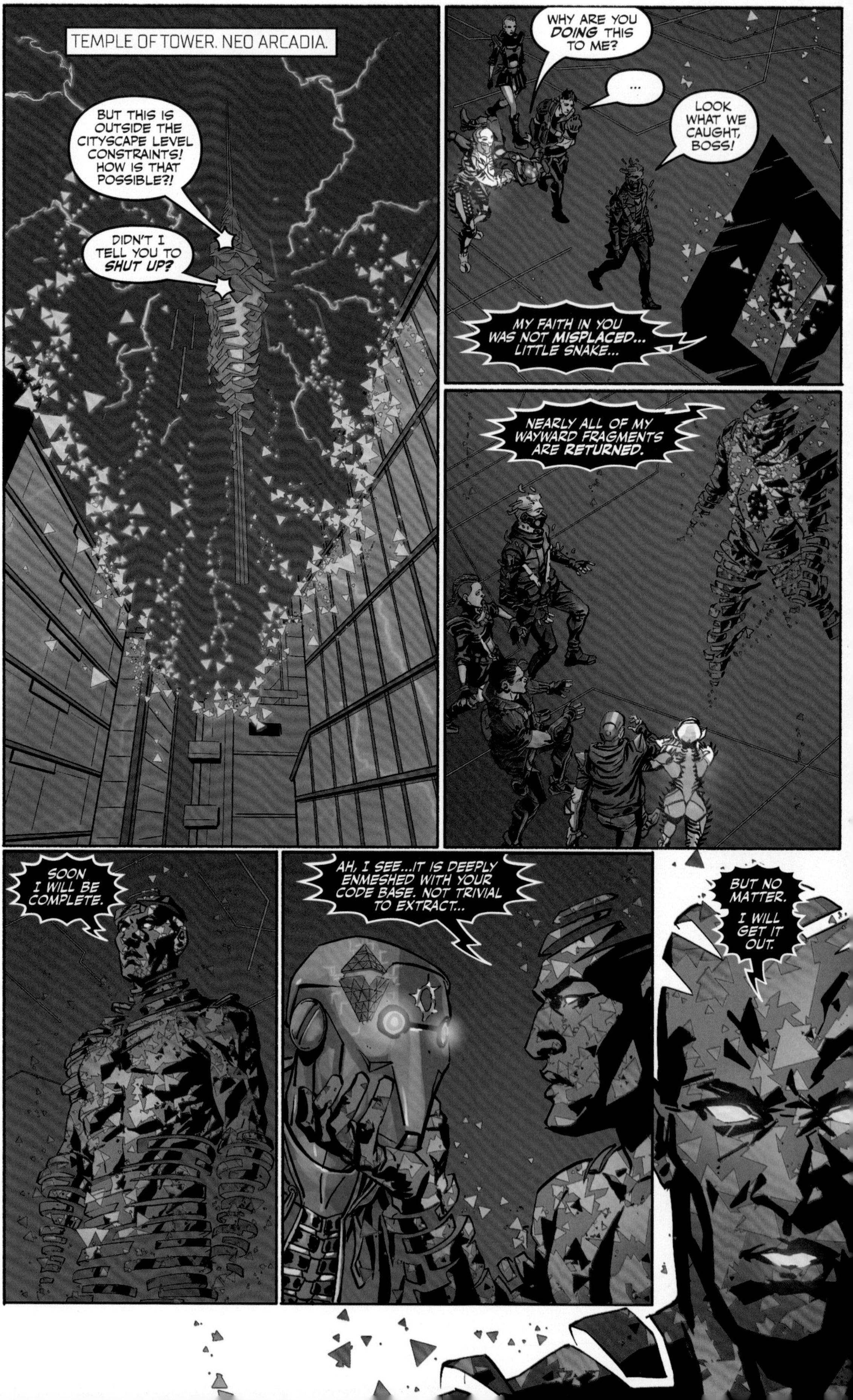
TEMPLE OF TOWER. NEO ARCADIA.
BUT THIS IS OUTSIDE THE CITYSCAPE LEVEL CONSTRAINTS! HOW IS THAT POSSIBLE?!
DIDN'T I TELL YOU TO SHUT UP?
WHY ARE YOU DOING THIS TO ME?
...
LOOK WHAT WE CAUGHT, BOSS!
MY FAITH IN YOU WAS NOT MISPLACED... LITTLE SNAKE...
NEARLY ALL OF MY WAYWARD FRAGMENTS ARE RETURNED.
SOON I WILL BE COMPLETE.
AH, I SEE...IT IS DEEPLY ENMESHED WITH YOUR CODE BASE. NOT TRIVIAL TO EXTRACT...
BUT NO MATTER. I WILL GET IT OUT.

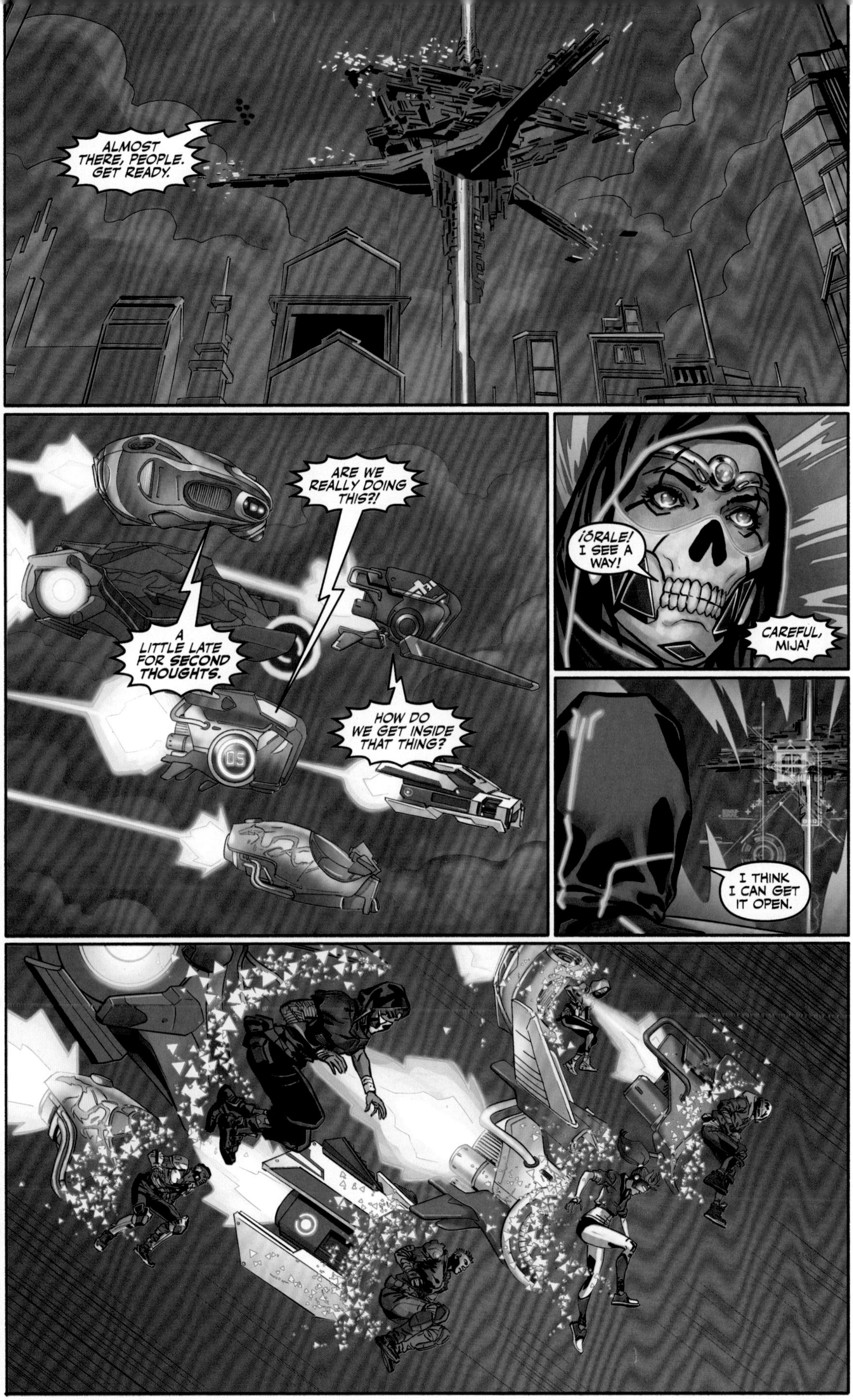
ALMOST THERE, PEOPLE. GET READY.
ARE WE REALLY DOING THIS?!
A LITTLE LATE FOR SECOND THOUGHTS.
HOW DO WE GET INSIDE THAT THING?
¡ÓRALE! I SEE A WAY!
CAREFUL, MIJA!
I THINK I CAN GET IT OPEN.

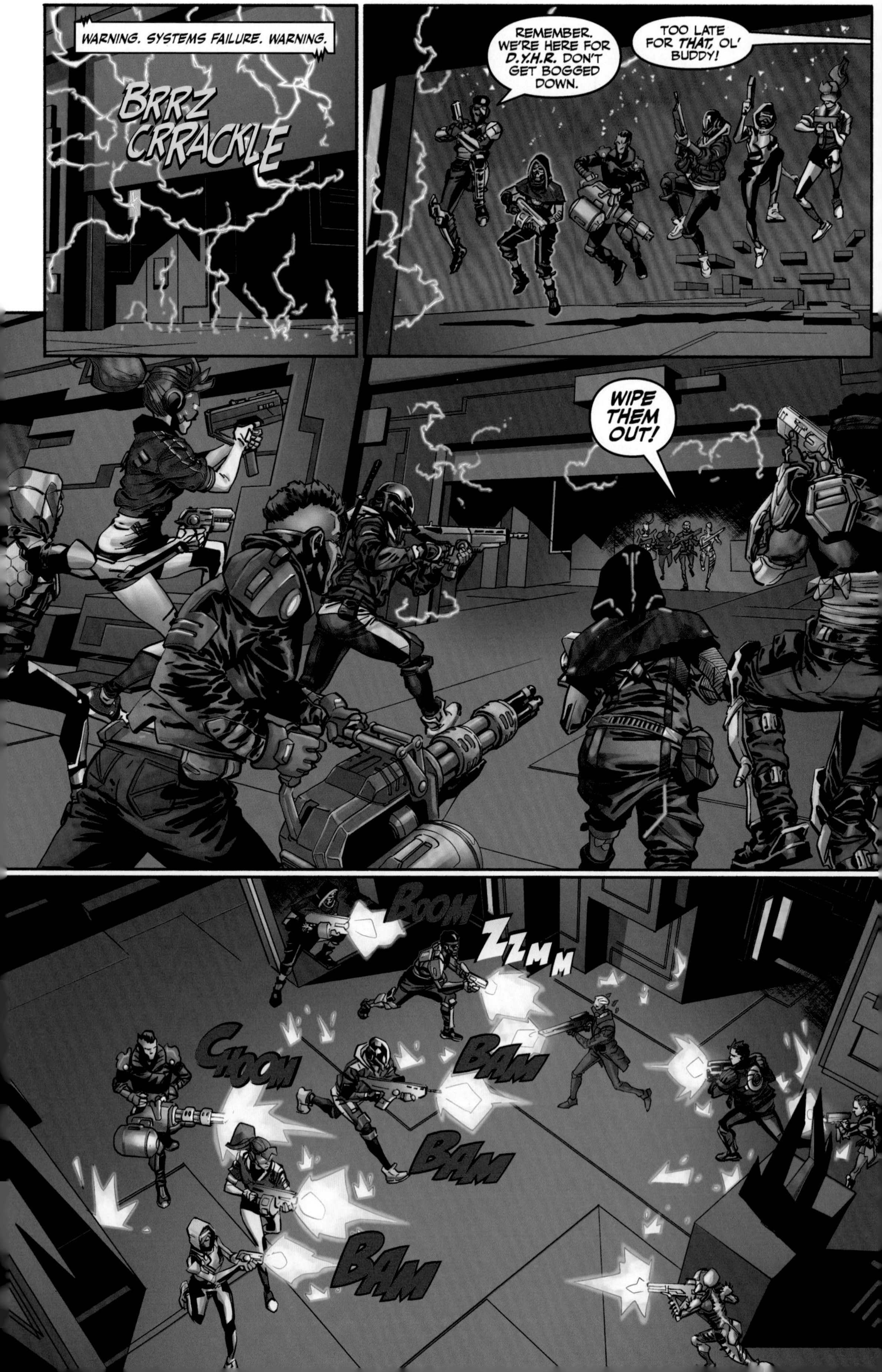
WARNING. SYSTEMS FAILURE. WARNING.
BRRZ CRRACKLE
REMEMBER. WE'RE HERE FOR D.Y.H.R. DON'T GET BOGGED DOWN.
TOO LATE FOR THAT, OL' BUDDY!
WIPE THEM OUT!
BOOM
ZZMMM
CHOOM
BAM
BAM
BAM

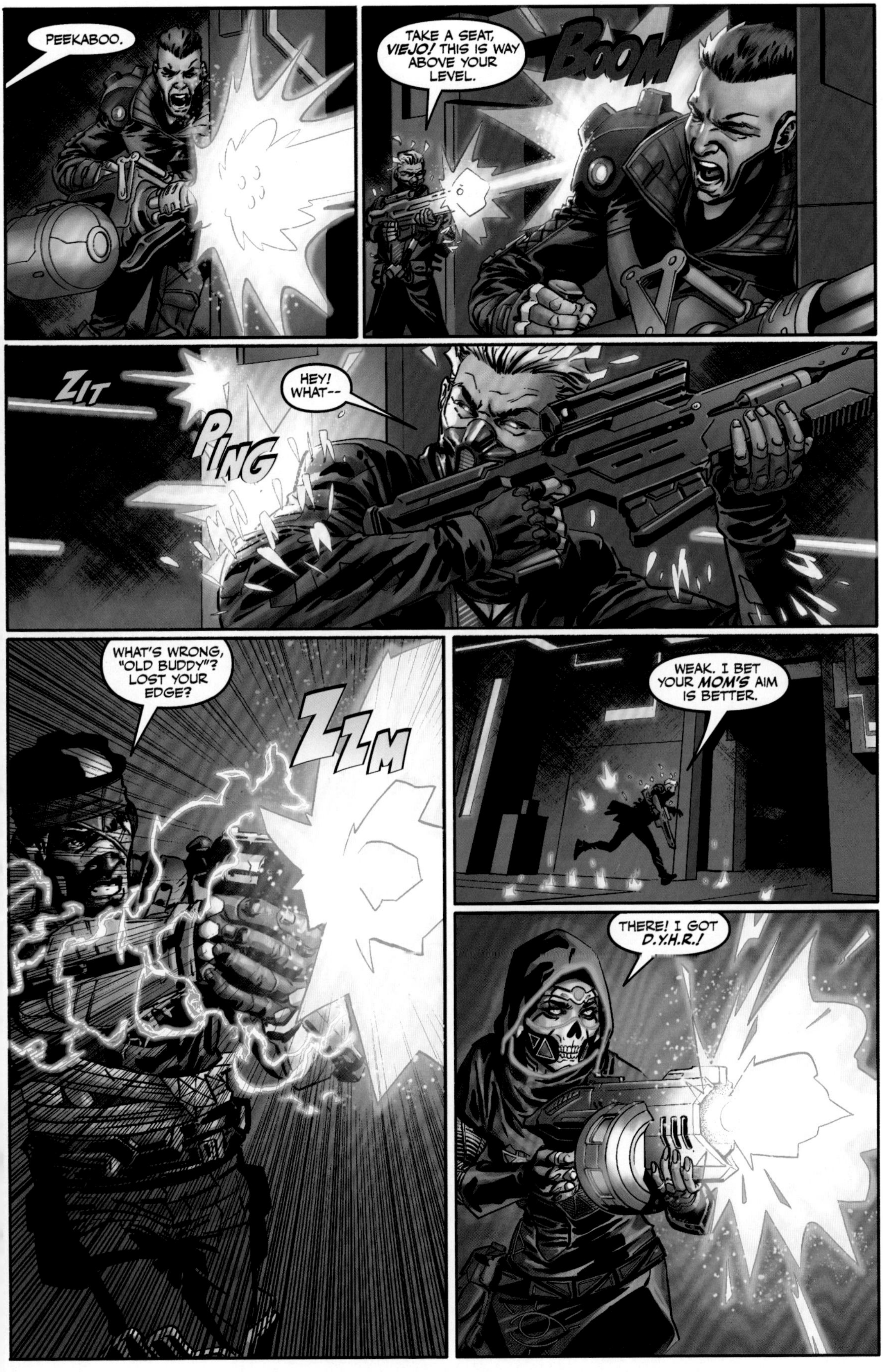
PEEKABOO.
TAKE A SEAT, VIEJO! THIS IS WAY ABOVE YOUR LEVEL.
BOOM
ZIT
PING
HEY! WHAT--
WHAT'S WRONG, "OLD BUDDY"? LOST YOUR EDGE?
ZZM
WEAK. I BET YOUR MOM'S AIM IS BETTER.
THERE! I GOT D.Y.H.R.!

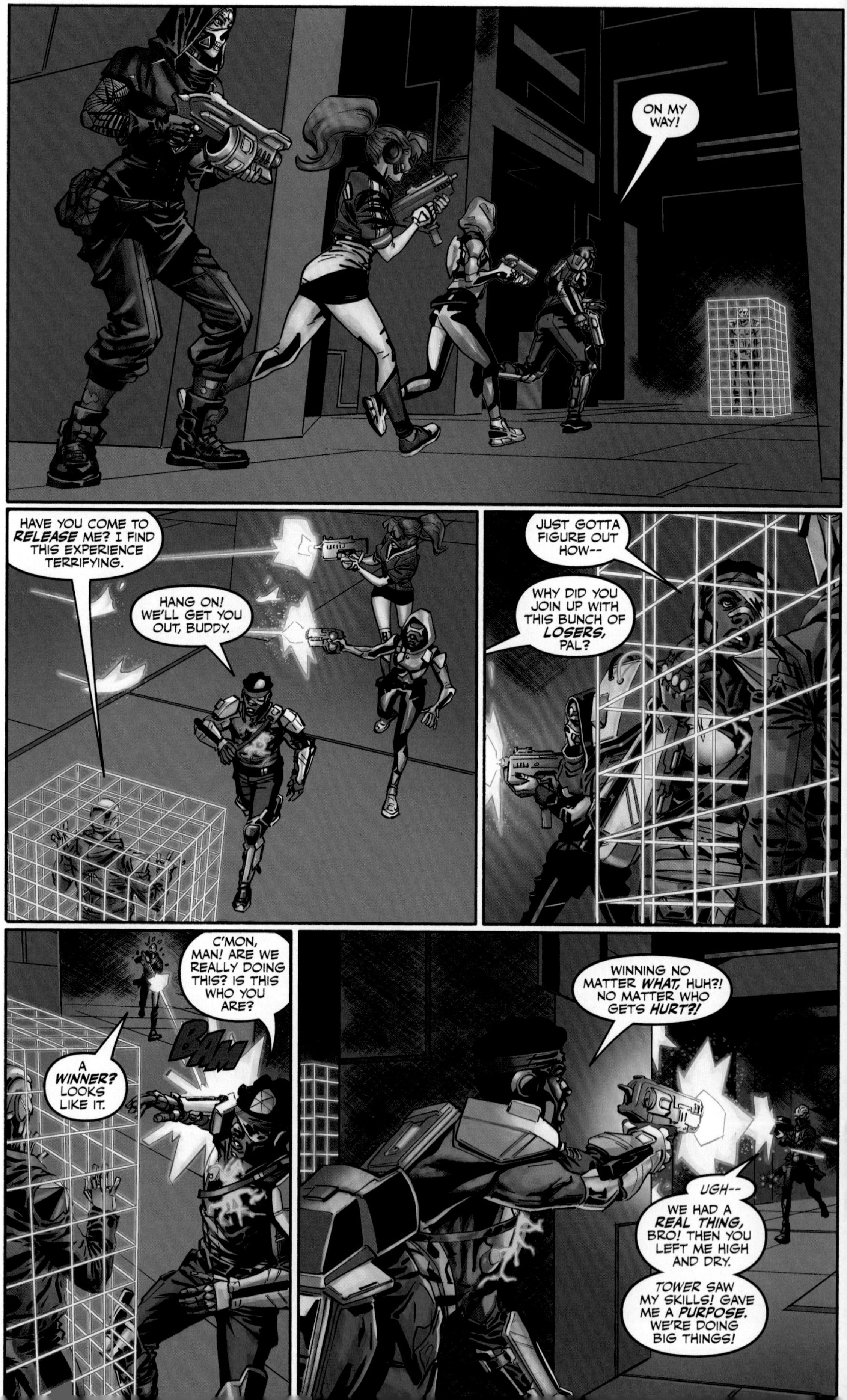
ON MY WAY!
HAVE YOU COME TO RELEASE ME? I FIND THIS EXPERIENCE TERRIFYING.
HANG ON! WE'LL GET YOU OUT, BUDDY.
JUST GOTTA FIGURE OUT HOW--
WHY DID YOU JOIN UP WITH THIS BUNCH OF LOSERS, PAL?
C'MON, MAN! ARE WE REALLY DOING THIS? IS THIS WHO YOU ARE?
BAM
A WINNER? LOOKS LIKE IT.
WINNING NO MATTER WHAT, HUH?! NO MATTER WHO GETS HURT?!
UGH--
WE HAD A REAL THING, BRO! THEN YOU LEFT ME HIGH AND DRY.
TOWER SAW MY SKILLS! GAVE ME A PURPOSE. WE'RE DOING BIG THINGS!

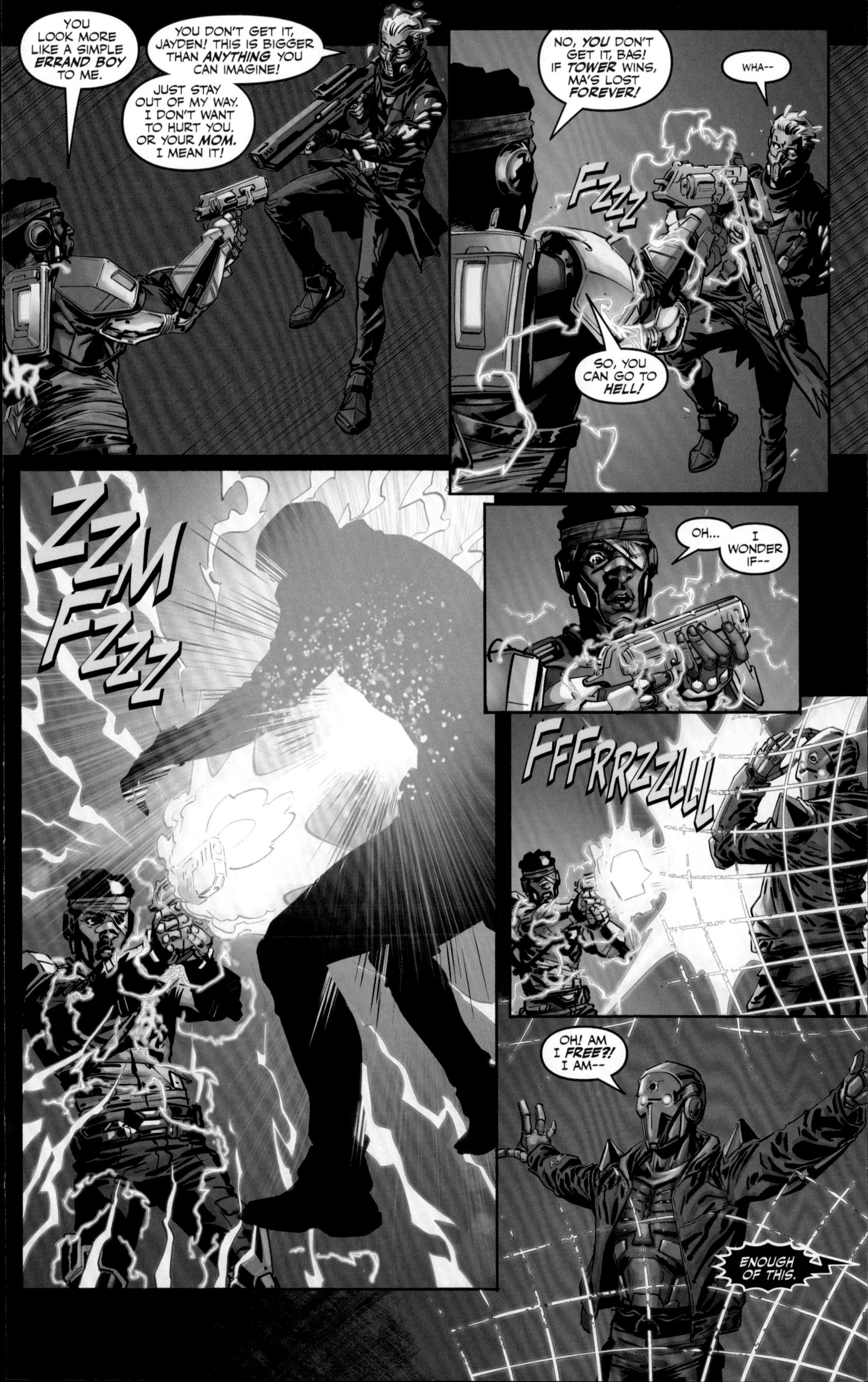
YOU LOOK MORE LIKE A SIMPLE ERRAND BOY TO ME.
YOU DON'T GET IT, JAYDEN! THIS IS BIGGER THAN ANYTHING YOU CAN IMAGINE!
JUST STAY OUT OF MY WAY. I DON'T WANT TO HURT YOU. OR YOUR MOM. I MEAN IT!
NO, YOU DON'T GET IT, BAS! IF TOWER WINS, MA'S LOST FOREVER!
WHA--
FZZZ
SO, YOU CAN GO TO HELL!
ZZM
FZZZ
OH... I WONDER IF--
FFFRRZZLLL
OH! AM I FREE?! I AM--
ENOUGH OF THIS.

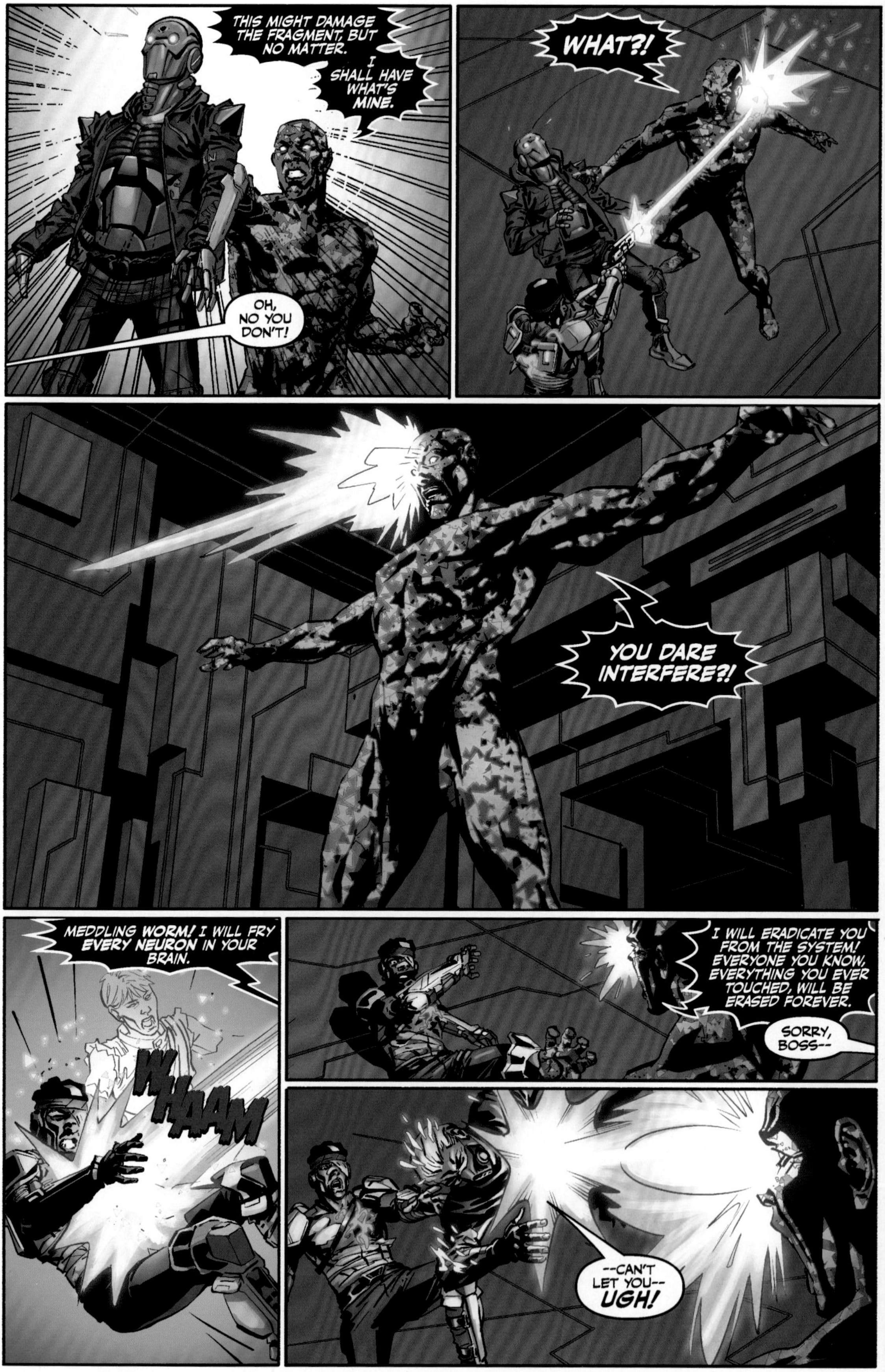
THIS MIGHT DAMAGE THE FRAGMENT, BUT NO MATTER.
I SHALL HAVE WHAT'S MINE.
OH, NO YOU DON'T!
WHAT?!
YOU DARE INTERFERE?!
MEDDLING WORM! I WILL FRY EVERY NEURON IN YOUR BRAIN.
WHAAM
I WILL ERADICATE YOU FROM THE SYSTEM! EVERYONE YOU KNOW, EVERYTHING YOU EVER TOUCHED, WILL BE ERASED FOREVER.
SORRY, BOSS--
--CAN'T LET YOU-- UGH!

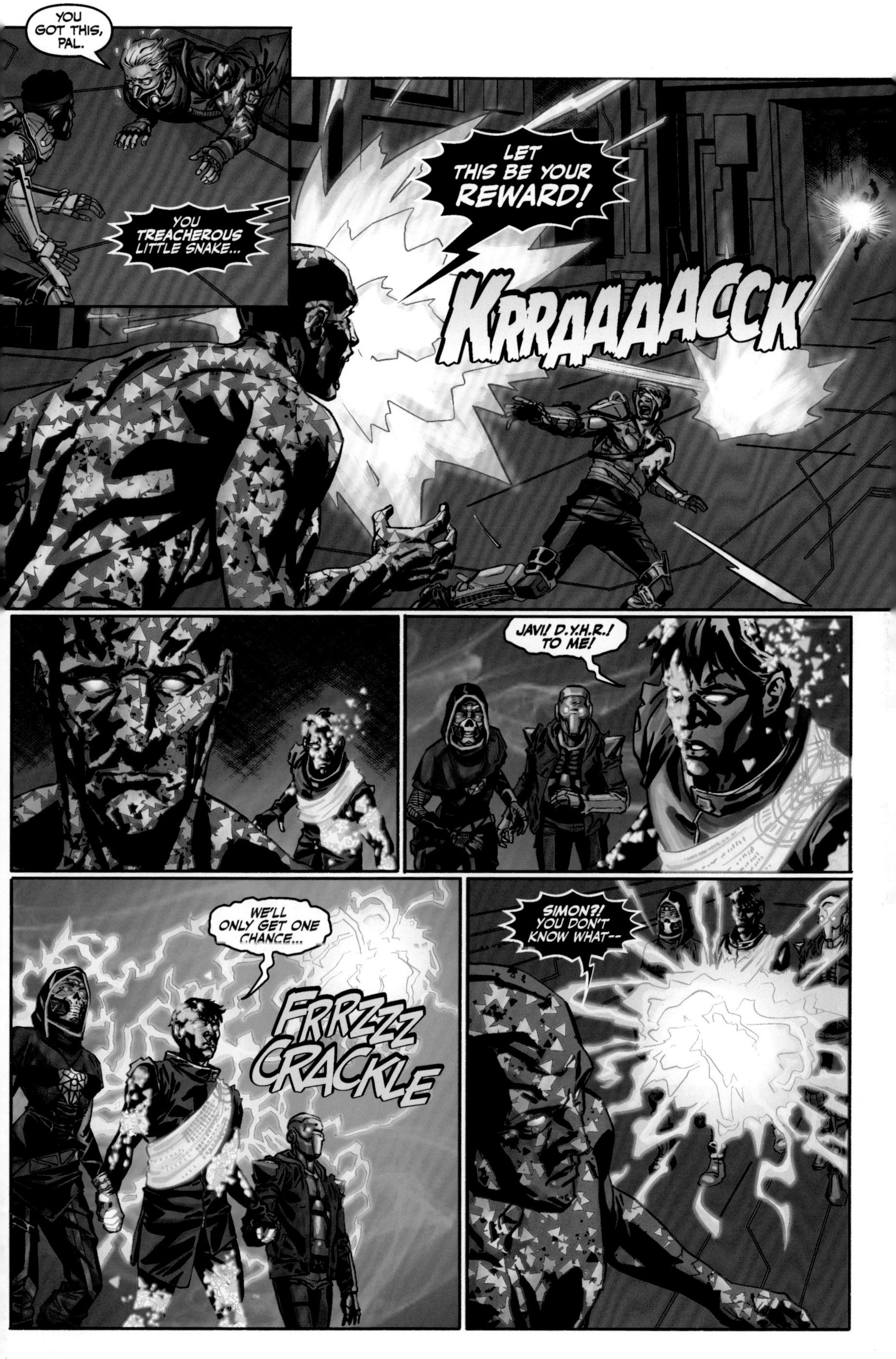
YOU GOT THIS, PAL.
YOU TREACHEROUS LITTLE SNAKE...
LET THIS BE YOUR REWARD!
KRRAAAACCK
JAVI! D.Y.H.R.! TO ME!
WE'LL ONLY GET ONE CHANCE...
FRRZZZ CRACKLE
SIMON?! YOU DON'T KNOW WHAT--

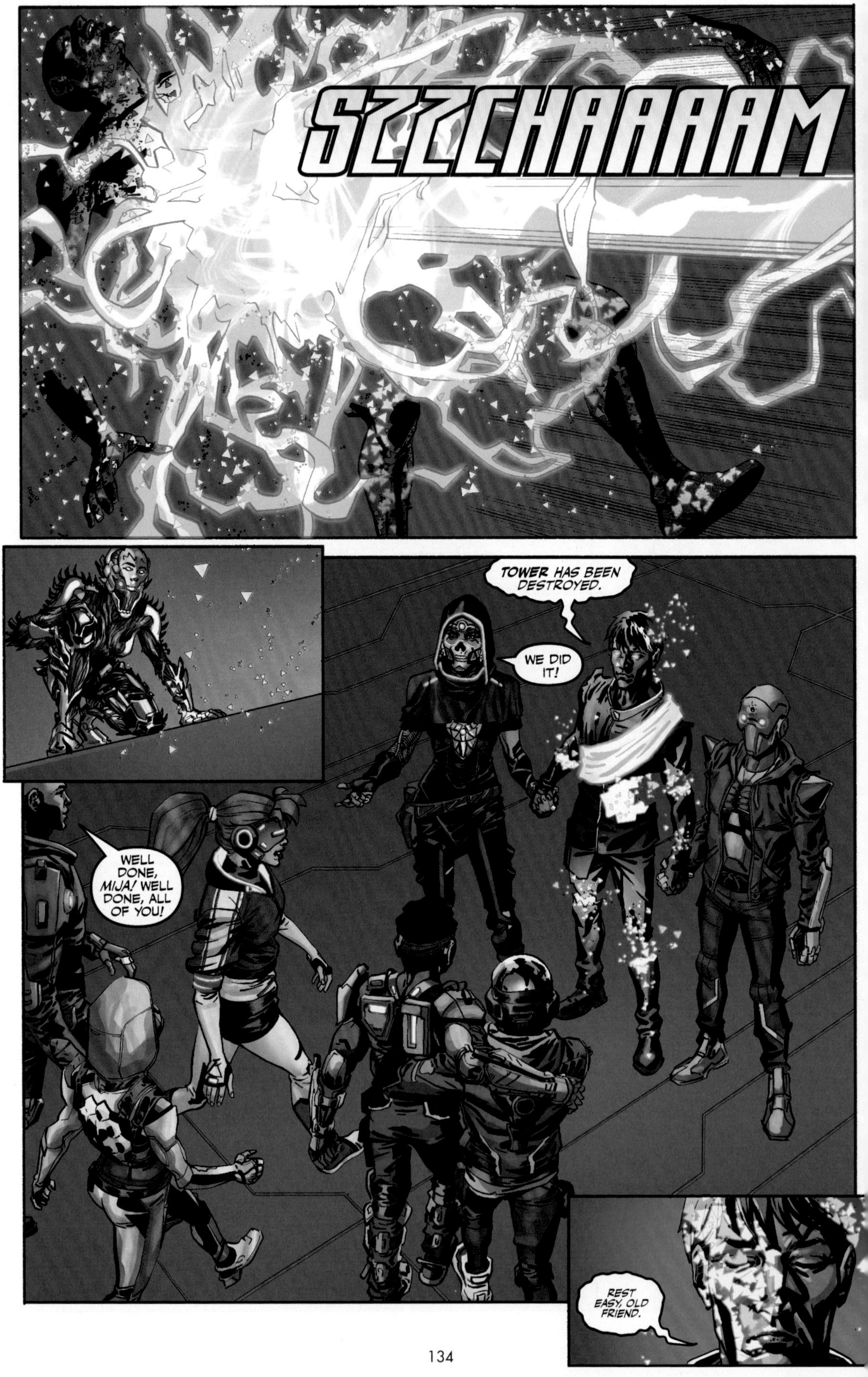
SZZCHAAAAAM
TOWER HAS BEEN DESTROYED.
WE DID IT!
WELL DONE, MIJA! WELL DONE, ALL OF YOU!
REST EASY, OLD FRIEND.

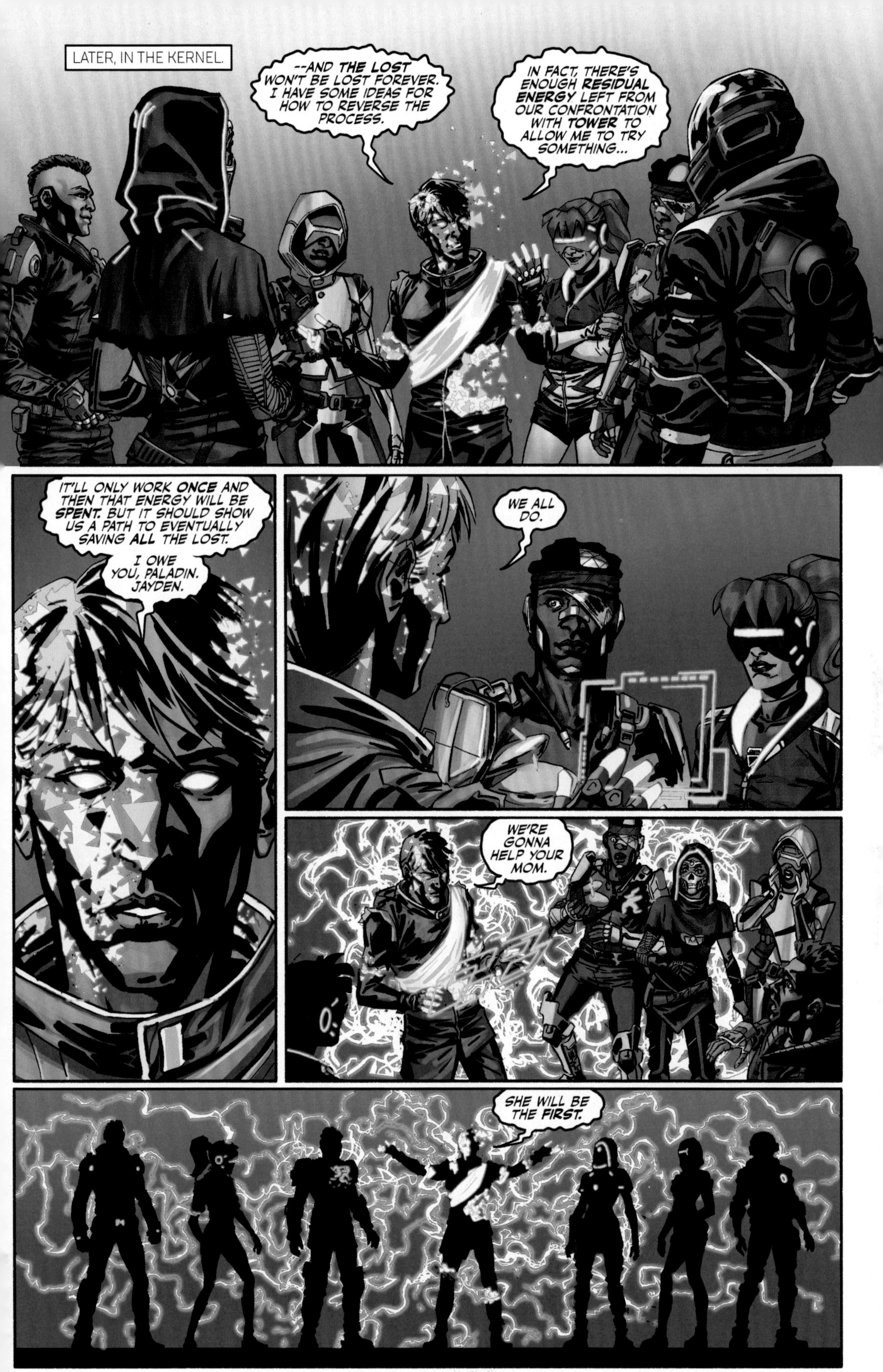
LATER, IN THE KERNEL.
--AND THE LOST WON'T BE LOST FOREVER. I HAVE SOME IDEAS FOR HOW TO REVERSE THE PROCESS.
IN FACT, THERE'S ENOUGH RESIDUAL ENERGY LEFT FROM OUR CONFRONTATION WITH TOWER TO ALLOW ME TO TRY SOMETHING...
IT'LL ONLY WORK ONCE AND THEN THAT ENERGY WILL BE SPENT. BUT IT SHOULD SHOW US A PATH TO EVENTUALLY SAVING ALL THE LOST.
I OWE YOU, PALADIN. JAYDEN.
WE ALL DO.
WE'RE GONNA HELP YOUR MOM.
SHE WILL BE THE FIRST.

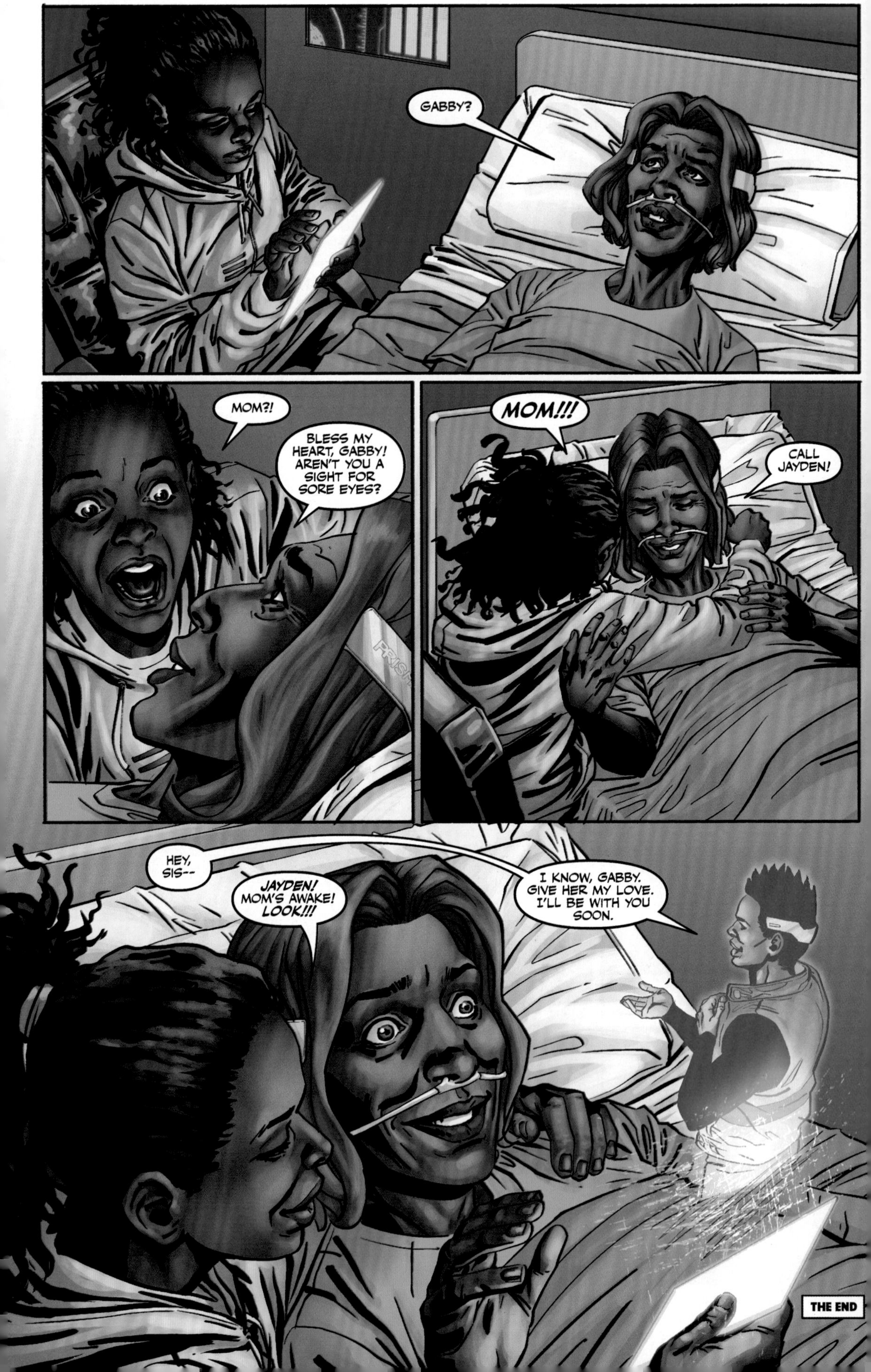
GABBY?
MOM?!
BLESS MY HEART, GABBY! AREN'T YOU A SIGHT FOR SORE EYES?
MOM!!!
CALL JAYDEN!
HEY, SIS--
JAYDEN! MOM'S AWAKE! LOOK!!!
I KNOW, GABBY. GIVE HER MY LOVE. I'LL BE WITH YOU SOON.
THE END

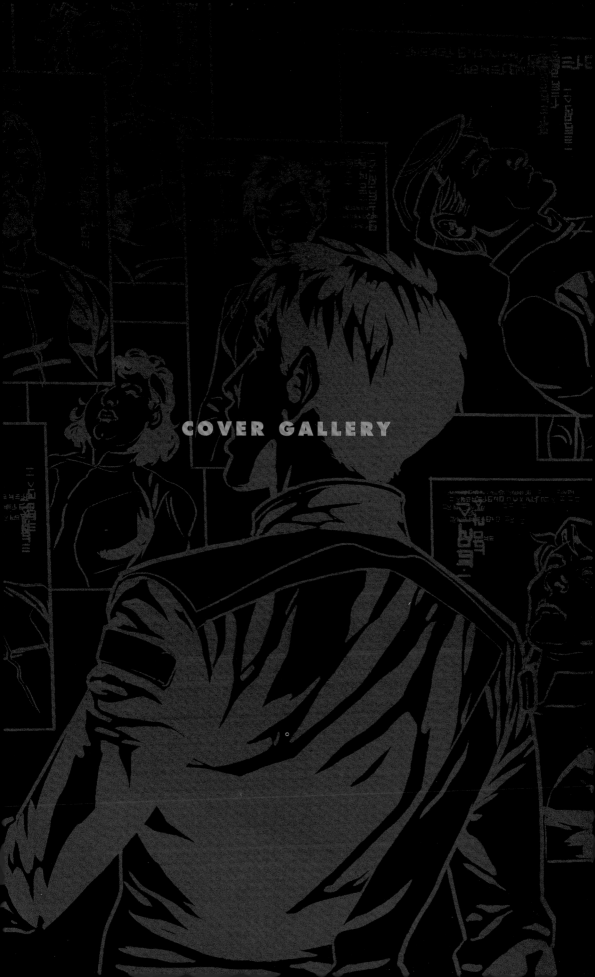

COVER GALLERY

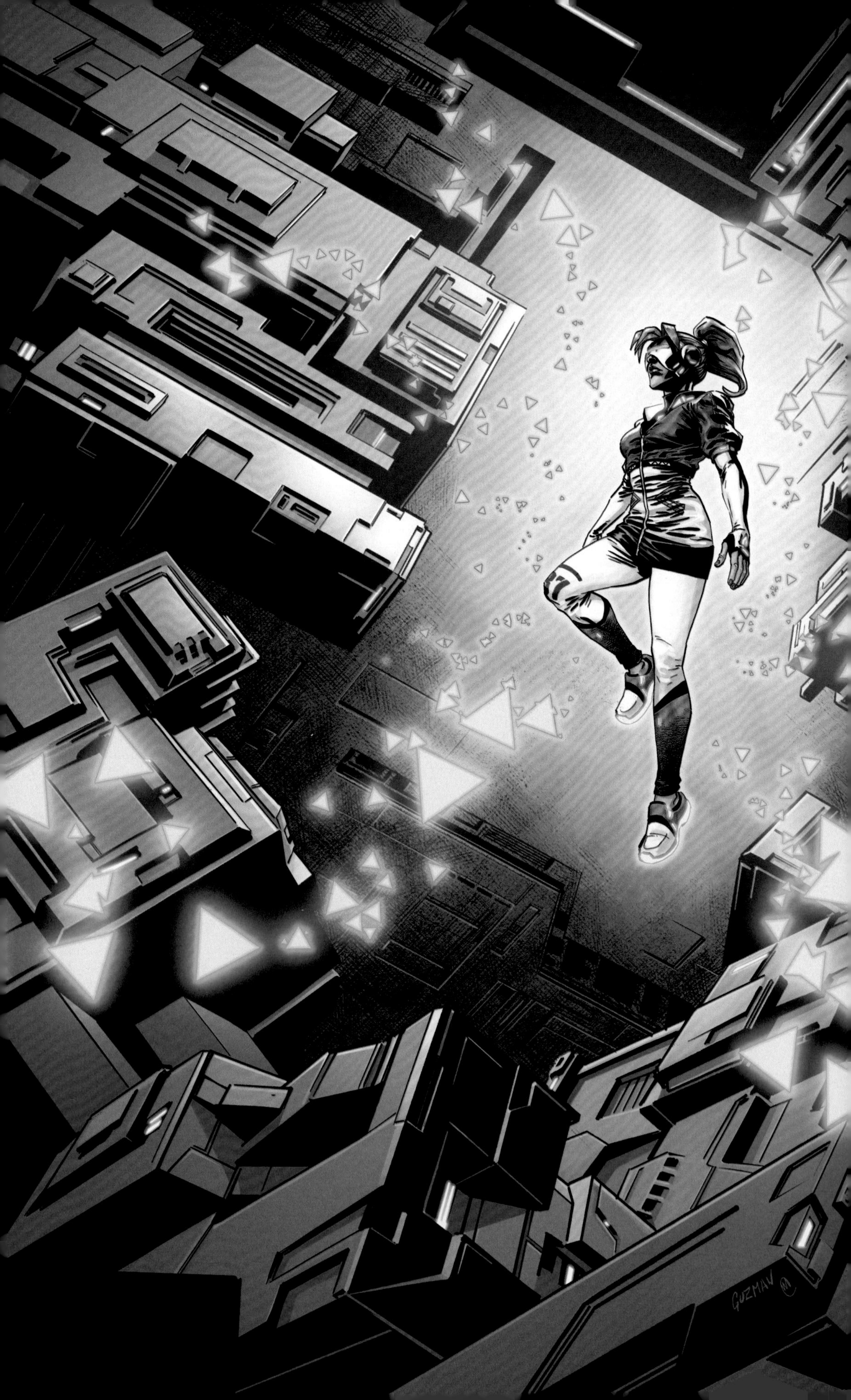
GUZMAN

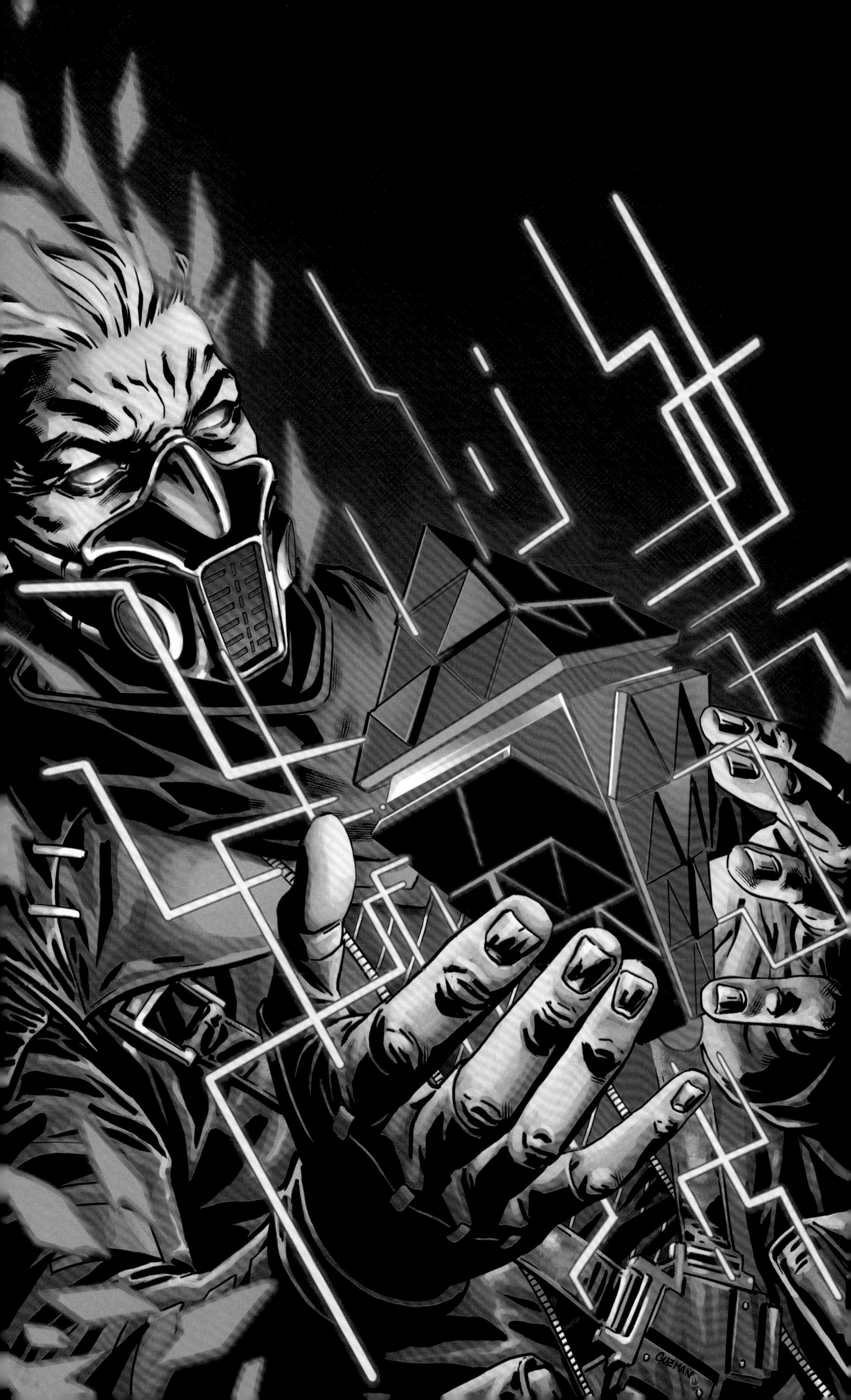
GUZMAN

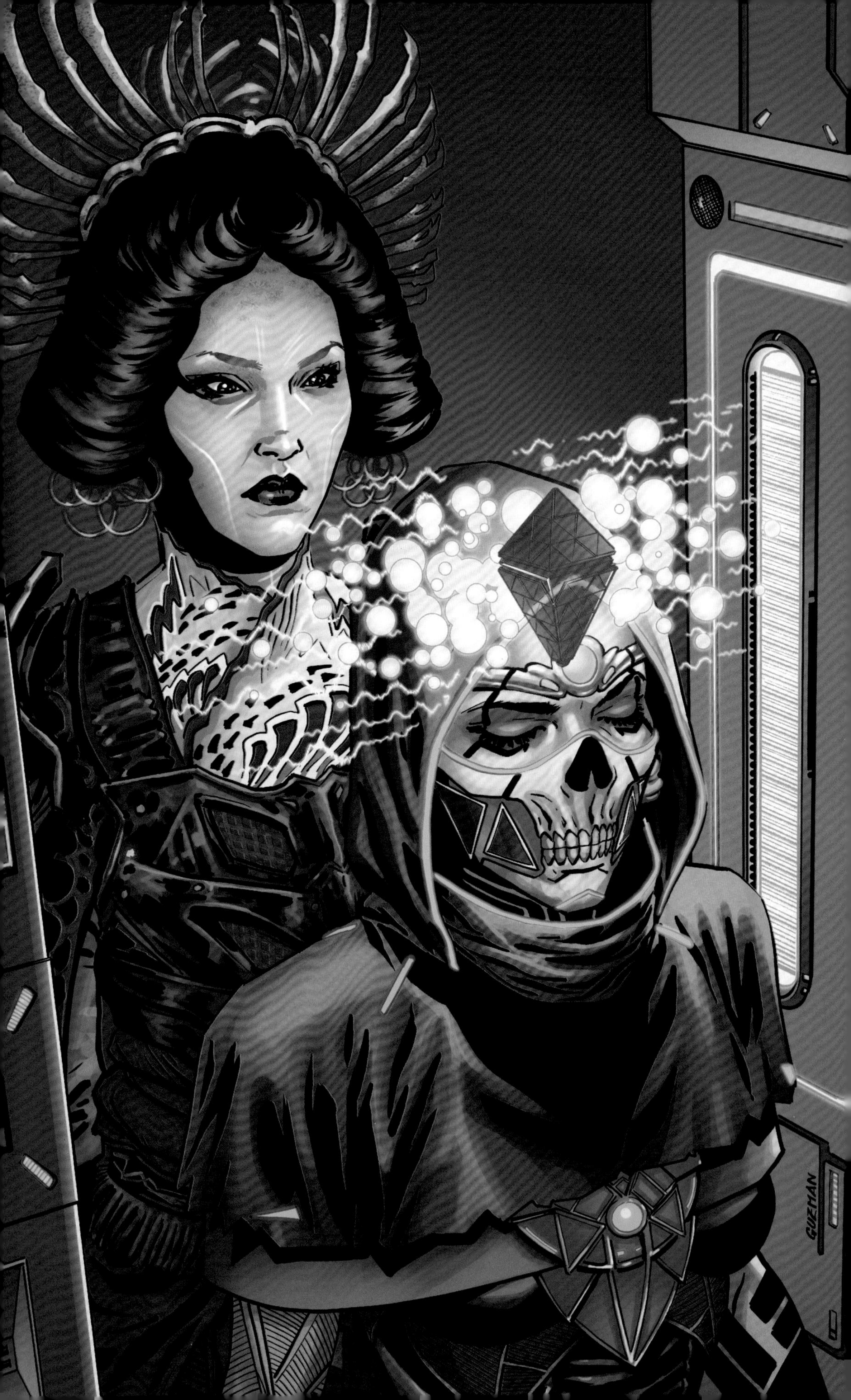
GUZMAN

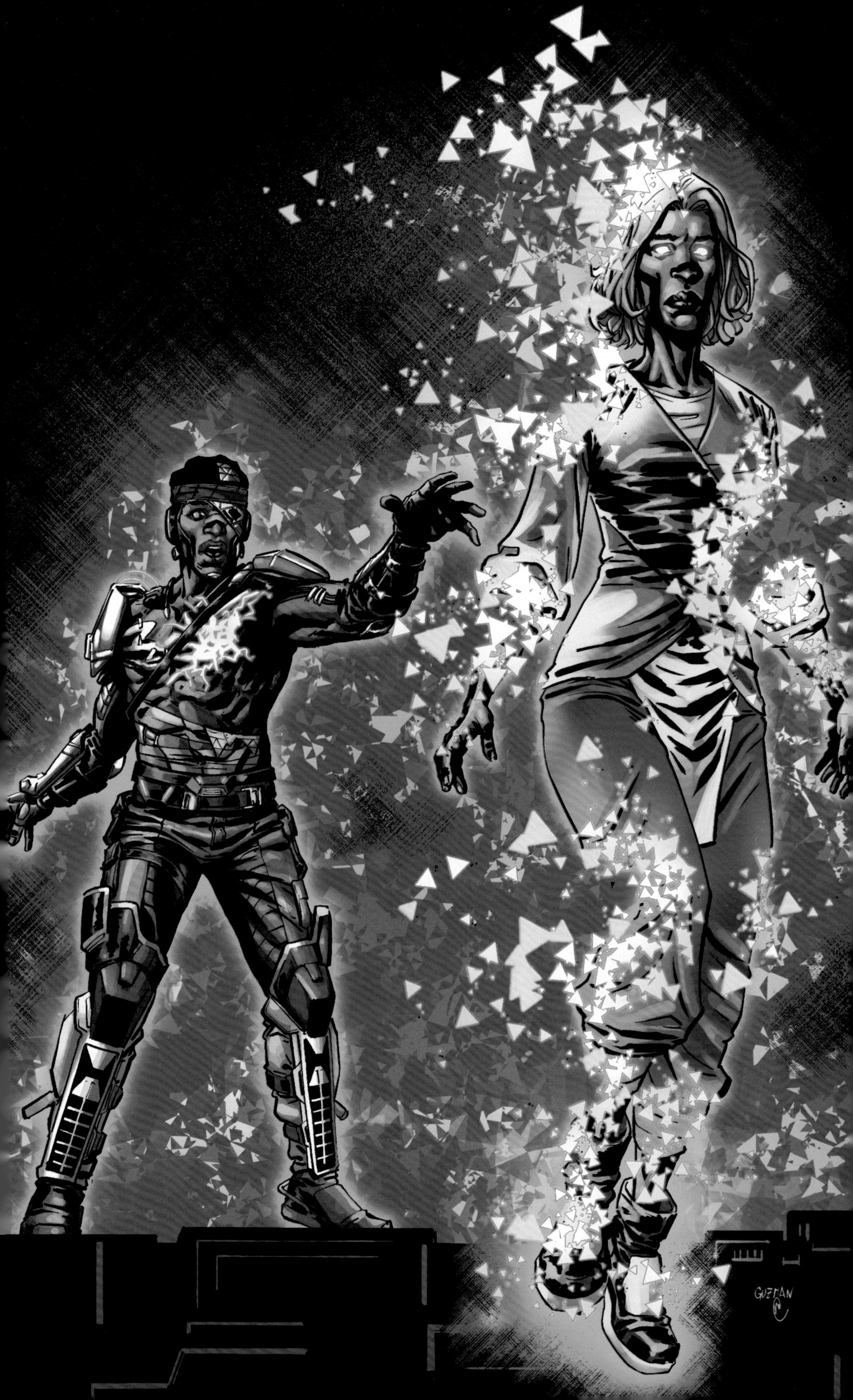
GUZMAN

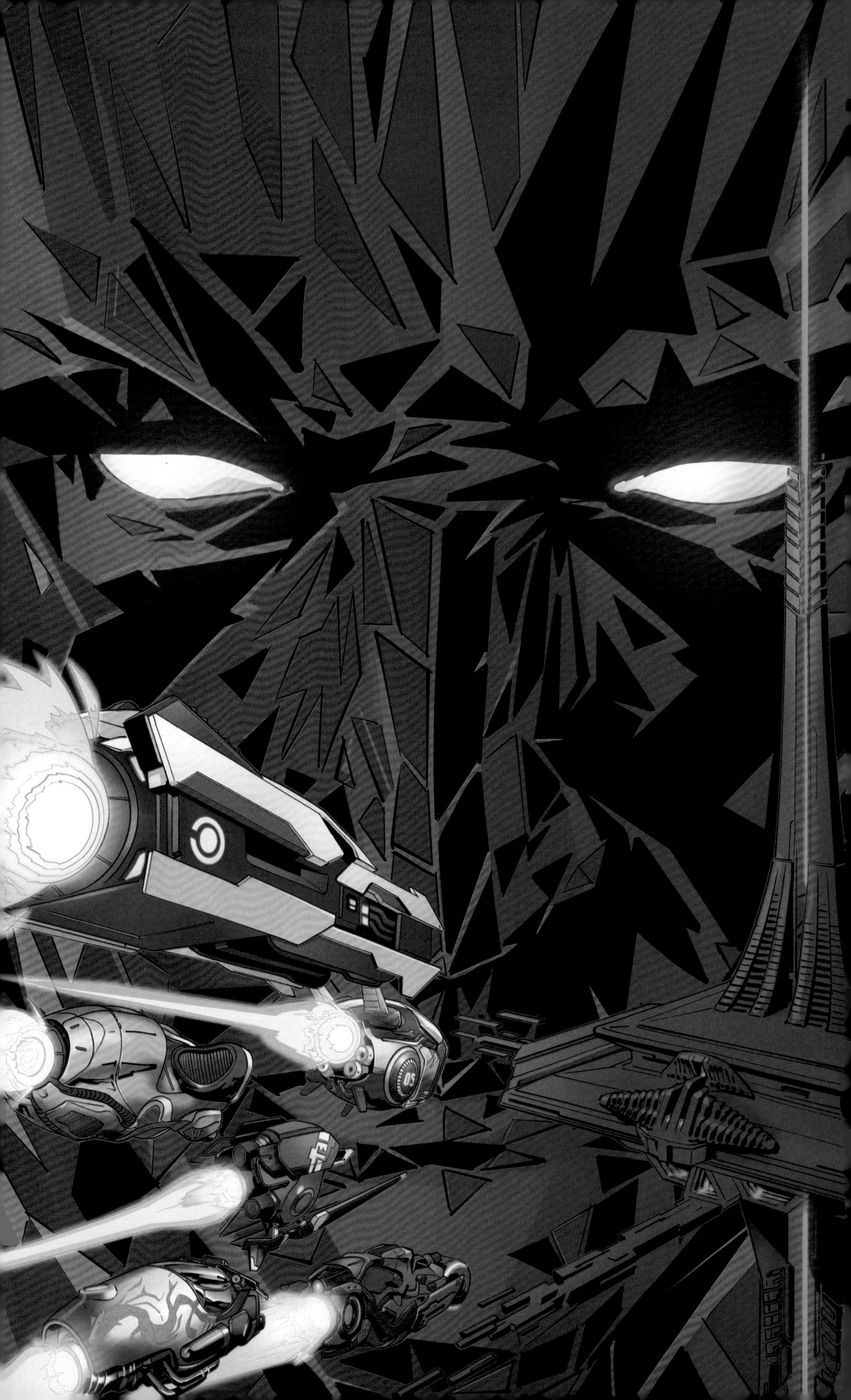

ENTER THE WORLD OF UBISOFT'S ASSASSIN'S CREED VALHALLA

ASSASSIN'S CREED VALHALLA: SONG OF GLORY

ASSASSIN'S CREED
VALHALLA
SONG OF GLORY

A prequel to *Assassin's Creed Valhalla.* Viking warrior Eivor seizes the attack on a neighboring village in her favor—but will her victory be a blessing? Elsewhere, another Viking searches for a different kind of prize.

978-1-50671-929-0 // $19.99

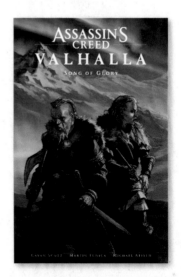

THE ART OF ASSASSIN'S CREED VALHALLA

THE ART OF ASSASSIN'S CREED VALHALLA (DELUXE EDITION)

This deluxe edition includes an exclusive cover, a decorative slipcase, and a gallery-quality lithograph art print.

978-1-50672-045-6 // $79.99

DARK HORSE BOOKS

UBISOFT

AVAILABLE AT YOUR LOCAL COMICS SHOP OR BOOKSTORE!

To find a comics shop in your area, visit comicshoplocator.com // For more information or to order direct, visit DarkHorse.com.

*Prices and availability subject to change without notice.

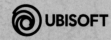

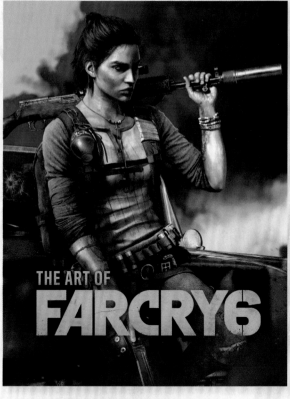

FAR CRY: RITE OF PASSAGE

El Presidente, Antón Castillo, takes his thirteen-year-old son on a journey, teaching him lessons in leadership and recounting cautionary tales he has heard about the undoing of three legendary men: Vaas Montenegro, Pagan Min, and Joseph Seed.

978-1-50672-629-8 | $19.99

THE ART OF FAR CRY 6

A full-color hardcover exploring the art and creation of *Far Cry 6*. Discover the vibrant island of Yara, a nation trapped in time. Meet its brutal dictator, Antón Castillo, and follow the guerrillas fighting to liberate the country. *¡Viva Libertad!*

978-1-50672-434-8 | $39.99

DELVE INTO UBISOFT'S
FARCRY ®